Running to the Top

Arthur Lydiard

Running to the Top

In Collaboration with Garth Gilmour

Meyer & Meyer Sport

British Library Cataloguing in Publication Data
A catalogue record for this book is available from the British Library

Arthur Lydiard: Running to the Top
In collab.with Garth Gilmour
Oxford: Meyer & Meyer Sport (UK) Ltd., 2007
ISBN 978-3-89124-440-1

© 1997 by Meyer & Meyer Sport (UK) Ltd.
2nd Edition, 2007
Aachen, Adelaide, Auckland, Budapest, Graz, Indianapolis, Johannesburg,
New York, Olten (CH), Oxford, Singapore, Toronto
Member of the World
Sport Publishers' Association (WSPA)
www.w-s-p-a.org
Printed and bound by: Burg Verlag Gastinger GmbH, Germany
ISBN 978-3-89124-440-1
E-Mail: verlag@m-m-sports.com
www.m-m-sports.com

Contents

Introduction

The Oxford dictionary defines running as the act of progressing by advancing each foot alternately, never having both on the ground at once. Chambers says running is the act of proceeding by lifting one foot before the other is down. Neither definition is particularly complicated and neither places any limitation on the degree of forward momentum attained.

The art and technique of running and the processes of talking and writing about running should be equally as simple. Running, after all, is as natural as walking. Once a child has learnt to walk, no one has to teach it how to run.

This book, then, is written to be as uncomplicated as the principle of putting one foot in front of the other without ever having both on the ground at once.

Its purpose is simple – to enable you go faster, and get both feet off the ground if you want to, or farther, or both faster and farther, according to your personal aims and aspirations. If you want to be an Olympic or world champion, this book is for you. If you merely want to jog in comfort around your neighbourhood in the interests of your physical wellbeing, this book is for you, too.

We set out the guidelines, the rationale, the simple principles behind the art and pleasure of running better; we offer schedules upon which to base your own programmes of training for whatever you aspire to.
The rest is up to you.

Like none other, Arthur Lydiard's philosophy of running training touches everyone who pulls on a pair of running shoes. He devised the principles of training now employed by leading coaches and athletes all around the world, in track and field and in many other sporting spheres; he invented the pure and simple exercise of jogging which has infected millions with its benign bug.

First tested and found successful in the 1950s, the Lydiard system has undergone some subtle refinements through the years. But it remains the same elemental theory that first placed a small handful of ordinary runners, from Lydiard's immediate neighbourhood in an Auckland, New Zealand, suburb, at the forefront of world middle and distance running for more than a decade and then, as Lydiard advanced from being a coach of runners to an international coach of coaches, spread around the running tracks and training centres of the entire world.

Arthur Lydiard turned a simple, practical faith in himself into a world-wide nostrum for everyone seeking a method of running better. His name and his methods have won instant recognition in many nations speaking many tongues. As gurus go in the modern world, he ranks among the greatest and, almost certainly, the most physically and psychologically effective.

For several years from the mid-seventies, the late great Japanese middle and distance coach Kiyoshi Nakamura brought teams of his top runners to New Zealand to spend months training in the remote vastness of the South Island back country behind Ashburton.

These were the famous runners who, in a sudden spasm reminiscent of the explosion of the Arthur Lydiard-trained team into international running in the sixties, became a dominant world force particularly over the longer distances. The stars were the Soh brothers, then Toshihiko Seko, the legend who won three consecutive Fukuoka marathons, ran world track records for 25,000 and 30,000 metres in New Zealand and took the 1981 Boston marathon in 2:09.26.

Nakamura, one of the most respected figures in Japanese athletics, had an association with New Zealand that stretched back to 1936, when he represented Japan in the historic 1,500 m which saw Jack Lovelock race away with a spectacular record-making gold medal.

But why, year after year, did he bring his teams of distance runners to New Zealand?

The first reason, he told 'New Zealand Runner' magazine's Tim Chamberlain in 1982, on his seventh visit, was that Arthur Lydiard lived in New Zealand.

Nakamura was one of the first Japanese to learn Lydiard's methods, the first to invite Lydiard to Japan in 1962. He read all Lydiard's books and came to believe he knew more about Lydiard's methods than Lydiard himself because his studies made a vital link between Lydiard techniques, Christianity and Zen.

That might be argued. What could not be argued was that Nakamura used Lydiard as the basis for his coaching methods and philosophy that fired Japan, for a time, into the forefront of international middle and distance running. He took his runners to nearly 20 Japanese records, several world records and a string of international successes.

Among the Japanese, Nakamura knew Lydiard best. When he died, the vital spark that lit Japan died with him but he had made the point: The Lydiard system, once understood, was the critical factor between success and failure.

Olympic marathoner and leading US coach Ron Daws was unashamedly a Lydiard fan. Lydiard's name appeared on page one of Daws' 'Running Your Best' with the quotation, "It's not the best athlete who wins, but the best prepared."

Of the Lydiard system, Daws wrote: "A few aspiring kids approach a neighbourhood shoe-maker to teach them to run. The shoemaker is a high school drop-out and retired distance runner whose own brand of torturous training methods have so far earned him little more than scorn and ridicule from the coaching community. He agrees to help and, although the runners are not the country's best, not even the city's best – just eager kids from the neighbourhood – the shoemaker promises them world records and Olympic medals if they can endure the workouts. The boy the shoemaker first publicly predicts will set a world record is crippled in one arm; and another runner, who the shoemaker says will be the best middle-distance runner ever, looks muscle-bound and awkward.

"A few years later, the country's entire contingent of distance runners to the 1960 Olympics is coached by the former shoemaker. Thirty minutes apart, the crippled one and the awkward one win gold medals; a day later, another of his runners, seemingly athleti-cally nondescript, takes a bronze. From these and other of the shoemaker's pupils come most of the world records from 800 metres to the one-hour run and two more golds and a bronze in the next Olympics.

Wild dreams? A fairy tale? Hardly, I'm just recounting the emergence of New Zealand's Arthur Lydiard, guru of distance runners, father of the jogging craze, prime mover and motivator of Olympians world-wide ... Lydiard has either directly coached or influenced more world record-holders and Olympics medalists than anyone. With see-mingly endless energy, he has lectured up one country and down another, pausing peri-odically to serve as national coach in Finland, Denmark, Mexico and Venezuela. Ironically, he is, like many prophets, largely ignored in official circles in his own country."

"When Peter Snell and Murray Halberg sprinted off with the gold in the 800 and 5,000 and Barry Magee won the marathon bronze in the 1960 Rome Olympics, the rest of the world was full swing into interval training. So ingrained is the Lydiard philosophy now, we almost have to force ourselves to recall that before him, the coaching of distance runners was aimed 180 degrees in the other direction. Lydiard was the beginning of a magic era; jogging became acceptable if not godlike ... Lydiard was the keystone and he never lets us forget that, as an unschooled layman, he did what physiologists, theorists and profes-sional coaches hadn't been able to do. He was unsophisticated but he was smart and he had the tenacity of a bulldog."

It was the Lydiard approach that turned my career around and it is the basis for my con-cept of efficient training.

Lydiard's methods are not geared towards immediate results. He speaks of progres-sing over several years and sacrificing early success to lay the groundwork for bigger vic-tories later. Even within each season, you would not reach your peak until the last possible moment. Both of these concepts are implied when Lydiard wrote: "You will come to your peak slower than many others and you will be running last when they are running first. But when it is really important to be running first, you will be passing them."

The March/April 1992 issue of 'Peak Running Performance', a US publication which presents running-related research information, was entirely devoted to a study of Lydiard's running philosophy.

"His legacy", it said, "can be seen in the training schedules of most of the world's best middle- and long-distance runners. While Lydiard's coaching days ended about a quarter-century ago, his breakthrough approach to training remains securely embedded.

"After his great coaching successes at the 1960 and 1964 Olympic Games, sports scientists and exercise physiologists around the world confirmed the scientific soundness of his methods. While Lydiard was not a scientist, his overall training approach was well ahead of the scientific community of his day."

Lydiard's programme epitomises one general but very critical concept related to exercise and sports physiology. This broad principle is gradual adaptation. While most athletes would call this "plain old common sense", experience tells us that common sense is not so common – especially among runners who have a strong desire to improve their running.

The magazine illustrates the concept with the legend of the Greek strong man who lifted a calf when it was first born and continued to lift it each day until it was a full-grown cow. The day to day increase in weight was hardly noticeable although the increase over time was significant. With the Lydiard system, it says, this process of gradual adaptation can produce astounding long-term results.

Garth Gilmour

Chapter 1: The Twentyone Factors

Twentyone factors influence the running athlete. Some are factual, some physical, the rest mental. All of them play a part in how well an athlete performs, how successfully he or she can reach whatever level of achievement he or she aspires to.

Here they are:
• The date of the race
• The challenge the race represents
• Age
• Talent
• Health
• Nutrition
• Drugs
• Hormones
• Body build
• Running technique
• Aerobic capacity
• Weight
• Body fat
• Training methods
• Coaching
• Tactics
• Self-discipline
• Track conditions
• State of the weather
• The opposition
• The balance between aerobic and anaerobic exercise

Some of them appear under more than one heading. For instance, your weight and body fat at any given time are facts but they are physical conditions which can be altered. And there are some physical conditions which are susceptible to mental influences or can influence mental attitudes. Each is an integral part of the whole athlete and his or her little personal encyclopedia of knowledge.

We have not given them any order of priority because none exists but, perhaps, the single most important factor of them all is the first listed – the date of the competition.

Think about it. You do not have to be an Einstein to see how significant that race date is. Whether the race is a club championship, a national title event or an Olympic Games final, everything that happens in the lead-up to it – and we're talking from weeks to years depending on the individual athlete's level of experience and ambition – is aimed at that single event. Anything else along the way is merely a stepping stone to the ultimate goal. So, everything the athlete does in that lead-up has to be timed correctly and precisely to produce the peak performance when the starting gun sounds on the big day. If you doubt that, listen to any group of athletes talking after a championship.

They are noted for their excuses after events and a great many excuses followed the 1990 Commonwealth and 1992 Olympic Games. A lot of those Olympic titles were won in times that very many competitors had comfortably bettered. Yet, on the day, they could not perform anywhere near their best. This was particularly so in the 10,000 metres. It was won in 27 m 46 s, yet there were runners in the field who had been close to 27 m flat and could not even break 28 m on the most important day of their running careers.

This demonstrates that the race date is indeed the key to correct training. I often tell young people, "Look, last year, you ran the best race of your career. Everything went right and you performed at your very best. Now, if you know why that happened and you put your training plan together properly to reproduce that peak performance again on the day of the first race you want to win this season, then I would say you know something about training.

"Until you can do that, you don't know a damn thing about it. You are just a good athlete who, one day, without realising why it is happening, will run a good race."

I often refer back to Lasse Viren, who, after his first Olympic triumphs, was injured and out of running for a couple of seasons but then came back as great as before. The American accused him of blood-doping, which was ridiculous. The reason was simply that I had taught the Finns how to construct a programme and follow it to achieve peaks when they wanted them – and the Finns had listened and learnt. Viren knew the programme that got him his first Olympic medal; all he had to do to win some more was repeat it.

Many of the medal winners in the 1992 Olympics were not the **best** athletes but they were the **best-prepared** athletes on the day of competition. I cannot emphasise this strongly enough: A world of difference lies between the two.

The 1992 Olympic 10,000 was the perfect example. Once you have achieved that peak, of course, that's not the end of it. You can go on, holding that peak from race to race, until your condition starts to deteriorate. Then you go back and rebuild.

So that, fairly succinctly, is what this book is all about: Guiding you to get all those 21 elements together in the right place at the right time for you to attain your selected goals in athletics.

Let's begin by considering why running is for everyone – from potential Olympic champion to the woman or man, girl or boy who merely wants to get that extra enjoyment and satisfaction out of life that spring from simple physical and mental fitness.

Chapter 2: Why is Running Valuable?

The key that opens the first door to that goal is oxygen. We can be healthy without being fit. Or we can be fit without being healthy. What we need to aim for is both fitness and health. The first fundamental we have to recognise, in trying to reach this happy combination of both, is that nearly every metabolic reaction in the human body depends, directly or indirectly, on oxygen. The key, therefore, is to achieve the best oxygen uptake level possible to feed the metabolic processes.

The second fundamental is that the only way we are going to get that higher oxygen uptake level is by steadily exercising over long periods – and the only way we can do that, day after day, is by maintaining the exercise at an aerobic level, not an anaerobic level.

What's the difference? Aerobic exercise requires the presence of oxygen; anaerobic exercise does not. A muscle can contract for a while under the anaerobic conditions of inadequate oxygen supply but, sooner or later, the restoration of an adequate oxygen supply is essential for the recovery of that muscle or it ceases to function efficiently.

Drs Laurence Morehouse and Augustus Miller in their 'Physiology of Exercise' say quite simply that aerobic metabolism is far more efficient than anaerobic metabolism because more energy is derived from a given amount of foodstuff when the reactions occur under aerobic rather than anaerobic conditions.

So it follows that aerobic activity can be sustained by drawing energy from the oxygen we supply to the operating muscles and, the more efficient the supply, the more efficient and enduring will be the activity.

This brings us to the heart, the large pumping muscle which transports oxygenated blood from the lungs through the bloodstream to supply those muscles. We have to teach that pump to work progressively harder to take more blood with more oxygen to where it's wanted. Only one set of the body's multitude of muscles can work long enough and hard enough to maintain a reasonably high aerobic pressure on the blood vascular and cardio-respiratory systems to achieve that desired result. They are the quadriceps, the large muscles at the front of the thigh.

An evaluation of various sports has proved that the activity that best produces this consistent aerobic pressure is cross-country skiing. It works all muscles but it works the quadriceps best. Not everyone is in a position to go cross-country skiing all the year round but, fortunately, next comes an activity which is available to virtually everyone – running.

Running lifts the body weight against gravity, largely using the upper leg and thigh muscles hard enough and long enough to get a better result even than cycling, which ranks next, rowing or walking.

Swimming, for instance, is well down the list because the body weight is buoyant in water. Once swimmers reach a level of endurance and technical skill, they can go through the water fairly well without too much strain and without exerting that required level of pressure on the heart that running achieves. Compare swimmers at the end of a 1,500-metre race with runners who have just competed over the same distance.

To use running as the cornerstone of fitness depends on the development of a programme that enables us to maintain that aerobic pressure at its upper limits – just short of tipping into anaerobic effort – for long periods.

You cannot build a house without a solid foundation; you cannot build good physical condition without a sound aerobic foundation. We can use a variety of exercises to develop muscular efficiency and strengh but we also need muscular endurance to acquire real fitness.

One of my favourite photographs is of two large German shotputters standing on either side of a girl marathon runner. Her weight is half that of the shotputters but tests determined that she had twice their cardiac output. These huge men, briefly, could move heavy weights a considerable distance but both had poor blood vascular and cardio-respiratory efficiency. The small girl's, developed by long aerobic running, was 100 per cent better.

Particularly as we get older, we need not only good muscular strength to keep our muscles toned, we also need to improve our cardio vascular system. We breathe in a lot of oxygen but, unless we have that efficiency, we also waste a lot. If we can improve the blood flow per minute from heart to lungs and back, we create the opportunity to assimilate more of that oxygen.

And, of course, once we get the extra oxygen into the body, we can improve the circulatory system. We know from testing older walkers, distance runners, cyclists and other athletes that their circulatory systems are very well defined and efficient; many times more developed than those of sedentary people.

To improve our ability to transport more oxygen and then use it and our blood sugars through muscular endurance, we need good capillary beds. These can be developed quite substantially by continuous aerobic use of muscle groups over long periods.

All living cells, plant and animal alike, contain mitochondria, aptly called the powerhouses of the cell system. Mitochondria metabolise carbohydrates and fatty acids to carbon dioxide and water and release energy rich phosphate compounds in the process. All the activities of life – growth, movement, irritability, reproduction and others – require the expenditure of energy by the cells but the number of mitochondria per cell may range from a few to more than a thousand. Mitochondria move, change size and shape and fuse with each other to form bigger structures or split apart to form shorter ones and are usually concentrated in the region of the cell with the highest rate of metabolism.

Living cells are not heat engines and cannot use heat energy to drive these reactions. Instead, they must use chemical energy, chiefly in the form of energy-rich phosphate bonds.

Adenosine triphosphate (ATP) is the chemical which is the source of our energy. The ATP stored in the working muscles is sufficient to work for only a few seconds but the muscles also contain creatine phosphate, which is there for rebuilding ATP. It, too, is limited – to about 15 to 20 seconds of strenuous exercise.

This is where the delicate balance between aerobic and anerobic exercise plays its part. A marathon runner, employing a moderate work-rate, can get enough oxygen to economically burn fat and glycogen. This enables ATP to be rebuilt as fast as it is being used and the trained runner, working aerobically, can continue for several hours – in the case of the elite ultra runner, for day after day of steady aerobic output.

What happens when the runner sprints or shifts his work-rate into the anaerobic phase is that oxygen is no longer absorbed fast enough for the fat and glycogen breakdown. The body will then cheat and break down glycogen without oxygen.

The difference is that aerobic metabolism produces innocent wastes, water and carbon dioxide; anaerobic metabolism produces lactic acid, which, as it accumulates, progressively prevents the muscles from contracting.

The anaerobic system will function temporarily even during a long run at a basically aerobic work-rate – when you tackle a tough hill or kick in a burst of speed, for instance – and certainly will when aerobic metabolism can no longer supply the energy you need to sustain your pace. In fact, even when you begin a run slowly, you are likely to be running anaerobically until your aerobic mechanism reacts and takes charge. This should be borne in mind to guard against going out too fast at the start of a race or training session or failing to warm-up adequately to prepare the aerobic mechanism.

No matter how hard or deeply you breathe, the oxygen your muscles can use is limited to your maximal aerobic capacity, or maximum oxygen consumption, known as VO_2. It is calculated by the amount of oxygen you can consume each minute divided by your fat free weight. All other things being equal, therefore, the large person can use more oxygen than the small one.

VO_2, naturally, varies widely. A normally active mid-twenties male can use between 44 and 47 ml of oxygen for each kilogram of fat free weight each minute. Top endurance runners can lift their capacity to more than 70 ml/kg/min. Women score, on average, lower than men because, pound for pound, their muscle mass is less. But the gap between male and female VO_2 capabilities is reducing rapidly as more and more women work to training schedules as tough as men's.

How widely the VO_2 can vary can be seen in any marathon race.

The top runners will be cruising aerobically on their high VO_2 at around five-minute miles; at the back of the field are runners who couldn't cover one mile at that pace because they would be completely anaerobic. Their lower aerobic capacity means they can run their consecutive miles only at a much slower pace.

In aerobic exercise, one molecule of glycogen forms 38 molecules of ATP. Anaerobic exercise yields only two. And Morehouse and Miller, in 'Physiology of Exercise', consider that severe anaerobic work is only 40 per cent as efficient as aerobic work.

The elite runner covers distances at high speeds aerobically because his or her muscles are able to break down and release fat from the fat cells and oxidise the fat as fuel.

During sub-maximal exercise, fat is the main fuel. When your muscles are metabolising mainly fat, the oxygen demand is greater than when burning glycogen, which means you either have to take in more air or slow down. Fat, therefore, is not the preferred fuel for fast running.

In shorter races, say, under 10 km, runners burn glycogen almost exclusively. When the marathon runner burns fat efficiently, the glycogen is conserved and is available for that fast finish over the last ten miles that wipes out the opposition.
Once you have established the base of muscular endurance, maintaining muscular strength and tone is attainable by developing the muscle fibre through the application of resistance – by lifting weights or running up stairs or hills.

Again, since the muscles contain both red and white fibres (otherwise known as slow twitch and fast twitch), you have to define exercises which work on both. No amount of exercise will change the balance of red and white fibres you were born with but you can improve their efficiency. The slow-twitch fibres are the best for aerobic metabolism, the powerful fast-twitch fibres for anaerobic metabolism.

The diaphragm and extensor muscles that maintain posture are red or slow twitch muscles; muscles in which the white fibres predominate, including most of the flexor muscles, are specialised for speed and tire more easily.

Essentially, we have to develop oxygen uptake to make our body machinery function better. The net results will be, hopefully, a delaying of the aging process and, certainly, an improvement in both muscular and mental endurance. We will find that, when we don't tire physically, we don't tire mentally either.

I have proved this in training high school boys and girls. Not only did they improve as athletes, they also became better students. They were able to study longer and more effectively without suffering from mental fatigue. Quite a few who became national athletic champions were also duxes or top academic pupils at their schools.

In Finland, one newspaper took me to task, declaring that the training programme I was laying out for high school boys was too severe and would affect their studies. Three of those boys won Finnish high school championship events and one of them became dux of his school.

There is no necessary distinction between the sporting jock and the academic swot; the one attribute goes hand in glove with the other. They can be the same person.
The high oxygen uptake levels of properly trained athletes feed a better oxygen supply to all parts of their bodies, including their brains.

Chapter 3: The Basic of Youth

The great Swedish coach Gosta Holmer, head Olympic coach in 1948, said that if you can get an athlete in his teens to train but not race until he is mature, you will have laid the foundation for an Olympic champion. It's an ideal I've always agreed with, the reason why I've always insisted on taking the long view with athletes who want to become champions in a hurry. There are no safe shortcuts.

I was in Kenya again recently and was reminded once more of the lesson the African athletes have given us since they began dominating middle and distance running around the world. Part of their way of life has been doing exactly what Holmer preached.

In Kenya, as in other African nations, many youngsters run to and from school every day of the school year. No cars, no buses, just their own legs. A youngster called Biwott, for instance, ran ten miles to school and ten miles home again five days a week – one hundred miles a week. He became an Olympic champion at the 1968 Games in Mexico, which illustrates how long the message of this great potential for success has been around. These kids run because it's the only way for them to go. They run with no pressure on them, no racing except in fun, and all the time they are laying a wonderful foundation of high oxygen uptake and endurance so that, when they finally turn out in a race somewhere, many of them produce fantastic times. We saw this in the 1988 world cross-country championships when the junior Kenyans proved far superior to anyone else. Now the Moroccans, Tunisians, Algerians and others who are moving into the international scene are also running fast times because they, too, have done so much aerobic running as youngsters that they have a huge natural base on which to build speed and proper technique.

In the US, when youngsters show any form at high school, the tendency is to put them on the track and pile the anaerobic work into them. Consequently, they don't develop.

We know that young people, before they reach puberty and go through that fast growth rate, have the ability to use oxygen more efficiently for their body weight than adults. They also have highly sensitive nervous systems so they are protected by nature to be able to continue activity for a long time at the aerobic level. But they cannot stand heavy doses of anaerobic training and pressure from coaching regimes to race a lot. This occurs in many of the affluent countries, usually because sporting success is as good for an educational institute as academic success and success means better funding. These youngsters, therefore, don't develop their aerobic capacity sufficiently so when, as adults – if they're still interested in running – they come up against the Africans, their relatively low oxygen uptake level is no match for their opponents' high level. When the pressure goes on in a race, they lose knee lift, they experience neuromuscular breakdown, they can't sprint at the end – and the Africans can.

It's an anthropomorphic fact, of course, that the Africans have the advantage over Caucasians of larger gluteal muscles. They can do things to get more power that white people can't. They can actually lean forward and still get their knees up; the Caucasian has to stay much more upright.

But the American publication, 'Running Research News', recently cast new light on Kenyan supremacy by reporting the results of a study by Swedish exercise physiologist Bengt Saltin, of the famed Karolinska Institute in Stockholm. He compared seven elite Swedish runners with students from Kenya's St. Parick's high school, which, with a roll of about 500 students, has produced six world cross-country champions, four sub-2.10 mara-thoners and more than a dozen Olympians.

Saltin, reported 'RRN's' Owen Anderson, PhD, reckoned that thousands of Kenyan runners were just as good as the top seven Swedes but discovered that St. Patrick's athletes follo-wed incredibly simple training plans, which included a considerable mileage run as fast as possible on six days of the week. Running to and from school added some 10 km to 30 km slower running to the plan.

Saltin found the Kenyans had a small advantage over the Swedes in total anaerobic capacity (about three per cent). The Swedes' VO_2 max ranged from 76 to 81 ml/kg/m; the Kenyans' from 79 to 87. Each group had equal slow twitch-fast twitch fibre ratios but then Saltin found a significant difference in what lay inside and around the Kenyans' muscles.

They tended to have more mitochondria per muscle cell and more capillaries draped round their fibres. The Swedish runners had four to five capillaries per muscle cell in their quadriceps but the Kenyans had seven to eight, quite similar, Saltin found, to the world's best cross-country skiers and giving them a greater capacity to use oxygen and a greater resistance to fatigue.

Inside their muscle cells, the Kenyans had a higher concentration of the enzymes which break down fat and greater quantities of citrate synthase, a critical enzyme needed to provide muscles with energy aerobically. Reverting to Biwott for a moment, the American 'Sports Illustrated' magazine ran a big article on him when he won his Olympic medal, showing him in his home village, which was largely mud and straw huts. Here, the magazine said, was an athlete who had never had a coach, wasn't trained properly and didn't even have the right food but won an Olympic gold medal.

If we look at the situation sensibly, Biwott didn't need a coach. He was better without one. He laid the basis for his success with all that running between home and school with no more pressure on him than the weight of his schoolbag. He trotted along at his own pace, playing as he went, as kids will do when left to their own devices – and there was the best training he could get. None of the American way: The guy with 'Coach' on his back, a clipboard and a stopwatch in his hands, shoving kids through repetitions until they are falling down with fatigue, blacking out and vomiting because the oxygen debts they are incurring are so great their central nervous systems are being attacked. Many of them, who got their college education only because they won sporting scholarships, have told me since that they dropped running as soon as they graduated although they slowly drifted back to jogging and social running with friends and family. They had all had the competitive edge drilled out of them.

There have been many examples in New Zealand of top high schoolboys who, on natural ability, could beat everyone in the distance races, the road races and the cross-country events but then, at twenty or so, were no longer champions. With maturity, people lose the high oxygen uptake which is natural in children and these top runners hadn't trained to develop or maintain that level as they grew older. But the boys they had been beating, who didn't have the natural talent but had worked harder and more sensibly at developing their running, and maintained a high oxygen uptake capability as a consequence, went on to be the champions.

Peter Snell was only the third best 800 metres runner at Mt Albert Grammar School in Auckland. The best broke Murray Halberg's national junior mile record, the second best was the national 800 metre junior champion but Snell went on to beat the world. The others dropped out and disappeared.

And, as far as food was concerned, Biwott never went to a supermarket and loaded up with processed grains from which the producers had taken out about 18 minerals and vitamins and put only three back. 'Sports Illustrated' pictured him surrounded by beautiful fields of grain. When they cropped that grain, they didn't process it. They broke it up and beat it up and cooked everything. And it's another fact that Africa is possibly one of the last places on earth where most of the soil is still properly balanced.

So Biwott had the best training and the best diet. That's why he won a gold medal, contrary to what 'Sports Illustrated' was trying to establish.

So, if we are going to train children, we've got to encourage them to see how far they can run, not how fast. We've got to get them trotting along and enjoying it, using the parks and roads and cross-country, enjoying running as a pleasant exercise within their limitations. Setting them out to beat the other kids is contrary to the development of future champions.

Children are better equipped than adults to run distances. They love to run, to jump, to throw things ... it's all a natural release of energy. If you went into a street and said to all the kids there, "Come on, let's all go for a jog", they'd probably all follow along. In most cases, kids who seem idle and lazy only need someone to motivate them. If they have nothing to do, they'll probably get into trouble; if someone can give them a goal like going running or a game of football or cricket, they won't.

Years ago, the kids at the Owairaka Club in Auckland would turn up on Saturday afternoons with the harriers, go out and run two or three miles across country, come back to the club but, instead of lying around, they'd immediately start playing chasing games around the shed. They wouldn't be tired from the run; when they did get tired or, more likely, too hot, then they eased down or stopped until they were ready to go again. The endurance of children is a huge natural resource.

Girls can run just as easily as boys; when they're young, they can often run better. But as they develop and, as many of them do, get wider hips, they can't run as well because their physical changes prevent them from bringing their legs through as easily or as straight. They start to get knock-kneed and throw themselves around a bit. The tall, willowy build, what we might call the Swedish type, is physically best equipped for running. This is no hard and fast rule – I've seen girls with markedly wide hips develop into excellent runners – but it's common.

Another fact, of course, is that women, again as a general rule, have more subcutaneous fat in the muscles than men and, when it comes to real endurance, they seem to have an advantage. It's a natural storehouse of energy which they can use before running into deficit.

In 1971 in Copenhagen, two doctors specialising in cardiology put on a 100 km run which drew about a hundred starters. It was the first ultra I had seen so I was keenly interested in the outcome. And it was most interesting to observe that, at the end of that race, most of the men were lying down and relaxing and the women were still standing up talking.

They still don't run as fast as men, of course, because they don't have the same muscle power – probably about thirty to forty per cent less – although there are the inevitable exceptions of weak men and strong women. I would say, too, that their oxygen uptake level isn't as high, so cardio respiratory efficiency isn't as great although their cardio vascular efficiency could be. I could be wrong in this but the evidence seems fairly convincing.

This means they don't have the ability to run marathons as fast as men because they cannot generate power, drive and speed as economically as a man with his greater oxygen uptake capability. There is no reason why a woman will not, sooner or later, run a 2:18 marathon but they have the same limitations that I predicted about 30 years ago for men. I said then that, at this stage of human evolution, it wasn't physically possible for a man to run under two hours for a marathon; 2:05 would be about as fast as they would go. I think we're stuck around about there now.

The best marathon times for women have improved faster than men's best times in recent years because, until ten or twenty years ago, not many women ran marathons. Now, many women run marathons and they are training as hard as men, which is bringing their times down rapidly in comparison with men. Not that you can always go by times in marathons.

I always quote the Boston marathon as an example of a point-to-point race fashioned to produce fast times, because runners fall two hundred feet in elevation and invariably have a following westerly wind to help them along. Some years ago, I took a girl, Maria Moran, to Boston to help me with some seminars. Maria came from a place called Taiko at the foot of a South Island mountain range and I had trained her to be the New Zealand junior secondary schools cross-country champion. She'd followed that with four years on a physical education course at Otago University in Dunedin, most of which is built on steep hills. So, while we were in the US, I suggested she should run the Boston. "I've never run a marathon", she said.
"Well", I said, "I've trained you so you can run a marathon. Just get in there and run it."

So Maria ran it. She wasn't a heel and toe runner, she ran on the balls of her feet but she still finished in around 3:12. She just jogged through and didn't look as if she'd run around the block.

That evening, at the after-race function, someone asked her: "This is your first time in Boston?".
"Yes", she said.
"Well, what did you think of Heartbreak Hill?" the guy asked.
She said, "I never saw any hills."

They make a big thing in Boston about that hill but to Maria, with her background in hill training, it was just a bit of a rise.

Children can be started as runners as young as five or six, around the parks, jogging with their parents and so on and there's no reason why they can't go into short sprints at school or with track clubs. Sixty or seventy metres is the desired distance; the sustained sprints, from 200 to 400 metres, are unwise. Most kids have strong hearts and they love to win and, over the longer distances, they run fine and hard until they get to the straight and it starts to hurt. The risk then is that they'll push themselves to please their parents on the side or to beat someone in front of them.

Anaerobic training is what destroys young runners. I've had people complain to me that kids shouldn't do all the running that I prescribe; but what I have them doing is all aerobic and that's good for them. I do not use anaerobic training.

Think again of the Africans. They are doing aerobic training all the time as kids – and lots and lots of it. It's the main reason why they're beating most people when they become mature runners.

Kids have been running through the centuries. They mostly run barefooted so their feet develop properly and naturally. They're not, in most cases, getting into these stupid running shoes with all the gimmicks wich lead to problems. Their bones aren't set, of course, until they're mature but as long as they're running easily, no problems arise.

They're not going to hurt themselves because running, as part of whatever they're doing, is natural. Obese kids are an exception; they could need some attention in the way of diet and so on.

Chapter 4: The Development of Fitness

If we next want to add speed to our endurance, we move from basic running because we now need to use muscle groups against fast resistance, such as in isotonic exercises. We must also give them good rest periods, because the white fibres, the fast twitch fibres which dictate our speed, lack myoglobin, a red pigment chemically related to the haemoglobin of the blood and probably important as a reserve store of oxygen and iron within the fibre or in the transport of oxygen and iron between cells. This pigment gives its name to the red fibres, which produce slow, powerful contractions and are not easily fatigued. Morehouse and Miller discovered that if the tendon of a red muscle was cut and then sewn to the tendon stump of a white muscle, forcing the red muscle to take over the white muscle's function, its myoglobin content and resistance to fatigue gradually diminished, indicating that the appearance and endurance of a muscle are largely the results of the type of work it must perform.

If we're going to develop muscle bulk through the red fibres, we can use weights and resistance exercises, progressively increasing the periods of exercise and the weights and resistance employed. The balance depends on the sporting activity in which we are involved and how we want to go about developing muscular efficiency, strength and power. But it must all be built on that solid foundation of endurance, of stamina.

A lot of people sign on at gyms, pay the annual subscription and think, "Now, I'm going to be fit." Certainly, some of them are going to sweat a great deal and they will improve their muscular efficiency and strength and physique but, unless they improve blood vascular efficiency, unless they raise their oxygen uptake levels, they are really not going to be as fit and healthy as they would be if they had climbed into a pair of shorts and running shoes or on to a bicycle, gone out into the fresh air and spent their time on steady aerobic exercise.

It is a mistake to think that working out in a gym with weights and other activities is going to give you good cardiac efficiency.

During the 1974 Commonwealth Games in New Zealand, Drs McDonald and McLauchlan, who have a physiological testing laboratory in Wanganui, tested various athletes and came across an Asian weightlifter, who had a huge body and was extremely powerful but an oxygen uptake level that was less than one litre a minute. He was getting barely enough oxygen into his body to keep him alive, let alone healthy, despite his ability to momentarily lift huge weights. He faced the prospect that, unless he did something about it, he could be an early cardiac patient.

A properly fit high school boy or girl would have an uptake level of around four litres a minute and it is common for top athletes in endurance sports to have an uptake level of around seven litres. Cross-country skiers would be highest because they use all their upper body muscles as well as their legs against hard resistance.

The use of cyclo-ergometers, treadmills and running machines is becoming popular as a testing ground but we would make the point here that they don't always produce accurate results in the individual. Even some very good athletes, once they are wired up and wearing oxygen masks, perform poorly on these machines; they find themselves in an unnatural and uncomfortable environment and can be affected by claustrophobia. The air they are breathing is very dry because the humidity is low, the throat constricts and the uppermost thought in the runner's mind is to get the damned mask off, instead of concentrating on running with freedom, particularly when the technician is demanding faster and faster responses.

The researchers, allowing for margins of error, can get significant information from testing programmes but, for the individual, the best way to test for personal fitness levels, quite simply, is to run. Cover a measured distance on a fairly regular basis and you soon establish a pattern of time and effort that gives a good indication of progress. After-run pulse checks at, say, 30-second or minute intervals will quickly chart whether your recovery rate is improving.

Heart monitors which record as you run are also enjoying a vogue in this age of gimmickry but there is an inherent risk in setting yourself to run consistently at a certain heart rate. Your condition changes day by day, so do the climatic factors, so you could force yourself too much in following the dictates of a piece of equipment. How you run should be governed by how you feel on the day and by the simple catch-phrase I invented years ago, "Train, don't strain."

We all know during conditioning when we are going too fast and getting beyond our limitations and that's when we should ease back.

For instance, if you are recovering from a previous run and then go out on an extremely hot day or in severely cold or windy conditions and try to keep pace with the inflexible requirements of a monitoring system, you could find yourself straining – and not training. You could push yourself into anaerobic running and that is undesirable on top of a previous day's hard work, particularly when you are in a conditioning stage of your development.

The Americans work to a different catch-phrase which is totally wrong – "No gain without pain" or "No pain, no gain." That is not the way to train for steady improvement and it's one of the reasons why a nation like America, 250 million people capable of producing millions of runners, doesn't succeed particularly well in Olympic and other international endurance events. They could dominate if they stopped applying so much pressure on their athletes from school age onwards.

Some years after jogging began in New Zealand and William J. Bowerman, the University of Oregon track coach, took it home from here, the American physiologist Dr Kenneth Cooper set up an aerobic testing system in which you ran for twelve minutes and then, according to your age, were given a certain fitness grading. But age doesn't enter into it. Many fit people in their sixties and seventies would leave a majority of university students behind in a running race. And plenty of evidence exists of people in their twenties and thirties who have collapsed and died, while running, from undetected cardiac disorders.

You cannot classify anyone by age. The fit and the unfit are there in all age groups.

Other factors must be considered when fitness testing. Fat-free body weight is an important one because running requires about 1.7 ml of oxygen per metre for every kilogram of fat-free body weight. If you are double my weight, you are going to be at a disadvantage. So, when we run a mixed bag of people for twelve minutes, without taking that factor into consideration, a lot of the light, skinny runners are going to run farther yet, fundamentally, they may be no fitter then the heavier runners they are leaving behind. They could even be considerably less fit.

So the Cooper test wasn't accurate in that context and I believe he deleted the age factor later and used other parameters.

Psychological reaction is another factor. The big runners in fun runs, particularly those over hilly courses, where you have to use more calories and need more oxygen than in level road running, will be mentally deflated when they are beaten by lighter runners, not appreciating that it isn't an indication that they're not as fit.

The most valuable way to test your fitness level initially is against yourself, by checking your progress over courses you run regularly, by noting your recovery rate after running. If you begin quite unfit, your rate of improvement could be surprisingly rapid at first; but it will level off gradually as you approach your optimum or maximum oxygen uptake level – not that there is any real maximum because it is a factor still with a measure of infinity. No one can say positively what the limits are in blood vascular or cardio-respiratory efficiency. With regular controlled running, the upper level in any runner can be extended for many years.

The 1984 Olympic marathon produced a classic example. I was lecturing in the US earlier and was asked if I thought Alberto Salazar, who was winning everything at that time, would win. He had just changed his training methods so I questioned whether anyone thought he would even make the team. I didn't think the training he was doing, running around with oxygen masks on for simulated altitude training and so on, was correct. That shocked them a bit. (Salazar did eventually make the US Olympic team by finishing second in their national championship.)

When I was asked who would win, if Salazar wouldn't, I named the Portuguese Carlos Lopez. Their reaction was: He's too old, he's 36.

I said that was to his advantage because over the years he had been developing greater and greater cardiac efficiency, better capillary development and finer muscular endurance and, given that all other factors were equal, he would win because he would be able to maintain his knee lift and leg speed best.

That is exactly what happened. Over the final kilometres, Lopez just ran away from the field. Salazar finished eleventh or twelfth. He was, without doubt, a great marathoner but he changed from a training programme that was successful and the change didn't pay off.

Lopez was a fine example of self-improvement and that's the main motivation for many people in fun runs. They know they haven't a hope of beating the fast runners so what they do is try to improve their own times; in a sense, they run their races against themselves. Fun runs, since they are usually of five or ten kilometres, are good testing runs.

I recommend that an aerobic run over five kilometres or a test of how far you can run aerobically in fifteen minutes are the best for checking fitness progress.

Check your pulse rate when you finish and then every thirty seconds or so and, if you're getting fit, you will find it is going to come down and recover to normal faster. You may not have run the distance faster but you will have run more efficiently.

The resting pulse rate can be unreliable as a guide because it's subject to emotional variations and so on. I was once asked by a man at a seminar in Pennsylvania whether, if he took his pulse every morning when he woke up, he would build a good indication of his fitness level. I said, jokingly, that is all depended on who he was sleeping with. I was trying to impress on him that, even in bed, the pulse rate is subject to varying factors – hot night, cold night, deep sleep, restless sleep and so on.

One woman runner in New Zealand told me that every time her doctor took her pulse it was much higher than she believed it should be. I took it and it wasn't high at all. Then I remembered that the doctor she was talking about was a very handsome young man. There was the difference.

Every sportsman and sportswoman needs stamina, by which I mean the highest possible uptake level and muscular endurance, the ability to keep the muscles contracting consistently. Once those muscles begin to tie up, performance drops. Very few runners, for example, can maintain a good knee lift throughout a race because they lack the muscular endurance which comes from well-developed capillary beds in the upper leg muscles. Once the knees go down, stride length shortens and leg speed dwindles. That was the factor that Lopez demonstrated so well; he maintained his knee lift all the way to the tape.

This applies in any sport. When the Olympic canoeist Ian Ferguson came to me in 1983 and asked me to look at his training programme because he wasn't succeeding as well as he should, I found he was a well-built man with large, powerful muscles – partly developed in the high surf of New Zealand as a lifesaver – but without endurance. I set out a programme which required him to do a great deal of steady, long distance aerobic paddling.

When he went to the next world championship against the East Germans, who had never been beaten, he won the world title. He knew more about rowing than I did but I knew more about training for it.

After Ferguson came back to New Zealand, the seven class canoeists we had in New Zealand worked on a refined programme of mine, went to the 1984 Olympics and won seven gold medals between them. They now had their technical skills founded on a strong aerobic base so they could come out day after day through the heats and the semis, row right up to their optimum and recover rapidly in time for the next race. The schedule was perfect in the sense that we got the aerobic and anaerobic sections right at the right time. Everything was co-ordinated and balanced to produce top form on the day of competition.

I did the same in San Antonio, Texas, with Greg Lousey, who, at 32, was the fencing champion of the US but had been told he was too old for the LA Olympics and wouldn't make the team. He was a big man but he went out and ran 100 miles a week to my schedule, rode his horses, did his cross-country work, swimming, shooting and fencing, and not only forced his way into the team but won a silver medal in the modern pentathlon. He was a perfect example of what a good foundation of endurance can do.

Dr Uhlenbruck, from the West German Sports School, made a study of ultra-marathoners, people of all ages who could run 50, 60 and 100 miles a day for day after day. Max Telford, of New Zealand, comfortably ran 240 miles without stopping. Siegfried Bauer, an ex-patriate German who then lived in New Zealand, never put his shoes on without going for a run of 40 to 100 miles.

Dr Uhlenbruck came to the conclusion that if you use muscle groups continuously for long periods, even at the low levels adopted by some ultra runners in training, you very quickly develop the dormant capillary beds and also establish new ones and, as well, a mitochondria that will be likely to remain indefinitely. This, he said, was unquestionably the secret of muscular endurance.

If a boxer punches a bag steadily for two hours, without stopping – not fast but fast enough to keep the blood flowing through the muscles at an elevated rate – he will build the muscular endurance which will enable him to throw those punches hard and fast for the length of a 15-round bout.

Lionel Spinks, who won the heavyweight championship of the world, was trained on a tape I made for the coach and physiologist who controlled his training. This required him to punch the bag for long, steady periods. When he went into the ring, he was still throwing effective punches when his opponents were tiring to the point where they not only couldn't match his punching ability, they couldn't get out of the way of his blows.

Of course, when he met Tyson, he didn't get the chance to throw a punch but the point had been made – he won his other fights with a continuous barrage of punches because his arms, trained for endurance and with highly developed capillary beds, didn't tire.

Whatever the event, physiology and mechanics don't change. The fundamentals must be followed.

In New Zealand, we have seen the effect in rugby football, our national winter game. Years ago, I lectured in Hawke's Bay and the flanker Kel Tremain, who was in the audience, was fired up to run 100 miles a week to see what happend. He found it was too much for him, so we refined a programme which had him running an hour every morning as part of a conditioning system. The effect was that he not only improved his endurance, he got into the All Blacks, the New Zealand national team, because, at the end of a game, he would be running as fast as he had been at the start. He established himself as a leading try-scorer.

Des Christian, a friend who was an All Black many years ago, once challenged, "Arthur, all this running is no good to an All Black. Rugby is sprint, sprint, sprint."

Trying to make him understand the point he was missing, I asked him how many times he could sprint the length of a football field. He said ten. I doubted if he could do six one after the other but I explained that, if he could do ten and then set out to develop a higher oxygen uptake level, he could probably do twenty. He could never understand that but Tremain proved it. Tremain also had a wonderful effect on the Hawke's Bay team of that time. They used a friend of mine, who was also a physical education teacher, to refine the Tremain programme for the whole team and quite soon won the Ranfurly Shield, New Zealand's premier rugby trophy. They were not a team of internationals but a collection of run-of-the-mill footballers who, collectively superfit, could play their best football all the time when other teams were falling apart with fatigue.

Most people never realise what their potential is or understand the simple truth that it is based on their ability to assimilate, transport and use oxyen. If we can appreciate that and then improve that ability, we lay a better foundation on which to build the technical skills and reach a tireless physical and mental state in which we can employ those skills and techniques much better and for much longer.

If, for instance, you are a skillful soccer player but too tired to get to the loose ball, you cannot make use of these skills efficiently.

The first group of joggers we had in this country, more than thirty years ago, were mainly obese businessmen. Many had had coronary attacks. Their recreation was usually golf. The interesting outcome with most of them, after they had been jogging for some months, was that, not only were they feeling physically and mentally better, they were beginning to reduce their golf handicaps. It was an unexpected bonus for them but it was perfectly logical – their concentration and co-ordination over the closing holes of a round were much better than they had ever been. They were no longer finishing in a state of tiredness.

Blood toning and diet play a part in the ultimate conditioning. When I was in Finland, exercise physiologists were keeping a close eye on their top marathon runner and testing him regularly because he had an abnormally low blood count and they thought he might have some blood disease. They gave him B 12 and iron and liver injections to try to improve his condition. They never succeeded but the guy went on beating everyone. This had them confused but the fact was that, because he did all this long running as a marathoner, the improvement in his cardio-respiratory efficiency was so great that he could pump huge quantities of blood between his heart and his lungs and gather in a lot of the oxygen that other people just breathe out. Even though his blood wasn't what everyone thought it should be, he transported and used all that oxygen with complete efficiency.

I was involved in an unusual experiment in Oshkosh, Wisconsin, on one of my trips to the United States. A number of schizophrenic patients of the University of Wisconsin Outpatient Psychiatry Clinic, most of them suffering from depression, were started on a jogging programme and, at the end of ten weeks, seventy-five per cent of them had recovered from their depression.

The goal of their therapy was simple: They were taught stretching before and after running and then filled 30 to 45 minutes with comfortable movement – not to cover a particular distance at a set pace, just to jog. The researchers, two associate professors of psychiatry at the university, John Greist and Marjorie Klein, a running therapist, Roger Eischens, and a Madison doctor, John Faris, were all joggers who had noted that their own momentary blues virtually always disappeared while they were running.

One of their conclusions: "If there is any secret to the success our patients have had in treating their depression with running, it is that they have tried to run each day in such a way that they would want to run again the next day."

As an exposition of training, not straining, it's an excellent vision.

We had already seen similar results in New Zealand because many of the people who joined the jogging movement were inclined to be neurotic. They were self-centred, disinclined to be outgoing and largely treated their neuroses with nicotine and liquor. This all changed once we got them interested in the routines of simple jogging. The smoking and drinking, the outward effects of their neuroses, were either drastically reduced or stopped altogether. They became more confident and self-reliant, they began to enjoy meeting new people and throwing off their inhibitions.

Chapter 5: How to Start Running

Right, you 've decided you want to get into an activity or sport that will give you what you need most to get more out of life – not bulging muscles or super strength but a state of fitness of the Lopez kind. First, have a medical check. Tell your doctor what you want to do so that he will give you the kind of examination that will show whether you should or you shouldn't. As we have said earlier, even young people have died in fun runs from unsuspected and undetected causes. Young children can have health problems – cases are recorded of children dying in sprint races because no one knew they suffered from heart defects.

Don't take the risk of adding to the number. Very few doctors these days don't recognise the value of restrained exercise or don't understand its benefits.

Having got the green light, consider whether you really want to run. Some people just don't. Consider the options and find something you'll be happy with because enjoyment is one of the critical requirements of this project.

If you're a big person, possibly overweight, consider that when you begin running, you'll be slow and all that weight means you'll be hitting the ground hard. The faster you run, the lighter you hit. The sprinter, for example, doesn't run heel and toe. His centre of gravity is carried forward so fast he is landing on the balls of his feet. His heel will make only light contact with the track before he springs off his toe into his next stride.

The jogger comes down nearly flat-footed on the outside of the heel, rolls through on to the ball of the foot and then, ideally, pushes off again with the toes. So the correct shoes are a vital piece of equipment to handle that pounding. We discuss that subject in more detail in a later chapter because you've got to fit your feet into something that will take the jarring and thumping properly or, eventually, your joints are going to suffer.

Cycling is a good exercise for cardiac development and general fitness if runing isn't your style. You can row and get excellent results because it employs a legs-arms, arms-legs action. Swimming is beneficial but it does lose some effect because your body weight is being supported against gravity in the water.

Whatever activity you choose, the main requirement is that you keep the exercise of that activity within strict limitations. Most people, unfortunately, are competitive by nature, particularly if they have a friend or neighbour down the road who can run or cycle or row faster. They can be lured into pushing themselves to inefficient and even dangerous efforts as a matter of pride or challenge.

Look at cardiac development as a progression which lasts for several years, even the rest of your life. We are going to develop further and further as we go, as long as we don't thrash ourselves competitively from the outset. Your objective must be to make yourself a fitter person, not to beat the chap down the road.

Seek out the advice of the best people you can in the activity you're taking up. Don't be afraid to go to the champions; they like to help people. Ask people who are successful coaches or have been in the sport for a long time. They have vast reservoirs of knowledge, which they may not realise, but tap them and you'll make your own progress that much easier because you'll know the right things to do and the wrong things to avoid.

A good coach, for instance, doesn't have injured athletes. He knows how to protect them from hurting themselves and that's a subject for much deeper exploration and explanation in other chapters.

The stranger to jogging or running will follow his medical check by running easily out for, say, five minutes and then turning for home. If he makes it back in the same time, he's already learnt to move aerobically. If he struggles, he's gone out too fast. But even if he feels good on the way back, he doesn't make the mistake of finishing with a sprint. The ideal way to finish is always to feel that you could run some more.

That five-minutes out-and-back routine should occupy a few days to accustom leg and arm and body muscles to the activity. The beginner can then start adding time on his/her feet.

When you can do 15 minutes every day, or at least every other day, step up to 30 minutes, followed by two days at 15 minutes, another 30, another two 15s and so on. Always give your body adequate recovery. Then go out to 45 minutes, with two 15-minute days in between, and then on to an hour plus two 15s when you can handle it. Then you can start to bring up the intermediate days – alternating an hour, two half-hours, an hour and so on.

Now you can extend that long run as you feel. This is the most effective way to do it. Some people start running 15 minutes a day every day, then 30 a day, then 45 a day. It seems to be the faster way to achieve fitness but it will take them three times as long to achieve the goals they would get if they used patience. You cannot neglect those vital recovery days.

As we have said, the world's first group of joggers, in Auckland, were about 20 businessman. Most had had mild heart attacks. They were aged from 40 up to 70 or so. Inside eight months, eight of them ran a full marathon. Since they couldn't run 100 metres when they started, their results demonstrate the reaction you can expect from a systematic approach. One 74-year-old had had several heart attacks and couldn't run 50 metres. Inside six months, he ran 20 miles without stopping and had lost 60lb in weight. A friend just up the road lost 60lb in a year and has already tackled and completed a full Ironman. He's 47 and he had done nothing before he started. He was a huge man then and he's still bigger than average – the difference is that he is now fit and confident.

He is not an unusual case. One of the remarkable aspects of jogging has been the discovery by so many who have taken up running, even late in life, of potential they didn't know they had to be quite successful athletes.

They have found that, provided they keep training systematically and don't suffer any major setbacks – like being knocked down by a car, for instance – they can continue to improve and can even run better 10 kms or marathons after ten years of running than they could after two. This is the most significant result of the continual build-up of the basic ingredient in running, endurance.

This has been reflected in a number of sports with the emergence in masters classes of quality athletes who are comparative newcomers.

When you start jogging, you are almost certainly going to get sore muscles. By all means, try massage; but the important thing is to out and jog again the following day, even if it's for only a slow ten or fifteen minutes at the most. Allow your heart to push the blood around and raise the blood pressure and use the exercise to flush out waste products which are causing the muscular discomfort. Let the heart do the gentle massage for you.

If you stop the exercise until the muscle ache disappears, you'll have to begin again and work through sore muscles again. You'll have gained nothing.

Hot baths help. So does turning a cold hose on your legs as soon as you finish a run; or a wade in the sea or lake. You can use ice packs if any soreness is bothering you and follow it with an application of heat. The cold brings the natural cortisone to the area, which stimulates the circulation and helps the recovery process. The heat prevents stiffness.

Another source of soreness is the tearing of muscle tissue when you first subject muscles to a new exercise. They will probably have been gummed together all the time you weren't training. Increased circulation is probably the best remedy for that kind of soreness.

Chapter 6: The Technique of Running

Whatever sport you're involved in, you've got to adhere to and understand the mechanics. I recommend here a very food book by Geoffrey Dyson, 'The Mechanics of Athletics', which explains the mechanics basically and simply.

If you're rowing or cycling, you've got to get the seat adjusted correctly, set the distances and the leverages accurately, taking into account body weight and arm and leg extensions. In swimming and running, technique is equally important. The position and action of the body, the arms and the legs all matter.

Once the nature of the activity and the fundamentals of technique are achieved, we can add the endurance and strength to get the optimal results out of the athlete. Running, for instance, entails getting the right stride technique and then adding a longer and faster stride to produce the results.

To run correctly at speed, we've got to get the knees up so that the thigh is as near horizontal as possible. Not only can we stretch out farther but we can also bring the foot up higher behind, which shortens the lever established by the knee. The shorter the lever, the faster the action. So, if your foot comes up close underneath your butt, it's going to move through much faster than if it stays low to the ground all the time.

One of the reasons Carl Lewis is such a fine sprinter is because, in full motion, his trailing heel comes right up on his butt and then whips through very quickly. Other runners who don't get that high backlift have to bring the foot through a greater distance at a lower level and therefore lose leg speed.

So, a foot coming through low to the ground gives a slow stride; a foot coming through high gives a fast stride.

The difference between the long-distance runner and the sprinter? You can test this easily: Hold one end of a three-foot rod and try to move it to and fro quickly; then do the same thing with a six-inch rod. The short lever will always be easy to move faster.

That's why you always see sprinters in training doing a high, bouncing knee action, fast, fast, fast, bringing the knees up, bang, bang, bang, with the heel hitting the butt.

The Caucasian, unlike the negro, can't get his knees up high with his hips back and the body leaning forward so he has got to learn to run upright. The less you bring your upper body into running, the better. You should run as you walk, with the arms loose and relaxed and moving in a straight line, flexing at the elbow with the hand coming just inside the shoulder.

Highly-developed upper body muscles are not necessary in the runner. Lasse Viren was very thin in the upper body, Murray Halberg ran with an arm that was withered because all the nerves had been cut in an operation after a football injury. He just tucked it in beside him and never lost any forward momentum.

If we clench our fists – and I often see people running with weights clenched in their hand – we tighten the upper shoulder muscles and, consequently, start to get a shoulder roll. Something has to go back when you're running; it should be your hand but put tension on those arms and the shoulder will begin to roll and that's undesirable. The rolling action throws kilos of weight from one side to the other and prevents high knee striding because you'll fall over if you try it. Instead of going straight along over your driving leg, you lose forward momentum. Relaxation is the key to good running.

You've got to learn to relax and let the arms come through in a loose, relaxed manner. Because our knee lift controls our stride speed, we must have strong upper leg muscles with full endurance. That enables us to maintain knee lift throughout a race, something very few runners can do. So we need exercises which are going to develop this area and overcome muscular viscosity. We don't want muscles like a weightlifter or a gymnast, we want muscles like a ballet dancer, springy and bouncy, with flexible, powerful ankles. We've got to be able to straighten the back leg and drive. We've got to learn to keep up tall and drive hard right off the front of the foot. A lot of runners run with their legs permanently bent. They never straighten into that proper driving line. They're losing power all the time. So we need exercises, such as striding or bounding up a hill or stairs, to correct that.

The ankles can develop more speed than a lot of people realise. If all runners had the ankle flexibility and power of ballet dancers, they would be so much faster. Again, that needs special exercises, which we discuss later.

Percy Cerutty used to advise people to lift themselves out of their pelvis. Bud Winter, the greatest sprint coach the world has seen, used to say, "You've gotta run tall." Both were saying exactly what I'm saying.

Try to make yourself six inches taller when you're running. Get that feeling of always being up, not sitting in a bucket. We' re fortunate today that we have videos to help us in our technique. You can tell a runner he's sitting in a bucket but he can't visualise it. Videotape him and he can immediately see what the fault is and do something about it.

When I was conducting training camps in America, I could change runners' form within a week. We used video tapes and in a week we'd have them running like Sebastian Coe, bounding along with their knees up and completely in control. Correct technique applies to every event because, if you have any kind of fault in your technique or in the equipment you're using, for cycling or rowing, for instance, you cannot capitalise on your fitness, however good that is. So seek out the best advice you can get on these matters or you could be wasting valuable potential.

We're not talking here about skills of the kind you get in tennis and other sports of that nature.

Very few people know their potential. Until they get cracking and exercise properly and start to get the benefits, they never will know. You can't tell potential by looking at people or taking tests because endurance can be developed in anyone, providing they have no medical or health problems.

How fast or efficiently we can move our muscles will always be a limiting factor. We can improve speed with better technique but we cannot basically make a slow person very fast. But when it comes to endurance, we can develop that in anyone.

I've often told audiences, however mixed, that there is no reason why anyone of them could not go out and become a reasonably good runner. Physiologically, there is no reason why they couldn't all be trained to run many miles in a day and get up again the next day, fresh, and do it again. It can be done with the proper training.

As we get older, we start to tighten up. We need more suppling, loosening calisthenics, to try to maintain suppleness.

The average person tightens up much faster at 40 than when he was younger. So it pays, to eliminate muscle injuries, to maintain suppleness. Spend 15 minutes a day on stretching and suppling – I'm no fan for much more than that – but it does become an essential requirement to avoid torn muscles and tendons. It gives support to the tendons.

You see a lot of injuries in some sports because the training the athletes do tends to get the quadriceps too strong for the hamstring muscles and, when they pull their legs through, they pop a hamstring. The hamstrings should be kept stronger than the quads.

Cycling or running up stairs and hills will eliminate that problem. This is one of the risks with weightlifting, which tends to build overstrong quads at the expense of the hams.

The fad in soccer, rugby and league these days is for players to wear elasticised bandages around their quads and hamstrings to support them because they've pulled them but they should never have pulled them in the first place. Invariably, it's because their exercising programme is giving them that muscle imbalance, with the quads too strong for the hams. That's why my athletes always ran up hills and stairs – to get that balance right. I never had any problems with runners.

The muscle sheaths and tissue around the muscles are going to be torn and will bleed internally a little when you begin training. What you've got to do is go about it gently and stretch gradually until you get more movement in the muscles. Gentle massage or applied heat, such as swimming or a sauna, alternating cold and hot, will help that suppling programme.

Muscles always hurt when you first use them but the pain wears off gradually if you keep at it. If you get sore muscles and stop training until they recover, you're going to have a continual problem. Try to run easily through a sore muscle, as long as it's not too serious. You probably won't be able to use a muscle at all if you tear it but most muscle soreness represents no barrier to running. There is nothing wrong with using weights to maintain muscle balance, as long as you get someone to tell you how to use them, which muscle groups to use them on and what intensity to apply and in what sequence. Make one set of muscles too strong for its counter-balancing set and you run into trouble.

Triathletes don't have much trouble because their cycling muscles, swimming muscles and running muscles all balance each other perfectly. Mark Allen, one of the finest triathletes in the world, has developed a beautifully muscled body and he's never lifted a weight in his life. And he's never pulled a muscle either. His secret is that he sets his bike in a high gear and heads up the hills. This gives him superb muscle balance.

Getting seriously hurt isn't the best motivation for a fitness programme. So, when you begin running, the only thing you should be thinking of is the development of muscular endurance, of building capillary beds, of regular, long, easy training periods, at least two hours or more if possible. Don't stop for more than 12 or 15 seconds. The East Germans have proved that stopping longer retards capillary development. It's a question of how far you go rather than how fast.

Once you've built that foundation, you can increase the speed a little, although this will come naturally because, as you get fitter and raise your oxygen uptake level, speeds that were low anaerobic become high aerobic.

Chapter 7: The Path of Full Potential

When the point has been reached when an athlete, keen to continue improving, finds he cannot do it on his own, he needs to seek advice from a good coach or the most knowledgeable person he can find in his particular field. Joining a club is the best first move and singling out the best coach in the club is the second. Look for the coaches who are being successful, not the ones who are not. Training is essentially an individual thing. No two athletes are exactly the same; they have different strengths and weaknesses and only the best coaches can evaluate those differences and set out a programme that will strengthen the good points and eliminate the weaknesses.

The athlete must understand the training schedule he is following, its mechanical and physiological effects and the reasons why its pattern needs to be followed as closely as possible, day by day, as a systematic method of developing full potential. If it's properly balanced, that progress can be moved along quite quickly without risk of injury or strain. Excellent results should be apparent in a matter of months. It cannot be hurried and it cannot be followed haphazardly.

This book will give you many clues as to what should be done but no athlete can reach his full potential by reading books or by trying to go it alone. This book isn't designed to do that; its purpose is to show you the right way to run, to explain why it is the right way, and to set you on the road to discovering your capabilities.

But, to be successful at the highest potential level as soon as possible, every athlete in any sport needs a coach. Trial and error will work but it could take years of effort when the answers could be found quickly by working with a coach. You cannot stand back from yourself and see exactly what you might be doing wrongly or how you might effect an improvement.

Most of us don't know how good we could be until we train systematically on balanced prgrammes for about three years. There will be improvement in the first year and even greater improvement in the second but the third year's results are likely to be quite marked. You tend to jump ahead at that stage and then maintain a steady rate of improvement.

Placing trust in your coach is essential but your own input – through reading all you can about your particular sporting area, by learning at least the basics of physiology and so on – plays an important part. It will help you to understand why you are doing a specific exercise or going through a particular phase of training, what reactions to expect from what you are doing and what is causing those reactions. It will also help you to understand why, sometimes, a particular exercise might not seem to be working for you; then you and your coach can re-assess it and steer you on to the right track.

Nothing happens overnight and quite often the best coaches take longer to produce the best results. The poorer coaches may get early results but they can't continue to develop their athletes' potential beyond that, usually because they have overdone the anaerobic training far too soon in the interest of achieving that early success.

This retards the margin of improvement. The athletes don't come on as well as their early success suggests they should and they become discouraged and even less likely to progress to their potential.

A smart athlete soon knows if he's being led along the wrong track. We all know our limitations, we know when we hit the wall. But only the smart ones learn how to handle that knowledge efficiently. If you go out to do a specific bunch of repetitions or a long hard run because that's what the coach has ordered, you'll know when the effort begins to get beyond you and you start thinking, "This is where I've got to quit."

Quitting then is what you have to do. Instead of going for hypothetical figures, such as fifteen 400 m reps in such-and-such a time, just run them until you feel, "Well, that last one got to me. Now I'm going to cool down and stop." This comes back to listening to your body as well as your coach. Coaches cannot always know exactly what everyone should do; they may be fairly good judges but the amount of anaerobic work a runner can handle will vary from day to day and from athlete to athlete.

Learning to quit when your body says it's had enough is important. There is no need to count how many reps you did or how far and how fast you ran; jog yourself cool and then give yourself a couple of easy days for recovery and come at it again. That way – doing an honest workout and stopping when you feel you've had enough – you'll build your anaerobic capacity without setbacks.

I would sometimes set goals for my athletes but we never counted what they were doing in repetitions and we never really knew whether they reached the goals, stopped short or went right past them. It didn't matter; the requirement was that they stopped when they honestly felt like not going on.

Cleaving strictly to a given schedule is not the way to progress. If your schedule says you are to run ten miles but you don't feel like running even one, don't. It's no good losing sleep if you were set to do twenty 400 m reps and did only nineteen. The goals in my schedules are optimum guidelines; they have to be modified to suit the conditions on the day, how you feel and so on.

This applies to all schedule training, not just the programmes in this book. They are merely guides. You quit when you've had enough. Your condition changes, the conditions outside change and that affects you and the times you're doing. Learning to make allowances is part of the mental approach to training efficiently. Slavish adherence to a schedule is inefficient. It's a wise move to learn what you can about what you want to do and write your own schedule. Then take it to a coach or a top athlete and ask for an opinion. They can explain how you can get perhaps better balance or be more systematic. This is a good way to do it because you begin to learn more about the objectives of training, to think more deeply about those objectives and their effects.

In building a schedule, you first must understand that one goal follows another. There is no value in going out and doing sprint training if you haven't conditioned the muscular system to handle sprint work. You cannot try to run fast five and ten kilometres if you haven't got the sound aerobic conditioning base.

The first step has to be to develop the cardio and blood vascular systems to high steady state and you 've got to get your muscular system into condition so you can add power and speed later without muscle pulls or other damage.

That means a big initial mileage. You concentrate initially for several months on purely aerobic running. Fast aerobic running if possible, keeping the effort just below that point where it can overbalance into anaerobic running. You must do as much of this aerobic running as you can. The minimum is three months. Four months is better, five is better still but anything less than three months is not enough.

During that period, you should be doing something about your muscular system. Get out and do some easy jogging as a supplement to your scheduled training and mix in a little bouncing, springing and running up hills or flights of stairs to apply resistance to the muscle fibres and develop more power and strength.

Hill running also helps flexibility. If you can't find hills or stairs, some stretching exercises and other calisthenics and weight training under a weights instructor will help. Approach them exactly as you do running – with caution. Don't try the first time to see how far you can stretch or how much weight you can lift. Apply gentle pressure and maintain it as you become more flexible and supple.

Chapter 8: How to set out a Schedule

After as many months of this that you can give it, you move into applying more resistance in your running and at a faster pace. This exercise, slightly anaerobic, involves hill training, up and down the hills, using three different exercises – bounding, springing and running – in a co-ordinated routine, and you'll employ some timed running over the hills as well. The purpose in all this is to use your body weight against gravity to build more powerful, springlike muscles; and to use the downhill running sections to build leg speed by striding out fast. At the bottom, you throw in some wind sprints to begin the development of your anaerobic capacity.

This is a transitionary phase of about four weeks so that, when you go into the proper anaerobic training phase, you will be able to handle some reasonable workloads without distress.

The heavy anaerobic period also lasts about four weeks and this is the time at which you develop anaerobic capacity to near maximum. It entails three days a week of heavy overload work and in this you can do any kind of anaerobic work you feel like. You can run straight-out long distance hard, say, three, five or ten kilometres; you can do hard repetitions over whatever distances you feel like; you can run hard on forest trails, if such luxuries are available to you.

You can run your repetitions anywhere. On the road, in a park – you don't need to measure the distance you're covering or count the number of times you run it. Keep on doing them until you hit the wall; your body tells you when it's had enough so you go and warm down and call it a day. The repetitions should be longish, at least 600 metres, to get the best reactions.

I have never used interval training because no one can determine exactly what anyone should do with intervals, distance run and numbers. You cannot do that successfully.

In conjunction with that anaerobic overload, you will work on your leg speed with typical sprint technique running and leg speed exercises.

Then, in the last six weeks, you get into co-ordination work, getting the body used to the speed and distances at which you plan to race. You do a number of things in this phase but you drop the long repetitions in favour of short ones and wind sprints to sharpen the whole body and its reactions. The short, sharp technique enables you to maintain your anaerobic capacity at the level you've achieved in the previous phases. You mix it with easy fartlek – striding up and down hills, jogging, doing exactly what you feel like and enjoying it, which is what fartlek (speed play) is all about.

You'll do development racing – under-distance and over-distance events – at least once a week with another race adjusted according to your reactions in the previous race and the mood you're in. You won't forget that every day of hard work has to be followed by a day of recovery and you will maintain your balance of preparation with sessions of long stride-outs, fast but relaxed, to help you to capitalise on the condition you've achieved and build your speed even faster.

Once a week, you go for a long, steady run of an hour or an hour and a half. Once you get into racing, you train to race, you don't train to train, so the work is very light and anything anaerobic is short and sharp. Any long running is not too far or too fast.

When you go into racing, you've got to appreciate that training is finished and the aim now is to keep fresh and sharp. It is important to recover from hard racing by jogging one day and the following day doing some easy stride-outs. Throw in some wind sprints if you think you're in need of more sharpening but your energy must be conserved for the races. If you have a good background of conditioning, you can hold your form for a long time, provided you make sure you recover fully from races. Cut the conditioning short and your recovery rate won't be so good and you won't be able to sustain good racing form for too long.

There are other ways of racing. If you are in good condition and have gone through a thorough training programme but plan either just one major race, a championship, for instance, or a season of social running, with five or ten kilometre runs most weeks, you can mix your training, keeping a balance, and you can maintain your form or even continue to improve it from the actual racing. I have set out a race week/non-race week schedule which can be used for cross-country, road racing or even track racing.

You bring in every element of training that's important; the week you are not going to race, you train harder, and the week you are racing, you back off. You do not want to be racing seriously every week on the road or cross-country. The hard week brings in some harder anaerobic volume work, some fartlek, some long aerobic running, some technique or actual speed training and probably a couple of trials run at less than full effort to bring about co-ordination. You do your longish run as well.

In the week you are going to race, you do some short, sharp wind sprints, a little easy fartlek work, an under-distance trial, maybe some stride-outs and some jogging. You cut your long, steady run down.

This is a programme designed for people who want to enjoy their running without aspiring to be champions and get a lot of fun out of racing consistently at a personally satisfying level. It doesn't pay to try to race 10 km every week but you could easily manage that distance every two or three weeks, with maybe 5 km races in between.

You can comfortably run a half-marathon once a month or every six weeks and you can run a marathon every couple of months, provided you make sure you get full recovery from hard racing. This is where the problem is: People think they are fully recovered when they are not and consequently start to pull their condition down. Race too often before fully recovering and you invariably suffer for it. You get injuries or fail to recapture the good form you had built up. You are pushed back into retraining, which represents a vast waste of time and effort. It is best, after a half or full marathon, not to do anything fast for about two weeks. Just jog nice and easily right through that period. You could add a little fartlek but don't get involved in anything too strenuous or exacting. The fear that you might be losing condition is unfounded.

We have seen a lot of good marathoners last for two seasons, then go down and never come up again because they race too often. They race a hard marathon and soon after are racing hard 10 kms, maybe because they are chasing money. They have about two good years before they go flat.

The school of thought that says you should not run more than two marathons a year is espousing a lot of rubbish. You can handle a lot of marathons; but when it's a question of racing a sequence of hard marathons there have to be some limitations. Anyone can go out and run a 42 km every week but when you race every marathon, which means you will come in very, very tired, you should aim at no more than one every two months at the most.

Again, the key is that you make absolutely sure you recover from one marathon effort before you begin setting yourself up for the next one.

New Zealand's John Campbell, probably for a period the best masters marathoner in the world, raced quite a few marathons a year and never seemed to have suffered from the effort. He tended to get faster.

Have a look at the backgrounds of some of the people who come up with these negative pronouncements and see who they've produced in the way of champions, what their authority is based on, what their experience is. Mostly, there is not a lot there.

The New Zealand ultra-marathoner Sandra Barwick made a valid point when she ran her first Sydney-Melbourne road race in about seven days and, in New York six weeks later, was the first woman to run a 1,000-mile track race. One long, steady, controlled race supported the other. In 1992 she made a 2,000 km charity run the length of New Zealand, timing it so that she arrived in Rotorua for the annual marathon round Lake Rotorua, completed that distance in 3:54 and then carried on with the rest of the charity run.

The previous three days she had run 100 km a day; the day after she ran 110 km, which took her over a range of mountains. Great marathon training. She had a best marathon time of about 3:20 before she switched to ultras, the kind of steady running that laid the basis for her extended running.

Chapter 9: Injuries

Most injuries runners experience come from running shoes and we discuss their defects that can lead to the injuries in Chapter 10.

I strongly recommend that anyone who is breaking in new shoes asks someone to run along behind for a while to check whether there is any sign of pronation or supination. Most people don't know they are doing either until it's too late and some damage is being done.

If there is evidence that your ankles are turning inward or outward, it doesn't necessarily mean you are a pronater or a supinater, it's probably simply because the lasts the shoes were made on weren't balanced and are pitching you one way or the other.

It's not normal for people either to pronate or supinate. When we all ran around with bare feet, we never needed orthotics; we didn't begin experiencing these troubles until we got into these specialised running shoes with stabilising bars and counters and all these things they put into them.

We trained on hard surfaces and did big mileages on hard surfaces. Invariably, we wore ordinary tennis shoes built up underneath with plenty of microcellular rubber because they were very flexible and allowed our feet to function normally.

It has to be recognised that, although they're expensive and make grandiose claims, a lot of these shoes are no good for the kind of training people are buying them for. They don't offer enough protection and in some ways retard the normal movements of the feet.

This can lead to the sides of the knees being strained and even the hips can feel the effects. If the resilience of the shoe sole isn't sufficient, it can lead to knee troubles, hip troubles, ankle troubles.

Some people might find the solution with a pediatrist but I don't believe as many need to go to pediatrists as do; all they need is a flexible shoe that's balanced and won't throw their ankles either inward or outward.

We talk about the loss of toenails and injuries to the feet generally. Let's move higher.

Runners get a lot of knee problems. This is because most of us do a lot of our running on cambered roads and if our shoes are not tightly laced on so they will not roll under our feet, damage can be caused to the miniscis and cartilage in the knees.

This won't occur immediately and may even take years to develop but it pays to think about it at the outset and protect yourself against the possibility.

If your shoes aren't resilient enough in the sole, all of us, when we start running, will hit the ground hard enough to risk some injury.

It follows that big people, particularly those carrying too much fat, will hit hardest and be at the greatest risk. They would be well advised to do all their initial running on grass until they lose some of their weight, can run faster and therefore more lightly and have developed a correct running technique.

Chondramalacia

A common knee injury is chondramalacia, which is felt just below the patella and is invariably brought about by runners not stretching their quadriceps before they exercise. The quads are powerful muscles and if they are still tight when you begin running, they will not stretch when you bend your knees and this will pull the tendons, which are anchored on soft bone under the knee, and hey presto, you're a chondramalacia victim.

The stretching is simple, either by doing squats or by standing alongside a fence or wall, supporting yourself against it and swinging the inside leg backwards and forwards, alternating between a bent and straight knee. Keep this exercise going for both legs until you feel comfortable and relaxed in the muscles and sinews of the upper leg.

Hamstring Pulls

Hamstring pulls are also common, usually because the quadricep muscles are too strong for the hamstring muscles. This is a common failing with people who lift weights because they develop the quads at the expense of the hams. Then, when they pull their legs through fast in sprinting, they pop a hamstring. Muscles have to be strengthened in a balanced way. One of the best ways to correct the imbalance between quads and hamstrings is hill or stair running, not fast but with a good knee lift so that you feel the resistance on the muscles you are trying to strengthen. This is not so much a bouncing action, which we do more for ankle strength and flexibility, but slow, positive running.

Many of the footballers you see playing with hamstring supports invariably would not need them if, during conditioning training, they ran up the stadium steps a few times each day. Regular attention to that kind of exercise would probably eliminate hamstring troubles altogether.

I used this technique for a gridiron team in the States who were experiencing a lot of hamstring breakdowns. The university was in a flat area with no hills so the coach built a ramp to a first floor balcony, covered it with coconut matting and ran the team up and down it. They also ran the stairs inside. The next season, they didn't have hamstring problems.

You're unlikely to damage a hamstring simply by jogging. It's when you start sprinting it hits.

Muscle Tear

This is damage to the muscle sheath. Unlike a strain or a sprain, which is general, you can usually place your finger right on the spot that's damaged and tender. The muscle, of course, won't contract and this can be quite painful, depending on how big the tear is.

The best thing to do is to make that area as cold as possible, with ice packs or cold water, to stop the internal bleeding because the more blood gets out between the muscle sheaths, the longer you are going to have in recovery. Avoid massaging muscle damage of this nature for at least four days. And don't use it either.

Sprains

Quite often, by slipping on the stairs, stepping in a hole or on a stone, we twist an ankle severely. It's going to swell up quickly, so again you should apply ice as quickly as possible and then bandage it quite tightly. Rather than elevate it, use it.

I have proved many times that a sprain recovers faster if it's used. I had a bad sprain in Munich the day before I had to be at the Olympic opening ceremony. My foot was so swollen I didn't think I could put it on the ground but I got out and walked on it that afternoon for some distance and the next day it was perfectly all right.

Minor sprains, which can occur frequently on jogging runs, can be run right through without risk. Just keep going; it may be quite painful for fifty or a hundred metres but then it will vanish. It is more likely to get worse if you stop and feel sorry for yourself.

Some of the leg problems can be quite complex in their cause and cure; it is best in that case to see your doctor or physiotherapist and follow his or her advice. Don't play around with an injury if you cannot analyse it properly and it doesn't recover quickly. Get expert attention.

Blisters

Be very careful with blisters that open up. Some you may have to open up yourself if they're large. But always bathe them with disinfectants and keep medications on them to prevent them becoming septic. Blisters are often traceable to the wrong kind of socks, if you wear them, or foot movement inside the shoes because you haven't laced them properly or they are the wrong size.

One cause of blistering under the foot – hot foot, we call it – is failure to put shoes on properly. When you put your shoes on, jam your heels as far back as they will go and then lace the shoes up firmly. If you start running with even an eighth of an inch gap between your heel and the back of the shoe, the movement can cause friction, which causes heat and the possibility of the skin breaking. That loose movement can be particularly damaging when you are running downhill because your foot will crush forward and you could lose a toenail.

Some tightness may be experienced after you've been running a while because the foot has swelled slightly but you can fix that by stopping and loosening the laces. I've never known swelling of the feet to be a problem, despite what the salespeople tell you about allowing for swelling when you buy shoes and trap you into buying shoes that are too big for you to get that second-skin fit you need. Any swelling will be sideways, not longways.

Chafing

Chafing in the crotch, across the chest or under the arms needs the same careful attention to avoid infection. It's better to anticipate chafing and use olive oil, petroleum jelly or some similar lubricant to prevent it.

Stitch

Running doctor Jack Sinclair, who was a New Zealand mile champion, investigated the stitch problem and found that people riding camels got stitch because their diaphragms were bouncing up and down with the camel's motion and extending the ligaments that hold the diaphragm to the skeleton underneath the rib cage.

You invariably get stitch when you're running downhill and jarring more. The solution is to make sure the stomach muscles just under the rib cage are not only supple but also firm. Many people do sit-ups to strengthen those muscles but they don't do back-bending as well to stretch them; the result is tight, inelastic muscles so, when the heart and lungs expand, they put pressure on the diaphragm. Strengthening the stomach muscles is excellent but you must also balance sit-ups with back-arching exercises. Chesting a table edge or similar exercises will stretch all that area where flexibility and elasticity are as necessary as firmness. Hip-rotation exercises are also good for suppling.

Back Problems

A lot of runners get back troubles and quite often they'll do a lot of forward stretching exercises, which are fine for the outer back muscles, but neglect the inner muscles closer to the spine, which must be stretched the other way. An excellent method of strengthening those muscles is uphill running as part of the training programme; or you can lift light weights. Again, the main requirement is back-bending but you need to hold the position for a minute or so to get real benefit.

This, combined with sit-ups, will produce very strong back muscles in the right places to eliminate back problems.

Cramp and Calcium

Cramp is a common problem. Very little calcium is used for muscle contraction and the central nervous system but if you don't have enough for both during sustained exercise it will be taken from the skeleton, which will weaken that structure. The calcium supply must be sufficient to keep up with your metabolism or you'll almost certainly experience cramps because the muscles won't contract.

The best way to assimilate calcium is with vitamin D as a catalyst and preferably in a gluconate form for easy absorption. I always get my athletes to use Calcium Sandoz before marathons or triathlons.

Stress fractures (see below) can be caused by a calcium deficiency. The metatarsals and shins are subject to stress fractures from the shock of hitting the road. The skeleton takes a tremendous pounding and if it is weakend by calcium loss the risk is aggravated.

Older people particularly need plenty of calcium. Older women are prone to osteoporosis – which can often start in someone quite young – so they need calcium to protect them while they are running and to guard against osteoporosis. It would appear, in fact, that running with a calcium deficiency could encourage the onset of osteoporosis.

Stress Fractures

You'll know when you've got a metatarsal stress fracture because you won't be able to run properly. It will hurt severely. An X-ray won't show immediately whether it is a stress fracture; you have to wait ten days or so. But, if you think you have a problem like a stress fracture, get to your physio or doctor quickly. You cannot fix it yourself.

Shin Splints

Shin splints can be caused several ways. Quite often, in my experience, athletes' shoes are too rigid so that when the heel strikes the ground, the whole foot claps down. This is particularly noticeable in steep downhill running. It seems to damage the tight front muscles of the shin. I guess the membrane between the muscle and the bone ruptures to a degree and the nerves start to get irritated. Another cause seems to be tight ankle muscles which prevent the ankle from flexing properly, or tight muscles under the calf, so that, when you run, the back and forth extension of the ankles pulls the muscles.

Circulation in the shin area is not good so it seems to take a lot longer to recover from shin splints. Once again, you must use ice and, if you want to run, stay on the flat, preferably on grass. Whatever you do, don't run downhill. Uphill running is okay but walk down to avoid jarring the legs. Recovery will be reasonably quick if you're careful and, again, your physio can help.

Because shin splints can be so troublesome for such a long period, prevention is eminently better than cure and the best prevention is flexible ankles. You have to work on them – a good method initially is by standing on a stair on the balls of the feet and lifting up and down to give full extension to the sinews and muscles both in front of and behind the legs. Later, when you are ready for it, hill bounding or springing will work exceptionally well. Like any other exercice, it's one that has to be worked at steadily. They are also good exercices for foot flexibility.

Bursitis

Bursitis at the back of the heel is caused by the backs of some running shoes biting in just underneath the achilles tendons. If you damage bone and flesh, you start to get a gristly growth an the bone and this can get bigger and become more and more troublesome until it starts to push on the achilles tendon itself.

Some people have bulbous heels, others are pretty much straight up and down – they are the ones likely to have a bursitis problem. More and more running shoes these days are made with a u-shaped cutaway at the heel to eliminate this problem. The first warning is when you feel pressure at the heel from the shoe.

A bursar that gets too big will require an operation for its removal. These are inevitably successful. If it's only a small bursar, avoid aggravating it and it won't get any bigger and you can probably live with it. It's a bit like the bunions women used to get through wearing shoes that were too tight for them and kept on getting bigger because they wouldn't change into shoes that were less fashionable but more sensible.

Bunions on runners' feet don't need to interrupt training. If you can't find a shoe with a wide enough fitting to accommodate the bunion, simply cut a hole in the shoe to let the bunion have its freedom; make sure the edges are softened and won't cause friction and carry on. It might not look much but its effective.

Heel Spurs

Heel spurs, which are growths on the bone itself, are an awkward problem. I developed one by jamming my heel down on some hard object. My doctor looked at the X-rays of the spur and said he'd operate but I told him there was no way he was going to operate on my feet. I went home and cut a hole in the inner bottom of the shoe so that the spur would fit into it. I ran my way through two pairs of shoes without any spur trouble; then forgot to cut the hole in my third pair and had been running for about a month before I realised I wasn't feeling the spur at all. It had gone.

If you have an acute spur problem and you can't overcome it the way I did, you're going to have to get medical advice. The condition is painful and can interfere too much with your activities to be left.

Cartilage

Cartilage and miniscis troubles in the knees occur in several sports, particularly in games such as football, which require quick twisting and turning at speed. What often happens is that, while the body is turning and rotating, the foot is firmly anchored to the ground by the sprigs of its boot. The miniscis, the pad inside the knee, and the cartilage, which goes around the bone, are forced to take the wrenching strain. Here again, they are not problems that occur in running, unless your shoes are not resilient enough and you experience a lot of jarring and pounding. This can wear the miniscis down and also weaken the grip between bone and cartilage.

Any pronation or supination is going to give you real trouble in the knees. It may not be the cartilage that is affected; it could be the ligaments or muscles around the knee that are strained.

The removal of a damaged miniscis or cartilage is sometimes necessary but I know many who have carried on running afterwards. The 1960 Olympic marathon bronze medalist Barry Magee, now in his sixties, is an example. His cartilages have gone but he still runs very well in masters events.

Elasticised Bands

Be careful if you wear elastic thigh, knee or ankle bands to protect weak areas. They can grip on the skin and rub it raw. They must be a type that flexes and won't curl up behind a joint and cause problems.

In America, they use a type of surgical stocking. It's like pantyhose material supplied in long rolls rather like cheesecloth. Cut a length off that and pull it on to your leg to cover any area you want to strengthen. You can double or treble the thickness if you want to. It doesn't move and it won't bunch behind your joints. If you're protecting, say, a hamstring during the recovery phase of an injury, it will enable you to run quite freely.

Chapter 10: Altitude

Immediately you step off a plane at high altitude, an increase will occur in your red blood cells. They will rapidly decrease again as soon as you return to sea level. This is a natural biological reaction which largely negates the apparent advantages of training at high altitudes for improved performances.

Two of the successes at the Mexican Olympics were the New Zealander Mike Ryan, who was third in the marathon, and the surprise winner of the 800 metres title, Dobell, of Australia. Both trained at sea level. They beat Mexico City's high-altitude problem because the name of the game in conditioning is to increase the steady state – the anaerobic threshold – to its highest possible level and they achieved that. They could push their pulse rate to a high level and maintain it there for a long time.

The moment you step off that plane, your steady state becomes lower, so you cannot train as fast and as far continually at altitude as you can at sea level. The pressure by the heart on the blood vascular system is lower, therefore the runner is not gaining as much benefit from the effort he is putting in as he would at sea level. So he would be better to be putting that effort in at sea level.

If you are a sea-level person, the best conditioning you can do is at sea-level – your natural habitat, if you like.

Anaerobic development is a limited factor. Only better conditioning preparation will give you a higher anaerobic threshold.

The best thing is to do all your conditioning at sea level and then go up. You can do speed work and so on during the six to twelve weeks needed for your normal blood change. Your anaerobic development will be commensurate with normal, though you may develop more red cells, but you are going to lose them quickly when you return to sea level.

When I was coaching in Venezuela, we ran a lot at Merida, which was 7,500 feet up in the Andes and at the bottom of a chairlift up to 15,000 feet. We would take that up to 11,000 or 12,000 feet, which was just below the snowline, and run back. A German doctor based at Merida told me many of his patients lived at 12,000 feet so I was interested in his views about altitude training and its benefits. He said he had concluded that if a sea-level person went up to 12,000 feet and had a family there, it would be three or four generations before offspring were born with systems which equalled those of people descended from a long line of mountain dwellers.

So, even if an athlete spent many months at a high altitude, the critical factor which would determine his success would be what happend to him when he returned to sea level. And what happens probably negates all the effort that has been made. Ryan and Dobell were far ahead of the altitude-trained athletes in Mexico. Only the Africans beat them.

I told the Soviets at the time that they were wasting their time concentrating on altitude training and the point was proved for me in Munich when their sea-level-trained runner Briginev proved their best runner.

The belief that you are at a disadvantage when you race against altitude-trained people is a psychological misconception, not a physiological one.

Chapter 11: Myths and Misconceptions

Hundred of thousands of words have been written about running for health. A great many of them are positive and a lot are pure myth and misconception. So let's look at some of the aspects of running that crop up in running conversation.

Running will help you to live longer

Well, it is safe to say that it can but we don't know for sure that it will. Seeing people now who, in the 1940s and 1950s, were athletes running a hundred miles a week in training, tends to confirm that it does because the physical appearance of most of them is relatively unchanged. Many are still highly physical and running extremely well in their fifties and sixties. Some of our original joggers from the early 1960s, and they were not young men and women then, are still running remarkable times.

What running does do – and we can say this with certainty – is make you aware of those things which are deterrents to enjoyable activity, such as smoking, drinking, eating the wrong kinds of food and so on; and if you change the pattern of your life by eliminating those, it's logical to argue that you're taking major steps toward adding, if not extra years, then at least better years to the end of your life.

This, of course, is the simplest effect of an increased oxygen uptake level. It's basic but it's a brilliant benefit – you do feel better.

Running will improve your mental capacity and confidence

Well, that's exactly so. There are instances all around us of people whose mental attitudes have been totally changed from depression to confidence and relaxation remarkably quickly. A friend of mine – we'll call him Bob – was in deep depression at the beginning of 1991 because his wife unexpectedly walked out on him after years of a marriage which, as far as he knew, was quite happy and stress-free. They'd just moved into a new home and he believed everything was okay. So the break-up really affected him badly.

I got him interested in running and within weeks he had completely shed all his hang-ups about the marriage and the reasons for its failure. He just wanted to get on with living his own life – and his first aim, after only a year of training and at the age of 47, was to compete in and finish an Ironman event. He did it, too. He had a great deal of bike trouble, including a broken chain, and five punctures during the 167 km ride, then lost his running shoes and had to borrow a pair which blistered his feet badly before he got his own back – but he finished inside the cut-off time and he was one of the happiest men on earth.

In the process of training that hard, he'd stripped of 27 kg of weight he didn't need and his whole nature changed. His former abrasiveness, caused by his depression, disappeared and allowed his sense of humour to take over.

I have seen this sort of thing happen so often through the years. One of the reasons, of course, is that people who take up jogging, whether it's just for jogging's sake or to help their golf or some other sporting activity, meet so many other people from all walks of life who have a common interest in just feeling good about themselves. This is an enormously important benefit.

When I conducted camps in America, we mixed up people in their seventies with teenagers. You'd think they wouldn't get on but when they sat down over lunch together you could see the common interest they were sharing break down all the traditional age barriers.

And class barriers vanished, too. We had lawyers and judges, carpenters and plumbers, college kids and school teachers and they all got along famously. The fact that a plumber could go out and beat a judge at running might have had something to do with it, if you want to take a cynical view, but it was really that common bond of fitness that got them all together. After all, the judge could probably beat the college kids – it works both ways.

Another basic is that we get into the habit of training because we feel so good after it and, if we don't train for a day, we get hit by a guilty conscience. We develop an abundance of mental and physical energy and we tend to protect that jealously and zealously by never missing training or hating ourselves when we do.

My friend Bob got to the stage where, as he said to me one evening recently, "Look, Arthur, it's getting late and I haven't run yet. I've got such a conscience about this, I've got to get out and do it."

Running should be avoided by anyone with heart problems

As we train, our blood pressure will invariably come down. Systolic pressure (the highest point at the height of the heart's contraction) and diastolic pressure (the lowest point when the heart is relaxing) will improve. It's because this is a direct effect of an improved blood vascular system that we put people with heart problems out jogging.

Careful jogging under close supervision from experts in heart problems, yes, but jogging nevertheless.

A pathologist in Hamilton, New Zealand, told me it was possible to develop the blood vascular system of a sedentary person twenty times because the body contains such a vast network of arteries, arterioles, capillary beds and small veins into which blood can be induced to flow by steady sustained exercise.

When I was directly training athletes in the fifties and sixties, some of them brought their resting pulse rates down by twenty to twenty-five beats a minute. Peter Snell's dropped from around sixty-eight to thirtynine or thereabouts.

This results in a significant effect on blood pressure. If the blood can move freely through an extended and expanded arterial system, the pressure is not going to build up in the aorta, which in turn eases pressure on the coronary arteries.

Cholesterol can kill you

Not so. We know now that there are good cholesterols and bad cholesterols, high density lipoprotein, which we have most of, and low. Some foods, even a little alcohol, can improve high density lipoprotein but exercise does help.

Modern testing of cholesterol levels can be quite misleading because the assumption is that the level has to be low or we're in trouble. But we all have to have cholesterol and some of us have a naturally high level.

I'm one of them. I remember Peter Snell, when he tested me in his laboratory in Dallas, Texas, got a shock at how high my level was. He started to look at me as if I was ready to drop dead any minute but I have always had that high level. It's not always an indicator at all of whether you're in good shape or bad shape.

Running heightens your sex drive

James Fixx said that sexuality is invariably heightened for both men and women when they get into shape through running. Well, I wouldn't be too sure about that; I question whether any man gets an erection every morning simply because he runs. And a lot of men who are by no means fit are pretty good at sex.

Dr Kerry Ragg, who used to be the physical education instructor for New Zealand air force in Auckland and is now in America, once produced figures which showed that fifty per cent of New Zealand men who died of heart attacks did so during sexual intercourse. He explained this to a group of air force ground and technical personnel who were so busy working computers and other equipment they didn't have time to think about keeping themselves fit.

They burst out laughing – but two of that group subsequently died of heart attacks while having sex.

I told this to Dr Uhlenbruck, the German doctor who went into muscle research relating to endurance and the capillary factor, and he said he didn't believe it. When I told him the facts were part of New Zealand Government official statistical data, he said thoughtfully, "Well, they couldn't have been having it with their wives."

Does running improve the ability to withstand pain associated with hard anaerobic exercise and competing?

Resistance to pain is largely governed by the organism's ability to stimulate the release by the pituitary gland in the brain of a pain-killing substance called endorphin. Some scientific evidence has now emerged that exercise helps in encouraging that release and may partly be the physical basis of the euphoria experienced by long-distance runners.

It's a natural genetic circumstance that some people can develop more endorphins than others. If you're one of them, you don't feel pain to the same extent.

If you have two people in a race who are equally fit, the one who can tolerate the highest level of pain is most likely to be the one who will succeed. When Ray Puckett and Merv Hellier, two of my early pupils, raced twenty miles cross-country for the Gold Cup in Wellington – I believe it's the longest cross-country race in the world – Puckett held about half a metre lead as they came on to the Trentham racecourse for the last mile.

Hellier tried all the way to get ahead but couldn't. Puckett reached the tape first, still only a half metre ahead, and dropped straight to the ground, completely out. Hellier, still running around, couldn't understand why Puckett was on the ground – but Hellier couldn't hurt himself like Puckett could. Puckett, because he could tolerate the pain, could run himself right out, which a lot of runners cannot do.

They can never do what Roger Bannister did in breaking the four-minute barrier for the mile. At the finish of that race, and again at the Empire Games in Vancouver, he ran himself out so that he could not stand up by himself. He had to be held up on his feet.

Because of the contribution exercise makes to the release of endorphin, you can handle that pain more easily when you have done a great deal of anaerobic training but that difference between two athletes of equal physical preparedness will always be there because that endorphin quality will stay more or less in the same ratio between them.

Is running bad for young children?

We have discussed the behaviour of children and their ability to use oxygen but they also, usually, have more common sense than the average adult. Adults will very often push themselves beyond their capabilities in the effort to succeed but a child, once he starts to hurt, will ease down a bit, even to a walk, and then start off again. At that age, winning isn't as important for most of them as it becomes when they are older.

We should all proceed like children in training, letting ourselves be guided by our own reactions. We should understand our limitations and keep within them. If we do that, particularly when we are training, we will get better results in the long run.
It's something children can teach us.

Do we need specific reasons to run?

That means motivation. We all need that, whether we intend just to get ourselves into a reasonable condition, or go out with friends who are social sportspeople or aspire to be great athletes. At all levels, we need to have our goals.

Good coaches can motivate people by assessing them accurately, appealing to their intelligence and making them realise their potential is far greater than they might have thought or, perhaps, lies in a more easily attainable direction. The runner who plugs away at miling without success might, for instance, be a winner over three or ten miles.
When we began the jogging revolution, the great motivation at the time was the wide awareness of the coronary problems that were afflicting many many people, mainly businessmen. Heart attacks were among the biggest killers. People knew in the back of their minds they should be doing something to protect themselves and they were inwardly worrying but they were doing nothing because they did not really know what to do that would safely distance them from the risk.

Once we explained the jogging programme and they understood that this was one activity within their reach that wouldn't, like many participatory sports, such as tennis or squash, place a heavy and potentially lethal strain on unfit bodies and hearts, they got out and started to do something.

This is one of the reasons why, if you're a jogger for the sole purpose of keeping yourself fit, it's much better to do it first thing in the morning, even if it means an early start to the day, because it gives a psychological boost to the rest of the day. You go off thinking, "Good, I've done my exercise for the day and I feel better for it."

There is nothing wrong with jogging in the evening, except that, if it's been a hard day, you have to drag the effort out of yourself and it becomes a temptation to start missing days. The psychological bonus is not there.

If a sedentary person can be motivated to run just fifteen minutes a day, he will immediately be winning back fitness. I know many of our early joggers had filled up on American statements that they needed to run an hour a day to achieve any progress; they were confused by the hundred miles a week regime followed by my leading runners; they were led to believe they needed to run a marathon before they could regard themselves as fit. But they calmed down once they were assured that if they ran for only fifteen minutes a day they would double their cardio-vascular efficiency within eighteen months.

We know now they can even throw in rest days and still get that remarkable benefit.

We know, too, that if we do more, we are going to get an even better reaction but it's important to know there's a happy minimum within reach of just about everybody.

Do we need to evaluate daily training and keep within our limitations?

This is one of the reasons why I found years ago that we had to alternate our training more than in our original schedules. It's necessary to switch more distinctly between easy days and hard days. It doesn't mean reducing total weekly mileage; it means that you run twenty miles one day and only ten the next or you run fast one day and slow the next over more similar mileages. It will pay off handsomely in much better results.
The longer runs produce better capillarisation of the blood vascular system, which in turn gives better recovery rates of the muscles. The shorter runs allow the muscles to recover more quickly, so it's a double benefit.

Breaking it down to the minimum requirements, this would mean covering, say, six to ten miles or kilometres one day and about half that distance the following day. Just think: Easy day-hard day, easy day-hard day or fast day-slow day, fast day-slow day – and work your personal goals from that. It depends on the type of training you're doing at any given time and it also depends on you listening to what your body is telling you and making adjustments accordingly.

It is also important, if you're into a heavy anaerobic section of your training, to give yourself a minimum of 48 hours, or more if possible, for recovery. This is vital when you are into a racing programme to allow the recovery of the central nervous system and the immune system, which can break down under a heavy anaerobic workload.

Is regularity in training in all conditions important?

This is again self-motivation and self-control, particularly if we get involved in training with other people. We have to use that training to suit ourselves, not anyone else. Let them train at their pace and their degrees of effort; you train at your pace and effort levels.

You will need strong self-motivation to get out and train in all sorts of weathers. But you'll soon discover that if you wear the correct protective clothing for the conditions, you'll be okay. And, again, it can be psychologically uplifting to know that you're out there doing it when other people are huddled inside. You can adjust quite easily to very hot or very cold conditions if you understand what effect those conditions are likely to have on you and how to protect yourself against any risks.

One benefit of training in this disciplined way is that you quickly find that discipline extending to other aspects of your life and, for most of us, that is a valuable bonus. I think most of us tend to be undisciplined in many areas.

And, if we run regularly, we get ourselves into such good physical condition we can afford to indulge ourselves with occasional excesses. You can, for instance, eat a whole chocolate cake in the comfortable knowledge that you're just replacing the calories you burned up on your last training run. We all have our weaknesses when it comes to foods that, in normal circumstances, would be bad for us. Usually, these are candies, cakes and other sweet foods; the jogging programme tends to create a desire for those things and we can happily satisfy that desire occasionally, knowing we're not going to do ourselves any harm.

We do need to be more selective with our food to some extent when we become runners and to increase our calory intake with wholesome foods, such as grain breads and starchy vegetables and the natural sugar source of honey. We don't pig out on chocolate all the time.

Training and not straining

If you want to do a lot of training or exercise to improve your physical condition without building up waste product, the effort has got to be aerobic. When respiration occurs, the chemical energy of carbohydrates and other molecules is transformed into a biologically useful kind of energy as these foodstuff molecules undergo oxidation. Cells metabolise foodstuffs such as glucose by a series of enzymic reactions and the energy present in the chemical bonds of the foodstuffs is transformed and conserved as the energy of ATP.

The ATP is the source of energy used by cells to transmit nerve impulses, to cause muscle contractions and all of the myriad life functions. Its importance in the athlete, therefore, is paramount.

Under aerobic conditions, one molecule of glucose makes thirty-eight molecules of ATP; but, when you train anaerobically, one molecule will make only two. So it is nineteen times more economic to run aerobically.

People constantly ask where the aerobic threshold is. Well, you know when you're crossing it? It's easy – if you're running, you know when you're getting uncomfortable; and when you begin to feel uncomfortable, you know you're starting to push beyond your limitations; and when you go beyond your limitations, you're running anaerobically. Your body isn't getting enough energy from the oxygen you're supplying, so it's delving into your reserves. No sudden turn of the switch is involved in moving from aerobic to anaerobic.

Naturally, the harder you work once you get into the anaerobic state, the greater the oxygen debt you create because the greater is the depletion of any reserves you may have tucked away.

What is happening while you train aerobically is that you are applying steady pressure on the heart to pump steadily increasing amounts of oxygenated blood and this forces your maximum aerobic capacity steadily higher – and that pushes the threshold ahead of it so that you can maintain a growing workload without going into oxygen debt. It's better to go a little too slow than too fast to keep this progression going in your favour. You must, initially at least, keep out of that anaerobic state.

Does running reduce weight?

A lot of people think that as soon as they start running, they are going to lose weight. Fixx said your weight would go down but that is not necessarily going to happen at all. Your waist and other measurements might go down but you could also replace any lost surplus fat with developed muscle to an extent that will actually increase your weight. Remember that fat may be bulky but it also floats so it's not the significant factor in weight that many imagine it to be.

And muscle, by comparison, is heavy, so it is possible for a little muscle to replace a lot of fat and maintain or even add weight.

So, if you plan to run as a means of losing weight, don't expect results at the start because you won't be burning off blood sugars until you get fitter and faster and can get into some form of anaerobic exercise. Then you'll burn off blood sugars 19 times faster than in aerobic exercises and you'll get a weight loss.

It is misleading to claim that basic jogging will reduce weight. People, because we are happily different, lose weight – or gain it – at different rates so it is impossible to lay down any hard-and-fast guidelines, except that extended running, once we are fit enough to do it, can help.

Another difference lies in the proportion of brown and white fat in the body. Brown fat will metabolise during sleep – so people with a high proportion of brown fat can eat a lot of food and never get fat. People with a low brown fat content can get fatter almost just by thinking about food, certainly by exceeding their calorific requirement only marginally. Animals, such as bears, which hibernate for months, have a high percentage of brown fat which their bodies metabolise during hibernation.

Do we need to control our calorie intake?

I've never done it myself but it is said that we all tend to eat too much and that if we can fast a little it will be beneficial to us. It seems a good idea to give the body an occasional rest instead of pumping food into it all the time but, if we're going into competition as athletes and are training a lot harder and expending more energy, then we are naturally going to have to take in more calories. The boiler has to be fuelled.

Our blood sugar level will come up mainly with carbohydrates. We can keep away from fats almost entirely although, when the training volume gets really high, some fat becomes essential. The polyunsaturated fats are less likely to cause us trouble than saturated fats.

The Americans put mayonnaise in their bread sandwiches, rather than butter or margarine, but I don't know how it compares in value.

We look at food more closely in later chapters on diet but it's perhaps sufficient to say here that, given certain healthy guidelines, it's common sense to balance your food intake, your proteins and carbohydrates, with the amount of exercise you are doing. Your body, being a smart piece of machinery, will let you know in most cases what it wants and what it doesn't want.

If a supplement is needed, I recommend honey. It's easy to digest, it has high calory value, it's not bulky and it doesn't cause gases. We found that, using honey as the supplement, we could eat perfectly normal meals and still have sufficient energy. Liquid glucose is another good substitute.

The best carbohydrates are in starchy foods, grains and so on but they can cause wind and, if the carbohydrate need is high, you could not eat eight potatoes at a sitting the night before a race without suffering for it.

Like carbohydrates, fats, or lipids, are also composed of carbon, hydrogen and oxygen but have much less oxygen in proportion to carbon and hydrogen. Each molecule of fat is composed of one molecule of glycerol and three of fatty acid.

Smoking and addictions

I don't know whether we have to talk about this. When we started people running, I didn't make any issue of it. I told them: Do what you normally do but just get out there and run. I knew what the psychological reaction would be. They stopped smoking because they started to take an interest in their own physical wellbeing and all the factors that influenced it – their food, their rest, their drinking habits, their smoking, all things that might be detrimental if they didn't use their common sense.

Once they began getting fit and a bit competitive – and most people are competitive – the thought naturally occurred, "If I can stop smoking, I can beat that guy."

Long-established habits that suddenly become transparently bad provide a powerful incentive to change.

Sports medicine testing

They're valuable, of course, but it's up to the individual to get his or her medical adviser to make the decisions on one. They are expensive and, probably, for most people they would be unnecessary.

Oxygen assimilation

A lot of people have the notion that you require great lung capacity to be a successful athlete but, unless you're an underwater diver, that's a lot of rubbish. Extra lung capacity is not going to enhance your athletic performance because that is dependent on your blood flow per minute. That is what dictates your ability to gather in oxygen, not your lung capacity. Blood tone is a factor but blood flow is the vital factor.

Exercise isn't going to affect your lung capacity much but it is going to vastly improve your cardio-vascular and cardio-respiratory efficiency.

Who can train?

We know there are people who have problems – sugar diabetes and so on – but that doesn't mean they can't exercise except that they need to be under medical guidance. That's an area we cannot and will not interfere with, apart from saying that the ability to exercise usefully is there. Talk to your doctor.

Natural attributes

These exist. We know that. People have different anthropomorphic measurements, different muscle size and conformation and efficiency and we can't change that. We know that the individual with more white muscle fibre – which means more muscle power, more drive – with physical measurements which give more leverage, high arches, more flexible ankles, stronger gluteal muscles and so on, is naturally faster than the person with flat feet and weak calf muscles and we know we can't change that.

But we can improve the endurance of the slower person and turn him into a good runner. As long as there is no health problem which would preclude a diet of sustained exercise, we can build endurance in anyone simply by improving their ability to assimilate, transport and use oxygen.

Their speed, their power, their reflexes, their natural adaptability to sporting activities are factors we can improve but cannot change dramatically. Some people are co-ordinated and some people are not – that's another aspect we can't change totally although we can improve the co-ordination factor to some extent. We cannot make naturally slow persons fast, although we can improve their speed, power and so on.

Do you have to be naturally good to succeed?

Nonsense. Not everyone is a natural athlete, with natural co-ordination. I can recall trying to get runners to do bounces and stride-outs and they'd start off by putting the right arm and the right leg forward together. How to run well has to be taught and practised.
Most people you see running don't know how to run. Invariably, they bring their arms up around their chests somewhere and roll their shoulders. It's a particularly bad habit of women. If you run that way, you lose forward momentum by throwing kilos of body-weight from side to side. Tight shoulders are another fault which wastes effort. Watch any fun run in progress and you'll see what we mean – just about every running style except a good one.

You do need to know how to run properly and how to develop a technique which will direct all your effort into going forward comfortably and as economically as possible.

The key to good running is relaxation. You must be nice and loose in the shoulders. The arms should be loose, relaxed and coming straight through as they do when you walk. The hands come from behind the hips and, when the elbow gets alongside the torso, the arms should flex so that the thumbs are in a line directly in front of the shoulder-blade.

Check your footfall by running on sand or across a dewy lawn. To be most effective, your feet should form almost a single straight line.

The most striking example of relaxed running was Flo-Jo. Even when she was running at world-record pace, all her muscles had the same loose movement and you could actually see her jaw flopping around.

I have seen advertisements advising people to hold weights in their hand while they're running. That's crazy. People who carry weights are upsetting their relaxation and creating extra tensions which eventually must disrupt their forward momentum – and, I repeat, that's what running is all about.

Do you need upper body strength?

That, again, is a lot of rubbish. I have a photograph of Viren and Vassala after they won three middle distance gold medals in Munich. They've just stepped out of the showers, stripped down with towels round their waists, and they look like a couple of plucked chickens.

A girl who was helping me with a seminar in Central Park in New York, a 28-year-old who ran a marathon in 3:12, told me she lifted weights. When I asked her why, she said she got excruciating pains in the back of her neck when she ran so decided she had better strenghten her upper body.

"Let's see you run", I said. Immediately she started, she got her fists up, clenched, and moving across her chest.
I called her back and said, "Have you ever stood with your arms up like that and your fists clenched across your chest for three hours?"
"Well, no", she said.
"Try it sometime", I said. "If you don't get a pain in the neck, there's something wrong with you."

Her neck trouble was entirely due to the tension she set up by her running style. So run with relaxed arms.

You've got to have your hips under your torso to get the correct knee-lift, which governs your stride speed. Remember that a higher knee-lift means your foot comes up higher, which shortens the lever action that brings your foot through. Try waving a three-metre stick to and fro and then a very short one and you'll see the difference between long and short levers. The simple mechanics of the action mean that you can't bring your knees up if you have your hips back and your hips will tend to go back if you don't run upright.

To get power, you have to avoid that running posture we call sitting in a bucket. This means you have to run tall and think running tall to keep your body straight and get full leg extension and drive.

These are style aspects we work on during speed and technique training for our athletes. They have to be observed.

You need to be strong in the upper legs, so you have to work on special exercises to develop that strength. You have to improve drive, so you need exercises to help that; and you need to practise routines which will lengthen your stride. None of these things come naturally.

A muddy cross-country course will show you who is running correctly and who is not. The runner with the bad technique will come in with mud all up his back; the good runner who was driving correctly over his hips won't.

Do we need fat?

We know it's better to have very little fat on the body if you want to perform at a higher level when you're running.

For example, I think John Walker's fat content was 3% when he broke the world mile record and most top marathon men have a content of about 5%. Women, through their reproductive organs, have more in their bodies than men – in marathoners, this is somewhere about 10-11%.

So with some exceptions, the good distance runners are thin and light. Some have more muscles but otherwise they tend to fit into a fairly specific body profile.

The problem with fat in a body is that every kilogram requires .17ml of oxygen to run every metre, which gives the light runner an immediate advantage. There is the possibility of compensation through muscular power, more drive and better stride and so on but over the longer distances the advantage becomes marked.

We have come a long way in the past thirty years as far as women's running is concerned. It was believed then they were incapable of seriously running 800 or 1,500 metres because in one race organised for them at the Olympics, they all fell over and fainted and God knows what. They were a big mess because they hadn't trained for it.

Now we know that women can train as hard as men. Not as fast as men but they do mileages as big, they can do all the other conditioning training that men do. The only thing they lack is the male's muscular power. I learnt years ago that there are no bars to women's ability to compete in running over all distances and to follow exactly the same schedules. If you really need proof, note how women emerged as a major force in ultra-distance running. In one 1,000-mile race on a circuit in New York, four of the first five finishers were women.

Is age a great barrier?

The advent of masters running has done a great deal to make people realise that, after forty, they're not as old as they felt. And they have learnt that one of the advantages of age in a runner is that you can have more endurance than younger athletes. Carlos Lopez, the LA Olympic marathon winner at 36, underscored that fact.

The top rank of men of forty and over can run marathons these days in 2:11 and so on and a great many have run under 2:20. Some of them have run very fast times on the track as well, especially over 5,000 and 10,000 metres.

It's an individual thing, a question of what you've done with your life as a younger man, whether you've kept in training and have the interest to be competitive, even if it is only with yourself. There is really no reason why people of quite senior years, who have not exercised or trained much before, cannot go out and learn to run long distances and enjoy fun runs.

A better cardiac system can be developed at any age. For instance, people with hardening of the arteries need not be discouraged from taking up active running because they undoubtedly have many other arteries which have never been developed and can be brought into service through a diet of regular controlled exercise. It's a bit like creating your own bypass system. Many of the good masters runners are proof of this because some of them did not begin until they were over forty.

I recall that when our original joggers in New Zealand were about to begin, a doctor warned that many of them had hardened arteries and the exercise might be unwise. One of the group was a man in his seventies who had just had all the varicose veins stripped out of his legs by this doctor. I asked the doctor where the blood was going to go now and he explained that the varicose veins were only ten per cent of the blood vessels in the legs; the other ninety per cent couldn't be seen because they were internal but the increased blood flow stimulated by running would develop them to replace the ones that had been removed.

I said, "One minute you tell me you can't develop the blood vascular system because you're too old and you've got hardened arteries and now you're telling me you can. So what do you really mean?"

I didn't get much of an answer from him on that one but I got an answer from those joggers because some of them, including men in their seventies, very quickly were able to run very well, regardless of the state of some of their arteries.

Feet and how to take care of them

The construction and functioning of the human foot are what uniquely set us apart from all other forms of animal life. Evolution has adapted a foot for the specific activities of the human, although no two pairs are exactly alike and some are naturally more efficient than others. Once we pass the crawling stage, we use our feet relentlessly and for a wide variety of purposes, usually with very little regard for their maintenance.

Between them, our feet do a remarkable job but, like the rest of us, they are only human; so, before we commit them to yet another role by taking up jogging, or running, let's pay them the attention they deserve.

Since the jogging boom spread from New Zealand and round the world in the sixties, it has spawned huge industries to supply all the gear runners need and a great deal they don't need but which look nice, give the sweaty activity a touch of fashionable class and make their designers and manufacturers comfortably rich. Aggressive shoe companies, mostly American, are locked in an endless battle for our attention and our dollars.

Since jogging took off, footwear to jog in has advanced from a basic sandshoe type of covering with a somewhat thicker sole than normal to provide protection between foot and running surface. We now have a staggering range of name-brand shoes with an even more staggering range of so-called aids to more traction, more cushioning, more recoil, less weight and a range of inserts and additions to counter pronating and supinating ankles – and, if the advertising claims are to be believed, generate greater speed.

Approach all the sales hype with a great deal of caution and suspicion.

For instance, if you told the average person of any age to take off his or her shoes and run down the hallway, you would almost always discover that the foot action contains no hint of pronation or supination. Those sideways flexings of the ankles begin only when people lace themselves into these running shoes because the construction of many of the shoes immediately alters the natural movement of the feet and sets up pressure and stress points.

More than twenty years ago, Californian researchers found 241 injuries in 100 middle-aged joggers, which coined a whole new range of anatomical classifications: Jogger's foot, jogger's heel, jogger's ankle, jogger's leg, jogger's knee and jogger's thigh, each with its own set of potential malfunctions and breakdowns.

For example, problems found to be associated with jogger's foot were: Blister, corn and callous; tenosynovitis (flexor and extensor hallucis longus and F. and E. digitorum longus); traumatic arthritis; hallux rigidus; longitudinal and anterior arch strain; and stress fracture. A similarly impressive range of other jogger's complaints spreads upward from ground level.

The point we are making is that paying several hundreds of dollars for the latest in hi-tech running shoes is no guarantee you'll avoid any of these injuries and can even guarantee that you **will** suffer from them in one form or another.

The first thing to realise is that the less we interfere with the natural movement of the feet, the better we are going to perform.

We develop a great deal of our speed from our feet and ankles; when I train athletes, I tell them they must emulate the ballet dancer, not a weightlifter or a gymnast. So we need a shoe that is very flexible and is little more than another layer of skin, if that is possible.

During my training camps, many people came to me to discuss running style, foot plant and so on and an amazing number told me they wore orthotics. When I asked why, they told me it was because they pronated or supinated. I have videotaped them running barefooted and shown them that, without shoes on, they neither pronate nor supinate. In other words; the orthotics are for the shoes, not the feet.

Some tell me they wear orthotics because of a high arch; others tell me they wear them because of a low arch, which is flat-footedness. I ask them if the podiatrist who fitted them with orthotics recommended any exercises to strengthen the foot and counteract the apparent fault and the answer is invariably in the negative.

I'm talking simple exercises such as balancing on the balls of the feet on a stair tread or a step or a thickish book and raising the heels up and down; or putting a rope or cycle tube round the front of the foot and gradually pulling upward at it; or picking up objects with the toes and so on. These all strengthen the muscles of the feet. They cost nothing.

But many podiatrists don't talk about exercises, they just fit the patients with orthotics and tell them, if the problem gets worse, to come back and get fitted for another orthotic. My advice ist that if people with foot problems don't exercise, they'll get to my age and they won't be able to walk, let alone run.

You'll never see a sprinter with a flat foot. Sprinters always have high arches. The arch acts somewhat like a spring and they exercise to coil the spring to its maximum.

With that need for a freely-springing arch in mind, consider that most running shoes made today are far too rigid in the arch. The makers insert things which seem actually to harden that area so that they won't flex at all, so your foot won't flex either and you'll immediately suffer a loss of potential speed. These inserts also tend to rapidly lose their resilience; ordinary EVA has far more bounce than the hi-tech inserts and aids now being offered.

So we want to learn to run faster and we're being fitted with shoes which won't flex to help us to do that. They'll flex at the joint of the foot all right but not at the arch, where flexing is a natural foot function. Put a board under each foot of an athlete and he couldn't even walk properly, let alone run, but that's very much how some of these running shoes affect the arches.

Another mistake is that shoe salesmen and some manufacturers insist that there should be a thumb's width of space between the toes and the front of the shoe or you'll lose your toenails. But the slowest runner in the world will push off with the end of his toes when he leaves the ground. If he's got flabby shoes, he's going to lose traction.

The reason you lose toenails is not because the toe is up to the front of the shoe but because the shoe last hasn't been made properly and the shoe hasn't been sprung properly. If the top line of the shoe around the top of the foot is too loose, your foot comes out. If it's too tight, it will pull in on the achilles tendon. When they cut the patterns and make the lasts, they've got to conform so that the tension is right in that area. That is the spring of the shoe; it has nothing to do, as someone once suggested, with the bounce of the shoe.

You need a last with not too much curve underneath. If you have a last like a canoe, it will flatten down when you put your foot in and the toe, instead of staying nice and round, will pull back like a vee. You've immediately got problems. That's when you lose your toenails.

Salesmen will say you need space in the shoe when you buy it because when you run and get hot your feet will swell. That's poppycock. Your feet might swell a fraction wider but they're not going to swell longways.

A lot of lasts are made too straight, some are too curved. The normal foot has a bit of curvature to it but it falls somewhere between straight and very curved. When you put your foot on the ground, the shoe should be right under it. You shouldn't have to have stabilising bars and foot counters to hold your foot in the shoe. That's more like having your foot in a gumboot and you'd probably run just as well in a gumboot as in some of these $300 and $400 shoes.

Look for a shoe that's flexible at the arch and has a good amount of resilient rubber underneath it to absorb the jarring. A shoe that feels comfortable with no pressure points. Forget the rest.

If you could just attach a rubber sole to your foot, with nothing on the top, you'd have the perfect running shoe.

Zola Budd, Abebe Bikila and Bruce Tulloch and many other good runners managed perfectly well in bare feet and never had any plantar fascia problems or any other troubles we have had with running shoes. Tulloch even ran superb races barefooted on cinders.

Many people suffer with plantar fascia, which is invariably caused by shoes which are too rigid under the arch of the foot.

Remember that some running shoe shops get incentives from different companies to promote their shoes so the advice you get from the salespeople isn't necessarily in your best interests. Find someone in your area or your club who has been running for a long time, who hasn't had any injury problems, who doesn't wear orthotics and ask them what shoes they wear. It's quite likely they've tried many makes of shoes and have been through all the problems themselves before finding the right shoes, so let their bad experiences save you from yours.

There are people who genuinely need orthotics to correct some malformation but there are not as many as we have been led to suppose.

It becomes difficult to know who to believe when world-famous athletes endorse running shoes and are quoted as saying that these are the finest you can buy. In the States, I often talked with athletes after the major road races and, because I was a shoe-maker and designer myself, I was interested in what shoes people were wearing.

"By the way", I would say over a beer, "So-and-So won the race today. What sort of shoes did he wear?"

The other runners not only didn't know, they didn't care. They were only interested in the shoes they wore.

Unfortunately, a lot of them will promote a brand of shoe while actually running in shoes which are nothing like the ones you would buy off the rack. They will have shoes specially made for them, with special lasts designed for their own feet. And you are quite likely to find that, within a year or so, they're promoting another brand anyway.

In my early days, we ran in canvas shoes. They were ideally flexible and we just put extra rubber on the soles. We didn't get plantar fascia, we didn't pronate or supinate; we might have lost a bit of skin from the rough canvas when we were running marathons but, generally speaking, we didn't have foot problems.

One of the problems with modern running shoe marketing has been that the Americans have fostered this notion that you need a protective shoe when you're training and a lighter shoe for racing. But think about it – when do you hit the road hardest? When you're training or when you're racing? Obviously, it's when you're racing so that's when you need the most protection. If you're going downhill in training, you can ease off; when you're racing, you can't afford that luxury, so the pounding you receive going down that hill will be many times greater, particularly if you're a big person.

As far as I'm concerned, you train and race in the same shoes and those shoes have got to be more like slippers than the hi-tech monsters they're producing these days – light, flexible mid-sole, plenty of resilient cushioning under the feet, allowing your foot to function as naturally as possible.

The shoe makers and salesmen aren't in the business to make champions; they're there to make money and if they can sell you two pairs of shoes instead of one they're laughing all the way to the bank.

Next time you go into a shop to buy a pair of shoes, if you haven't got a recommendation from someone whose judgement you trust, try all the shoes available for lightness, then find out which ones bend easily at the arch – in the middle – both ways, upwards and downwards. Look for the shoes that don't have too much on the uppers. You don't want stabilising bars and all this paraphernalia; the less you have on the top the better. As we said earlier, the perfect running shoe would be a resilient rubber sole that you could just stick under your foot with no uppers at all.

Try them next for shape. Some of the lasts shoes are made on are not right and never will be right, no matter how many models and designs they make off them or how many gimmicks they add to make them sound scientific. Lasts which are too straight cause pronation or, if they trap the foot with hard counters at the back, supination. Shoes which are too curved will also lead to supination.

Having got that far and brought the selection down to a short list, put the shoes on. You should be able to have your toe close to the end of the shoe but the shoe should not pull down on it as you move. If it does, it means the shoe is oversprung and will give you trouble.

The shoe for you should not have any pressure points at all. Close your eyes and concentrate; if you feel any pressure anywhere, that's where the shoe is likely to give you trouble, so it's not for you. Don't accept assurances that the shoes will stretch and pick up the shape of your foot; that's not true.

You should be able to put on a brand-new pair of running shoes and go out and run for an hour or two and have no marks on your feet at the end of it. A properly made running shoe does not need breaking in.

Having soles which are too thick and elevate you too high off the ground are a potential source of problems because they can lead to instability when you're running.

When Peter Snell went to the Rome Olympics in 1960, he was a comparative novice who had learnt to run on grass tracks because New Zealand then had no hard tracks. We were aware we faced a particular problem. Cinder and other hard surface tracks can be severe on middle-distance runners who run heel and toe until they sprint. Snell, unused to hard tracks, was scheduled to run four tough races in three days, which we knew could knock his legs around and cause severe muscle tightness and soreness.
So I made him a special pair of spikes and added a small rubber lift on the heels. When he reached the finals, we found that Adidas had persuaded the rest of the finalists to wear its shoes but, unfortunately, they must have decided Peter had no chance at all because they didn't bother to approach him. He climbed on the winners's dais wearing his plain white spikes, which can't have been the effect Adidas had in mind.

However, they were curious about the shoes' construction so we explained the heel had been padded to avoid damage to the red cells in the blood, which would gather in the veins and capillaries and cause progressive breakdown in the legs. Out of that experience, Adidas produced what became known as interval shoes, with a special rubber heel.

Shoe lacing is far more important than most runners realise. They should be threaded so that when they are tightened they don't pull down on the sinews and metatarsals on the top of the foot. A simple matter like incorrect lacing can prevent the foot from functioning freely and, because it may be straining against restrictive points, the foot can be damaged. We have included a lacing diagram showing how it is done to use the shoe itself to protect you from lacing pressure.

Watch heel wear on your shoes closely. Excessive wear leads to stress right through the leg and hip and can also cause bone wear. Lost heel rubber should be replaced regularly, even as often as once a month.

I'm not alone in my concern about the possible damage caused by some modern running shoes. A leading article in 'Sports Medicine 9 (2) 1990' by Steven E Robbins and Gerard J Gouw, of the Human Performance Group in the Mechanical Engineering Department at Concordia University in Montreal, reviewed a considerable volume of research into the subject through the 80s to measure shock levels experienced by runners in bare feet and in a variety of shoe platforms.

A significant discovery ot this research was that barefoot running in normally shod subjects resulted in greater shock-moderating behaviour than when wearing any running shoes tested, suggesting that the shock when running with bare feet may be lower than when wearing shoes.

Some have concluded that chronic overloading during locomotion is inevitable in modern man because of inherent lower extremity fragility. Accordingly, footwear, such as running shoes, which attempt to attenuate shock waves through the interposition of yielding layers between the plantar surface of the foot and the ground, are presumed essential for safe running, and are also promoted for use during walking. However, this supposition seems inconsistent with reports indicating that habitually unshod humans are not subject to chronic overloading during running.

"By taking this into account, the lower extremity must be inherently durable and chronic overloading must be a consequence of wearing footwear and probably due to increased shock with their use."

Summarising the data, the authors concluded: "The conclusion that modern athletic footwear makes the durable bare foot vulnerable to injury is supported by: (a) a report indicating that running related injuries are uncommon in barefoot populations (Robbins and Hanna 1987); (b) a report showing that modern athletic footwear produces sensory illusions (Robbins et al 1988); (c) the demonstration of diminished impact-moderating behaviour with modern footwear compared with the barefoot condition (Robbins et al 1988a); and (d) work reviewed in this paper showing that modern running shoes are not superior and are sometimes worse than the unadapted bare foot in attenuating shock during running (Snel et al 1985; Luethi et al 1987).

"The notion that more expensive athletic shoes from major manufacturers are particularly dangerous to use is supported by Marti et al (1989), who found a significantly higher incidence of injuries in those using more expensive shoes and in those who stated they had a brand preference, with all major brands showing a similar incidence.

Stated conversely, wearers of inexpensive shoes and those without a brand preference were protected better."

What the research was saying is that the excessive cushioning and gimmicks employed in modern running shoes create illusions of protection which trick the body into not making the shock-absorbing reactions normal when running in bare feet and may also lead the athlete to run with greater impact, increasing the shock effect and the risk of damage.

Chapter 12: Setting out Your Schedule

The method of setting out a schedule is fairly simple. Begin by counting the number of weeks between now and the first important race you intend to contest. Any races in between will become part of your training programme.

Allow the last six weeks for co-ordination training.
Four weeks before that for anaerobic and speed development and four weeks for hill exercise running and muscular efficiency and conditioning.

Any weeks left begin now and are for aerobic mileage to develop a high as possible aerobic threshhold. The more weeks the better. The conditioning starts with only aerobic mileage, on flat and hill courses. As you near the second phase, hill training occurs two or three days a week, with one long aerobic run and leg speed and fast relaxed runs over 100 metres on the others. Some wind sprints every 15 minutes during hill training.

Anaerobic training is also two or three days each week, plus one long aerobic run and days of sprint training sessions and easy running.

The co-ordination training consists of sharpeners, trials, development races (under and over the target distance), pace judgement training, fast relaxed striding and, if needed, fast anaerobic 300 and 500 m runs.
It ends with a freshening up phase which leads into the target race.

Remember that schedules are only for guidance because athletes have varying strengths and weaknesses, different training backgrounds and different levels of fitness. Treat the figures as hypothetical and use them in relation to your individual fitness and training background. Training, not straining, is the controlling factor; it is better to go too slowly than too fast.

Assess your day-to-day reactions and adjust the schedule within the guidelines and train accordingly.

The importance of the guidelines is that they are designed to progressively develop potential and control the ultimate form attained. So the aerobic base or anaerobic threshhold is of vital significance. The stronger it is, the better the foundation on which the rest of the preparation is based.

Anaerobic exercise must not enter the conditioning phase, although a sprinter should do some training for speed in some form through the whole schedule, possibly by conditioning muscles with isotonic resistance or exercising to improve flexibility and power, and should also work on technique. This could involve some speed sessions of an anaerobic nature which should be followed by easy jogging to allow for full recovery.

In each stage of development, I have included exercises that prepare the athlete for the next stage. For instance, during the aerobic phase, some hill training is suggested which will prepare a runner for the intensive hill phase which follows; and the hill phase includes some short, sharp sprints to prepare for the anaerobic phase which follows when you come off the hills. Not much, just enough to be effective and to make the transition from one phase to the next easier.

This balance in training is of utmost importance if the best results are to be achieved, whether your preference is to do the minimum amount in each session or the maximum, whether you want to be a champion or just a better, fitter fun runner. Always remember that it is not the best athletes who succeed in important competitions but the best prepared.

So, one development follows another, everything you do is important and patience is the guiding quality.
Training terms used include:

Wind Sprints

For sharpening and developing the ability to become accustomed to changes in pace in racing. Place markers at 25 m, 45 m and 25 m, sprint hard the 45 m, jogging the rest before sprinting again. 100 m sprints every 200 m are similar but more effective aerobically. Sprint the straights and float the bends.

Hill Springing

To strengthen the legs generally, particularly the ankles. Use a gentle slope and, after warm-up, use a bouncing action with slow forward momentum, pushing hard off the toes to lift the centre of gravity. Land on the toes, flexing the ankles to stretch tendons and muscles. Your bodyweight acts as a form of resistance and helps to develop the fast twitch or white muscle fibres. Do only what you feel your legs can take – a little often is best.

Leg Speed

Run about 100 m fast, concentrating on pulling the legs through fast, rather than on driving off the back leg, by using the quadriceps and lower stomach muscles. Try to maintain a near-normal stride and move the legs fast. Jog 300 m before repeating. Always run the fast work with the wind.

Long Aerobic Running

A strong aerobic effort, between jogging and racing – in theory, 70% to 99% of your aerobic capacity to finish in a pleasantly tired state.

Pace Judgement Running

Used over 400 m in reps of four to six, trying ro run at the speed you intend to average in your racing. Take whatever interval you feel you need for recovery because it is important to run the exact time if possible.

Relaxed Striding

It is important to try to relax during races and training by running varying distance from 100 m to 300 m. Keeping the upper body relaxed and concentrating on running with a good technique will help you to run faster times without being basically fitter.

Repetitions

For anaerobic capacity development. Run one and jog one.

Sprint Training

Use about 100 m with the wind, if any, and use this sequence, each one twice, after warm-up.

1. With slow forward momentum, raise the knees high and fast alternately in a running action so the quadriceps start to feel tired. Do what you feel you can; jog easily back and repeat.
2. With high knee lift, long-striding action with the arms being forced through and driving hard off the back foot. Do 100 m twice with good recovery interval.
3. Running tall exercise, keeping high on the toes, lifting the knees high and stretching the body upwards, trying to lift the torso from the pelvis. 100 m twice with recovery. The running speed should not be too fast.
4. Try to combine the three exercises and run the 100 m twice, as fast and relaxed as you can. After these exercises, run up to six laps, using one straight to run fast and relaxed with 300 m jogging interval.

Steep Hill or Steps Running

Used mainly to strengthen the upper leg muscles. Knee-lift is important in running, from sprints to marathons, and the quadriceps or front upper leg muscles often tire and cause the runner to lose stride length and speed. Run up a fairly steep hill or steps, bringing the knees up to make the back leg drive fairly hard. Don't try to go too fast uphill; make your legs feel the workload. As a variation, use a more gentle slope and, with long high knee-lifting strides and forcing the arms through, run up quite fast. Take a good recovery jogging interval before striding downhill. The hill should be 100 m or more. Do what you feel you can manage, with good recovery before attempting any more.

Time Trials
To co-ordinate the training.
Run at about seven-eighths effort, maintaining the same effort throughout. Don't sprint at the end.

The following is a schedule for cross-country and road race preparation. The variations in time, distance and so on are the minimums and maximums, governed by how the runner feels from day to day.

Conditioning
Monday:	Aerobic 45/60 minutes.
Tuesday:	Aerobic 60/75 minutes.
Wednesday:	Run hilly course 30/60 minutes.
Thursday:	Aerobic 60/90 minutes.
Friday:	Jog 30/60 minutes.
Saturday:	Run hilly course 30/60 minutes.
Sunday:	Aerobic 60/120 minutes.

Monday:	Run hilly course 30/60 minutes.
Tuesday:	Aerobic 60/90 minutes.
Wednesday:	Trial 2,000/3,000 metres.
Thursday:	Aerobic 60/90 minutes.
Friday:	Relaxed striding 200 metres 4/8 times.
Saturday:	Trial 3,000/5,000 metres.
Sunday:	Aerobic 60/120 minutes.

Hill Training
Monday:	Leg speed 100 metres by 6/10 times.
Tuesday:	Hill exercises 15/60 minutes.
Wednesday:	Fast relaxed running 100 metres 6/10 times.
Thursday:	Hill exercises (or jog) 15/60 minutes.
Friday:	Leg speed 100 metres 6/10 times.
Saturday:	Hill exercises 15/60 minutes.
Sunday:	Aerobic 60/120 minutes.

Anaerobic Training

Monday: Sprint training.
Tuesday: Reps.
Wednesday: Easy fartlek 30/60 minutes (jogging and striding and sprinting accor-
               ding to mood).
Thursday: Reps or jog.
Friday: Relaxed striding, fast and easy.
Saturday: Reps.
Sunday: Aerobic 60/120 minutes.

Co-ordination Training

Monday: Sharpeners.
Tuesday: For middle distance – fast relaxed striding or sprint training.
               For distance – 2,000/3,000 metre trial.
               For either – Easy fartlek or aerobic run up to 60 minutes.
Wednesday: Development races or trials; a sprint and middle distance.
Thursday: Fast relaxed striding – pace judgement – easy fartlek– fast runs in repe-
               titions over 300 m by 3 or 500 m by 2.
Friday: Jog 30 minutes.
Saturday: Development races over or under target distance.
Sunday: Aerobic 60/90 minutes.

Continuation of Training and Racing

Monday: Windsprints 50 metres 12/20.
Tuesday: Easy fartlek or aerobic 60 minutes.
Wednesday: Trial over race distance **(fast)**.
Thursday: Fast relaxed striding 100 metres by 6.
Friday: Jog 30 minutes.
Saturday: Race or trial over half race distance.
Sunday: Jog 60 minutes.

Monday: Windsprints 50 metres by 10/16.
Tuesday: Trial 400/600/1,500 metres.
Wednesday: Fast relaxed striding 100 metres by 6.
Thursday: Jog 45 minutes.
Friday: Jog 30 minutes.
Saturday: **The first important race.**
Sunday: Jog 60/90 minutes or more.

Many people run today for fitness and health. Some are middle-aged, some are old and some are quite young. None of them are concerned about being champions but enjoy fun runs and the social pleasures of being with people in a shared interest.

But, while they may not be highly competitive, invariably they like to see their times over different distances improving. They are racing against themselves rather than against others. The schedules followed by aspiring champions disconcert them; they are far too tough. What they want is a programme that will enable them to race every one, two or three weeks and will keep them improving and free of injury.

The non-race/ week schedule which follows makes that possible, providing a reasonable conditioning base has been established and the runner does not race over testing distances such as 10 km week after week. The longer races should be interspersed with shorter distance races and the runner should allow for recovery from any testing races by merely jogging each day until back to normal.

This schedule has worked well for some high schools in the United States and New Zealand, which have programmes of continuous cross-country races.

Cross Country Non Race Week
Monday: Reps 1,500 metres by 3 or 800 metres by 6.
Tuesday: Aerobic run 60/90 minutes.
Wednesday: Trial 2,000/3,000 metres.
Thursday: Aerobic run 60/90 minutes.
Friday: Fast relaxed striding 100 metres by 10.
Saturday: Trial 2,000/3,000 metres.
Sunday: Aerobic run 90 minutes or more.

Race Week
Monday: Windsprints 100 metres by 6/10.
Tuesday: Easy fartlek 45/60 minutes.
Wednesday: Trial 1,600/2,400 metres.
Thursday: Fast relaxed striding 100 metres by 6.
Friday: Jog 30 minutes.
Saturday: **Race**
Sunday: Aerobic run 90 minutes or more.

Road Racing Non Race Week
Monday: Reps, either 1,500 by 3 or 800 by 6.
Tuesday: Aerobic run 90 minutes.
Wednesday: 5,000 metres time trial.

Thursday:	Aerobic run 60/90 minutes.
Friday:	Fast relaxed striding 100 metres by 6/10.
Saturday:	5,000 metres trial.
Sunday:	Aerobic run 90 minutes or more.

Race Week

Monday:	Windsprints 100 metres by 6/10.
Tuesday:	Easy fartlek 45/60 minutes.
Wednesday:	1,500 metres time trial.
Thursday:	Fast relaxed striding 100 metres by 4/6.
Friday:	Jog 30 minutes.
Saturday:	**Race**
Sunday:	Aerobic run 90 minutes or more.

Fun Run Schedule for Beginners

For Six Weeks

Monday:	Jog 15/30 minutes.
Tuesday:	Jog 30/60 minutes.
Wednesday:	Jog 15/45 minutes.
Thursday:	Jog 30/45 minutes.
Friday:	Rest or jog 30 minutes.
Saturday:	Jog 15/45 minutes.
Sunday:	Jog 30/60 minutes.

For Four Weeks

Monday:	Relaxed striding 100 by 4/6 times.
Tuesday:	Jog 30/60 minutes.
Wednesday:	Time trial 3,000 metres.
Thursday:	Jog 30/60 minutes.
Friday:	Rest or jog 30 minutes.
Saturday:	Time trial 5,000 metres.
Sunday:	Jog 45/75 minutes.

Four Weeks

| Monday: | Relaxed striding 200 by 4/6 times. |
| Tuesday: | Jog 30/60 minutes. |

Wednesday:	Time trial 3,000 metres.
Thursday:	Easy fartlek running 30/45 minutes.
Friday:	Rest or jog 30 minutes.
Saturday:	Time trial 5,000 metres.
Sunday:	Jog 60/90 minutes.

Four Weeks

Monday:	Repetitions 800 by 2/4 times.
Tuesday:	Jog 30/60 minutes.
Wednesday:	Time trial 3,000 metres.
Thursday:	Easy fartlek running 30/45 minutes.
Friday:	Rest or jog 30 minutes.
Saturday:	Time trial 5,000 metres and 10,000 metres in alternate weeks.
Sunday:	Jog 60/90 minutes.

Two Weeks

Monday:	Repetitions 1,500 by 2/3 times.
Tuesday:	Jog 30/60 minutes.
Wednesday:	Time trial 5,000 metres.
Thursday:	Fast relaxed running 100 by 4/8 times.
Friday:	Rest or jog 30 minutes.
Saturday:	1st week time trial 5,000 metres; second week time trial 10,000 metres.
Sunday:	Jog 60/90 minutes.

One Week

Monday:	100 metres windsprints every 200 metres by 6/8 times.
Tuesday:	Jog 45 minutes.
Wednesday:	Time trial 2,000 metres.
Thursday:	Fast relaxed running 100 by 4/6 times.
Friday:	Rest or jog 30 minutes.
Saturday:	Time trial 3,000 metres.
Sunday:	Jog 45/60 minutes.

One Week

Monday:	Fast relaxed running 100 by 6/8 times.
Tuesday:	Time trial 1,000 metres.
Wednesday:	Jog 45 minutes.

Thursday:	Jog 30 minutes.
Friday:	Jog 30 minutes or rest.
Saturday:	**Fun run.**
Sunday:	Jog 45/60 minutes.

800 Metres

For as long a time as possible
Monday:	Long aerobic running 30/60 minutes.
Tuesday:	Long aerobic running 60/90 minutes.
Wednesday:	Long aerobic running 30/60 minutes.
Thursday:	Long aerobic running 60/90 minutes.
Friday:	Long aerobic running 30/60 minutes.
Saturday:	Long aerobic running 60 minutes.
Sunday:	Long aerobic running 90 minutes or more.

Four Weeks
Monday:	Hill springing/bounding/steps running 30/60 minutes.
Tuesday:	High knee lift exercise, long striding and running tall.
Wednesday:	Hill springing/bounding/steps running 30/60 minutes.
Thursday:	Leg speed 100 metres by 6/10 times.
Friday:	Relaxed striding 200 metres by 6 times.
Saturday:	Hill springing/bounding/steps running 30/60 minutes.
Sunday:	Long aerobic running 90 minutes or more.

One Week
Monday:	Repetitions 1,600 metres by 3 times.
Tuesday:	Easy fartlek running 45/60 minutes.
Wednesday:	Repetitions 800 metres by 6 times.
Thursday:	Fast relaxed running 100 metres by 10 times.
Friday:	Jogging 30 minutes.
Saturday:	Repetitions 1,000 metres by 4 times.
Sunday:	Jogging 60 minutes.

One Week
Monday:	Repetitions 800 metres by 6 times.
Tuesday:	Easy fartlek running 45/60 minutes.
Wednesday:	Repetitions 1,600 metres by 3 times.

Thursday:	Fast relaxed running 100 metres by 10 times
Friday:	Jogging 30 minutes.
Saturday:	Repetitions 600 metres by 6 times.
Sunday:	Jogging 90 minutes.

One Week

Monday:	Repetitions 600 metres by 6 times.
Tuesday:	Easy fartlek running 45/60 minutes.
Wednesday:	Repetitions 300 metres by 3 times fast.
Thursday:	Fast relaxed running 100 metres by 10 times.
Friday:	Jogging 30 minutes.
Saturday:	Repetitions 400 metres by 8/12 times.
Sunday:	Jogging 90 minutes.

One Week

Monday:	Repetitions 800 metres by 6 times.
Tuesday:	Easy fartlek running 45/60 minutes.
Wednesday:	Repetitions 300 metres by 3 times fast.
Thursday:	Fast relaxed running 100 metres by 10 times.
Friday:	Jogging 30 minutes.
Saturday:	Repetitions 400 metres by 8/12 times.
Sunday:	Jogging 90 minutes.

One Week

Monday:	100-metre windsprints every 200 metres by 6/10 times.
Tuesday:	Easy fartlek running 45 minutes.
Wednesday:	Time trials 200 and 600 metres.
Thursday:	Fast relaxed running 100 metres by 10 times.
Friday:	Jogging 30 minutes.
Saturday:	Time trial 1,500 metres.
Sunday:	Jogging 90 minutes.

One Week

Monday:	100-metre windsprints every 200 metres by 6/10 times.
Tuesday:	Easy fartlek running 45 minutes.
Wednesday:	Time trials 200 and 600 metres.
Thursday:	Fast relaxed running 100 metres by 10.
Friday:	Jogging 30 minutes.

| Saturday: | Time trial 800 metres. |
| Sunday: | Jogging 90 minutes. |

One Week

Monday:	100-metre windsprints every 200 metres by 6/10 times.
Tuesday:	Easy fartlek running 45 minutes.
Wednesday:	Time trials 200 and 1,000 metres
Thursday:	Fast relaxed running 100 metres by 10 times.
Friday:	Jogging 30 minutes.
Saturday:	Time trial 1,500 metres.
Sunday:	Jogging 60 minutes.

One Week

Monday:	100-metre windsprints every 200 metres by 6/10 times.
Tuesday:	Easy fartlek running 45 minutes.
Wednesday:	Time trials 200 and 600 metres.
Thursday:	Fast relaxed running 100 metres by 10 times.
Friday:	Jogging 30 minutes.
Saturday:	Time trial 800 metres.
Sunday:	Jogging 60 minutes.

One Week

Monday:	45-metre windsprints every 100 metres by 20 times.
Tuesday:	Easy fartlek running 45 minutes.
Wednesday:	Time trial 800 metres.
Thursday:	Fast relaxed running 100 metres by 10 times.
Friday:	Jogging 30 minutes.
Saturday:	Time trial 600 metres.
Sunday:	Jogging 60 minutes.

One Week

Monday:	45-metre windsprints every 100 metres by 12 times.
Tuesday:	Easy fartlek running 30 minutes.
Wednesday:	Time trial 400 metres.
Thursday:	Fast relaxed running 100 metres by 6 times.
Friday:	Jogging 30 minutes.
Saturday:	**First important race.**
Sunday:	/

1,500 Metres

As long a time as possible
Monday:	Long aerobic running 30/60 minutes.
Tuesday:	Long aerobic running 60/90 minutes.
Wednesday:	Long aerobic running 30/60 minutes.
Thursday:	Long aerobic running 60/90 minutes.
Friday:	Long aerobic running 30/60 minutes.
Saturday:	Long aerobic running 60 minutes.
Sunday:	Long aerobic running 90 minutes or more.

Four Weeks
Monday:	Hill springing, bounding, steps running 30/60 minutes.
Tuesday:	High knee lift/long striding/running tall exercises.
Wednesday:	Hill springing, bounding, steps running 30/60 minutes.
Thursday:	Leg speed 100 metres by 6/10 times.
Friday:	Relaxed striding 200 metres by 6 times.
Saturday:	Hill springing, bounding, steps running 30/60 minutes.
Sunday:	Jogging 90 minutes or more.

One Week
Monday:	Repetitions 1,600 metres by 3 times.
Tuesday:	Easy fartlek running 45/60 minutes.
Wednesday:	Repetitions 800 metres by 6 times.
Thursday:	Fast relaxed running 100 metres by 10 times.
Friday:	Jogging 30 minutes.
Saturday:	Repetitions 1,000 metres by 4 times.
Sunday:	Jogging 90 minutes or more.

One Week
Monday:	Repetitions 800 metres by 6 times.
Tuesday:	Easy fartlek running 45/60 minutes.
Wednesday:	Repetitions 1,600 metres by 3 times.
Thursday:	Fast relaxed running 100 metres by 10 times.
Friday:	Jogging 30 minutes.
Saturday:	Repetitions 600 metres by 6 times.
Sunday:	Jogging 90 minutes or more.

One Week
Monday:	Repetitions 600 metres by 6 times.

Tuesday:	Easy fartlek running 45/60 minutes.
Wednesday:	Repetitions 300 metres by 3 times fast.
Thursday:	Fast relaxed running 100 metres by 10 times.
Friday:	Jogging 30 minutes.
Saturday:	Repetitions 400 metres by 8/12 times.
Sunday:	Jogging 90 minutes or more.

One Week

Monday:	Repetitions 800 metres by 6 times.
Tuesday:	Easy fartlek running 45/60 minutes.
Wednesday:	Repetitions 300 metres by 3 times fast.
Thursday:	Fast relaxed running 100 metres by 10 times.
Friday:	Jogging 30 minutes.
Saturday:	Repetitions 400 metres by 8/12 times.
Sunday:	Jogging 90 minutes.

One Week

Monday:	100-metre windsprints every 200 metres by 6/10 times.
Tuesday:	Easy fartlek running 45 minutes.
Wednesday:	Time trials 200 and 600 metres.
Thursday:	Fast relaxed running 100 metres by 10 times.
Friday:	Jogging 30 minutes.
Saturday:	Time trial 800 metres.
Sunday:	Jogging 90 minutes.

One Week

Monday:	100-metre windsprints every 200 metres by 6/10 times.
Tuesday:	Easy fartlek running 45 minutes.
Wednesday:	Time trials 200 and 1,000 metres.
Thursday:	Fast relaxed running 100 metres by 10 times.
Friday:	Jogging 30 minutes.
Saturday:	Time trial 1,500 metres.
Sunday:	Jogging 90 minutes.

One Week

Monday:	100-metre windsprints every 200 metres by 6/10 times.
Tuesday:	Easy fartlek running 45 minutes.
Wednesday:	Time trials 200 and 600 metres.
Thursday:	Fast relaxed running 100 metres by 10 times.

Friday:	Jogging 30 minutes.
Saturday:	Time trial 800 metres.
Sunday:	Jogging 60 minutes.

One Week

Monday:	100-metre windsprints every 200 metres by 6/10 times.
Tuesday:	Easy fartlek running 45 minutes.
Wednesday:	Time trials 200 and 1,000 metres.
Thursday:	Fast relaxed running 100 metres by 10 times.
Friday:	Jogging 30 minutes.
Saturday:	Time trial 1,500 metres.
Sunday:	Jogging 60 minutes.

One Week

Monday:	45-metre windsprints every 100 metres by 16/20 times.
Tuesday:	Easy fartlek running 45 minutes.
Wednesday:	Time trial 1,200 metres.
Thursday:	Fast relaxed running 100 metres by 10 times.
Friday:	Jogging 30 minutes.
Saturday:	Time trial 800 metres.
Sunday:	Jogging 60 minutes.

One Week

Monday:	45-metre windsprints every 100 metres by 12/16 times.
Tuesday:	Easy fartlek running 30 minutes.
Wednesday:	Time trial 400 metres.
Thursday:	Fast relaxed running 100 metres by 6 times.
Friday:	Jogging 30 minutes.
Saturday:	**First important 1,500 race.**
Sunday:	/

3,000 Metres

As long a time as possible

Monday:	Long aerobic running 30/60 minutes.
Tuesday:	Long aerobic running 60/90 minutes.
Wednesday:	30/60 minutes.
Thursday:	Long aerobic running 60/90 minutes.

Friday:	Long aerobic running 30/60 minutes.
Saturday:	Long aerobic running 60 minutes.
Sunday:	Long aerobic running 90 to 150 minutes.

Two Weeks

Monday:	Easy fartlek running 30/60 minutes.
Tuesday:	Long aerobic running 60/90 minutes.
Wednesday:	Easy fartlek running 30/60 minutes.
Thursday:	Long aerobic running 60/90 minutes.
Friday:	Relaxed striding 200 metres by 6 times.
Saturday:	Long aerobic running 60 minutes.
Sunday:	Long aerobic running 90 to 150 minutes.

Monday:	Hill springing, bounding, steps running 30/60 minutes.
Tuesday:	Long aerobic running 60/90 minutes.
Wednesday:	Hill springing, bounding, steps running 30/60 minutes.
Thursday:	Easy fartlek running 30/60 minutes.
Friday:	Relaxed striding 200 metres by 6 times.
Saturday:	Hill springing, bounding, steps running 30/60 minutes.
Sunday:	Long aerobic running 90/120 minutes.

Monday:	Repetitions 800 metres by 6 times.
Tuesday:	Easy fartlek running 45/60 minutes.
Wednesday:	Time trial 5 kms.
Thursday:	Sprint training.
Friday:	Jogging 30 minutes.
Saturday:	Time trial 400 metres by 8/12 times.
Sunday:	Jogging 90/120 minutes.

Monday:	Repetitions 1,500 metres by 3 times.
Tuesday:	Easy fartlek running 45/60 minutes.
Wednesday:	Time trial 5 kms.
Thursday:	Sprint training.
Friday:	Jogging 30 minutes.
Saturday:	Repetitions 200 metres 8/15 times.
Sunday:	Jogging 90/120 minutes.

Four Weeks

Monday:	Repetitions 1,000 metres by 4 times.

Tuesday:	Easy fartlek running 45/60 minutes.
Wednesday:	Time trial 5 kms.
Thursday:	Sprint training.
Friday:	Jogging 30 minutes.
Saturday:	Repetitions 400 metres by 8/12 times.
Sunday:	Jogging 90/120 minutes.

One Week

Monday:	Repetitions 800 metres by 6 times.
Tuesday:	Easy fartlek running 45/60 minutes.
Wednesday:	Time trial 5 kms.
Thursday:	Fast relaxed running 100 metres by 10 times.
Friday:	Jogging 30 minutes.
Saturday:	Repetitions 200 metres by 8/15 times.
Sunday:	Jogging 90/120 minutes.

One Week

Monday:	100-metre windsprints every 200 metres by 8/12 times.
Tuesday:	Easy fartlek running 45/60 minutes.
Wednesday:	Time trials 200 and 800 metres.
Thursday:	Fast relaxed running 100 metres by 10 times.
Friday:	Jogging 30 minutes.
Saturday:	Time trial 300 metres.
Sunday:	Jogging 60/90 minutes.

One Week

Monday:	100-metre windsprints every 200 metres by 8/12 times.
Tuesday:	Easy fartlek running 45/60 minutes.
Wednesday:	Time trials 200 and 1,000 metres
Thursday:	Fast relaxed running 100 metres by 10 times.
Friday:	Jogging 30 minutes.
Saturday:	Time trial 1,500 metres.
Sunday:	Jogging 60/90 minutes.

One Week

Monday:	100-metre windsprints every 200 metres by 8/12 times.
Tuesday:	Easy fartlek running 45 minutes.
Wednesday:	Time trials 200 and 800 metres.
Thursday:	Fast relaxed running 100 metres by 10 times.

Friday:	Jogging 30 minutes.
Saturday:	Time trial 3,000 metres.
Sunday:	Jogging 60 minutes.

One Week

Monday:	100-metre windsprints every 200 metres by 8/12 times.
Tuesday:	Easy fartlek running 30/45 minutes.
Wednesday:	Time trials 200 and 1,000 metres.
Thursday:	Fast relaxed running 100 metres by 10 times.
Friday:	Jogging 30 minutes.
Saturday:	Time trial 3,000 metres.
Sunday:	Jogging 60 minutes.

One Week

Monday:	45-metre windsprints every 100 metres by 15/20 times.
Tuesday:	Easy fartlek running 30/45 minutes.
Wednesday:	Time trial 3,000 metres.
Thursday:	Fast relaxed running 100 metres by 10 times.
Friday:	Jogging 30 minutes.
Saturday:	Time trial 1,500 metres.
Sunday:	Jogging 60 minutes.

One Week

Monday:	45-metre windsprints every 100 metres by 12/16 times.
Tuesday:	Time trial 800 metres.
Wednesday:	Fast relaxed running 100 metres by 6 times.
Thursday:	Jogging 45 minutes.
Friday:	Jogging 30 minutes.
Saturday:	**First important 3,000 race.**
Sunday:	/

3,000 Metres Steeplechase

Training warm-ups should include the use of five hurdles, placed as for the steeplechase but using one hurdle in place of the water-jump. Run eight laps easily, practising technique. Using hurdles instead of steeplechase fences means they all have to be cleared without placing a foot on the top.

As long a time as possible

Monday:	Long aerobic running 30/60 minutes.
Tuesday:	Long aerobic running 60/90 minutes.
Wednesday:	Long aerobic running 30/60 minutes.
Thursday:	Long aerobic running 60/90 minutes.
Friday:	Long aerobic running 30/60 minutes.
Saturday:	Long aerobic running 60 minutes.
Sunday:	Long aerobic running 90/150 minutes.

Two Weeks

Monday:	Easy fartlek running 30/60 minutes.
Tuesday:	Long aerobic runing 60/90 minutes.
Wednesday:	Hurdles practice.
Thursday:	Easy fartlek running 30/60 minutes.
Friday:	Relaxed striding 200 metres by 6 times.
Saturday:	Hurdles practice.
Sunday:	Long aerobic runing 90/120 minutes.

Four Weeks

Monday:	Hill springing/bounding, steep hill/steps running 30/60 minutes.
Tuesday:	Long aerobic running 60/90 minutes.
Wednesday:	Hill springing/bounding, steep hill/steps running 30/60 minutes.
Thursday:	Hurdles practice.
Friday:	Relaxed striding 200 metres by 6 times.
Saturday:	Hill springing/bounding, steep hill/steps running 30/60 minutes
Sunday:	Long aerobic running 90/120 minutes.

One Week

Monday:	Repetitions 800 metres by 6 times.
Tuesday:	Easy fartlek running 45/60 minutes.
Wednesday:	Time trial 5 kms.
Thursday:	Sprint training, hurdles practice and water jump practice.
Friday:	Jogging 30 minutes.
Saturday:	Time trial 400 metres by 8/12 times.
Sunday:	Jogging 90/120 minutes.

One Week

Monday:	Repetitions 1,500 metres by 3 times.
Tuesday:	Easy fartlek running 45/60 minutes.

Wednesday:	Time trial 5 kms.
Thursday:	Sprint training, hurdles practice and water jump practice.
Friday:	Jogging 30 minutes.
Saturday:	Repetitions 200 metres by 8/15 times.
Sunday:	Jogging 90/120 minutes.

One Week

Monday:	Repetitions 1,000 metres by 4 times.
Tuesday:	Easy fartlek running 45/60 minutes.
Wednesday:	Time trial 5 kms.
Thursday:	Sprint training, hurdles practice and water jump practice.
Friday:	Jogging 30 minutes.
Saturday:	Repetitions 400 metres by 8/12 times.
Sunday:	Jogging 90/120 minutes.

One Week

Monday:	Repetitions 800 metres by 6 times.
Tuesday:	Easy fartlek running 45/60 minutes.
Wednesday:	Time trial 5 kms.
Thursday:	Fast relaxed running 100 metres by 6 times, hurdles practice and water jump practice.
Friday:	Jogging 45 minutes.
Saturday:	Repetitions 200 metres by 8/15 times.
Sunday:	Jogging 90/120 minutes.

One Week

Monday:	100-metre windsprints every 200 metres by 8/12 times.
Tuesday:	Easy fartlek running 45/60 minutes.
Wednesday:	Time trials 200 and 800 metres.
Thursday:	Fast relaxed running 100 metres by 10 times, hurdles practice and water jump practice.
Friday:	Jogging 30 minutes.
Saturday:	Time trial 3 kms.
Sunday:	Jogging 60/90 minutes.

One Week

Monday:	100-metre windsprints every 200 metres by 8/12 times.
Tuesday:	Easy fartlek running 45/60 minutes.
Wednesday:	Time trials 200 and 1,000 metres.

Thursday:	Fast relaxed running 100 metres by 10 times, hurdles practice and water jump practice.
Friday:	Jogging 30 minutes.
Saturday:	Time trial 3,000 metres steeplechase.
Sunday:	Jogging 60/90 minutes.

One Week

Monday:	100-metre windsprints every 200 metres by 8/12 times.
Tuesday:	Relaxed striding 45 minutes.
Wednesday:	Time trials 200 and 800 metres.
Thursday:	Fast relaxed running 100 metres by 10 times, hurdles practice and water jump practice.
Friday:	Jogging 30 minutes.
Saturday:	Time trial 3,000 metres.
Sunday:	Jogging 60 minutes.

One Week

Monday:	100-metre windsprints every 200 metres by 8/12 times.
Tuesday:	Easy fartlek running 45 minutes.
Wednesday:	Time trials 200 and 1,000 metres.
Thursday:	Fast relaxed running 100 metres by 10 times, hurdles practice and water jump practice.
Friday:	Jogging 30 minutes.
Saturday:	Time trial 3,000 metres steeplechase.
Sunday:	Jogging 60 minutes.

One Week

Monday:	45-metre windsprints every 100 metres by 15/20 times.
Tuesday:	Easy fartlek running 30/45 minutes.
Wednesday:	Time trial 2,000 metres steeplechase.
Thursday:	Fast relaxed running 100 metres by 6 times, hurdles practice and water jump practice.
Friday:	Jogging 30 minutes.
Saturday:	Time trial 1,500 metres.
Sunday:	Jogging 60 minutes.

One Week

Monday:	45-metre windsprints every 100 metres by 12/16 times.
Tuesday:	Hurdles practice and time trial 800 metres.

Wednesday:	Fast relaxed running 100 metres by 6 times.
Thursday:	Jogging 45 minutes.
Friday:	Jogging 30 minutes.
Saturday:	**First important steeplechase.**
Sunday:	/

5,000 Metres

As long a time as possible
Monday:	Long aerobic running 30/60 minutes.
Tuesday:	Long aerobic running 60/90 minutes.
Wednesday:	Long aerobic running 30/60 minutes.
Thursday:	Long aerobic running 60/90 minutes.
Friday:	Long aerobic running 30/60 minutes.
Saturday:	Long aerobic running 60 minutes.
Sunday:	Long aerobic running 90/150 minutes.

Two Weeks
Monday:	Easy fartlek running 30/60 minutes.
Tuesday:	Long aerobic runing 60/90 minutes.
Wednesday:	Easy fartlek running 30/60 minutes.
Thursday:	Long aerobic runing 60/90 minutes.
Friday:	Relaxed striding 200 metres by 6 times.
Saturday:	Long aerobic running 60 minutes.
Sunday:	Long aerobic runing 90/150 minutes.

Four Weeks
Monday:	Hill springing/bounding, steep hill/steps running 30/60 minutes
Tuesday:	Long aerobic running 60/90 minutes.
Wednesday:	Hill springing/bounding, steep hill/steps running 30/60 minutes.
Thursday:	Easy fartlek running 30/60 minutes.
Friday:	Relaxed striding 200 metres by 6 times.
Saturday:	Hill springing/bounding, steep hill/steps running 30/60 minutes
Sunday:	Long aerobic running 90/120 minutes.

One Week
| Monday: | Repetitions 800 metres by 6 times. |
| Tuesday: | Easy fartlek running 45/60 minutes. |

Wednesday:	Time trial 5 kms.
Thursday:	Sprint training.
Friday:	Jogging 30 minutes.
Saturday:	Time trial 400 metres by 8/12 times.
Sunday:	Jogging 90/120 minutes.

One Week

Monday:	Repetitions 1,500 metres by 3 times.
Tuesday:	Easy fartlek running 45/60 minutes.
Wednesday:	Time trial 5 kms.
Thursday:	Sprint training.
Friday:	Jogging 30 minutes.
Saturday:	Repetitions 200 metres by 8/12 times.
Sunday:	Jogging 90/120 minutes.

One Week

Monday:	Repetitions 1,000 metres by 4 times.
Tuesday:	Easy fartlek running 45/60 minutes.
Wednesday:	Time trial 5 kms.
Thursday:	Sprint training.
Friday:	Jogging 30 minutes.
Saturday:	Repetitons 400 metres by 8/12 times.
Sunday:	Jogging 90/120 minutes.

One Week

Monday:	Repetitions 800 metres by 6 times.
Tuesday:	Easy fartlek running 45/60 minutes.
Wednesday:	Time trial 5 kms.
Thursday:	Fast relaxed running 100 metres by 10 times.
Friday:	Jogging 30 minutes.
Saturday:	Repetitions 200 metres by 8/15 times.
Sunday:	Jogging 90/120 minutes.

One Week

Monday:	100-metre windsprints every 200 metres by 8/12 times.
Tuesday:	Easy fartlek running 45/60 minutes.
Wednesday:	Time trials 200 and 800 metres.
Thursday:	Fast relaxed running 100 metres by 10 times.
Friday:	Jogging 30 minutes.

Saturday:	Time trial 3 kms.
Sunday:	Jogging 60/90 minutes.

One Week

Monday:	100-metre windsprints every 200 metres by 8/12 times.
Tuesday:	Easy fartlek running 45/60 minutes.
Wednesday:	Time trials 200 and 1,000 metres.
Thursday:	Fast relaxed running 100 metres by 10 times.
Friday:	Jogging 30 minutes.
Saturday:	Time trial 3 kms.
Sunday:	Jogging 60/90 minutes.

One Week

Monday:	100-metre windsprints every 200 metres by 8/12 times.
Tuesday:	Easy fartlek running 45 minutes.
Wednesday:	Time trials 200 and 800 metres
Thursday:	Fast relaxed running 100 metres by 10 times.
Friday:	Jogging 30 minutes.
Saturday:	Time trial 10 kms.
Sunday:	Jogging 60 minutes.

One Week

Monday:	100-metre windsprints every 200 metres by 8/12 times.
Tuesday:	Easy fartlek running 45 minutes.
Wednesday:	Time trials 200 and 1,500 metres.
Thursday:	Fast relaxed running 100 metres by 10 times.
Friday:	Jogging 30 minutes.
Saturday:	Time trial 5 kms.
Sunday:	Jogging 60 minutes.

One Week

Monday:	45-metre windsprints every 100 metres by 15/20 times.
Tuesday:	Easy fartlek running 30/45 minutes.
Wednesday:	Time trial 5 kms.
Thursday:	Fast relaxed running 100 metres by 10 times.
Friday:	Jogging 30 minutes.
Saturday:	Time trial 1,500 metres.
Sunday:	Jogging 60 minutes.

One Week

Monday:	45-metre windsprints every 100 metres by 12/16 times.
Tuesday:	Time trial 800 metres.
Wednesday:	Fast relaxed running 100 metres by 6 times.
Thursday:	Jogging 45 minutes.
Friday:	Jogging 30 minutes.
Saturday:	**First important 5,000 race.**
Sunday:	/

10,000 Metres

As long a time as possible

Monday:	Long aerobic running 60 minutes.
Tuesday:	Long aerobic running 60/90 minutes.
Wednesday:	Long aerobic running 60 minutes.
Thursday:	Long aerobic running 60/90 minutes.
Friday:	Long aerobic running 30 minutes.
Saturday:	Long aerobic running 60 minutes.
Sunday:	Long aerobic running 120 minutes.

Two Weeks

Monday:	Easy fartlek running 60 minutes.
Tuesday:	Long aerobic runing 90 minutes.
Wednesday:	D 45 minutes.
Thursday:	Long aerobic runing 90 minutes.
Friday:	Relaxed striding 200 metres by 6 times.
Saturday:	Long aerobic running 60 minutes.
Sunday:	Long aerobic runing 120 minutes.

Four Weeks

Monday:	Hill springing/bounding, steep hill/steps running 30/60 minutes
Tuesday:	Jogging 90 minutes.
Wednesday:	Hill springing/bounding, steep hill/steps running 30/60 minutes.
Thursday:	Easy fartlek running 60 minutes.
Friday:	Relaxed striding 200 metres by 6 times.
Saturday:	Hill springing/bounding, steep hill/steps running 30/60 minutes
Sunday:	Jogging 90/120 minutes.

One Week

Monday:	Repetitions 800 metres by 6 times.
Tuesday:	Jogging 90 minutes.
Wednesday:	Time trial 3,000 metres at 3/4 effort.
Thursday:	Easy fartlek running 60 minutes.
Friday:	Jogging 30 minutes.
Saturday:	Repetitions 400 metres by 12 times.
Sunday:	Jogging 90/120 minutes.

One Week

Monday:	Repetitions 1,500 metres by 3 times.
Tuesday:	Jogging 90 minutes.
Wednesday:	Time trial 5,000 metres at 3/4 effort.
Thursday:	Easy fartlek running 60 minutes.
Friday:	Jogging 30 minutes.
Saturday:	Repetitions 200 metres by 15 times.
Sunday:	Jogging 90/120 minutes.

One Week

Monday:	Repetitions 1,000 metres by 4 times.
Tuesday:	Jogging 90 minutes.
Wednesday:	Time trial 3,000 metres at 3/4 effort.
Thursday:	Easy fartlek running 60 minutes.
Friday:	Jogging 30 minutes.
Saturday:	Repetitions 400 metres by 12 times.
Sunday:	Jogging 90/120 minutes.

One Week

Monday:	Repetitions 800 metres by 6 times.
Tuesday:	Jogging 90 minutes.
Wednesday:	Time trial 1,500 metres.
Thursday:	Easy fartlek running 60 minutes.
Friday:	Jogging 30 minutes.
Saturday:	Time trial 3,000 metres.
Sunday:	Jogging 90/120 minutes.

One Week

Monday:	100-metre windsprints every 200 metres by 12 times.
Tuesday:	Easy fartlek running 60 minutes.

Wednesday:	Time trial 5,000 metres.
Thursday:	Fast relaxed running 100 metres by 10 times.
Friday:	Jogging 30 minutes.
Saturday:	Race 5,000 metres.
Sunday:	Jogging 90 minutes.

One Week

Monday:	100-metre windsprints every 200 metres by 12 times.
Tuesday:	Easy fartlek running 60 minutes.
Wednesday:	Time trial 3,000 metres.
Thursday:	Fast relaxed running 100 metres by 10 times.
Friday:	Jogging 30 minutes.
Saturday:	Race 10,000 metres.
Sunday:	Jogging 90 minutes.

One Week

Monday:	100-metre windsprints every 200 metres by 12 times.
Tuesday:	Easy fartlek running 60 minutes.
Wednesday:	Time trial 5,000 metres.
Thursday:	Fast relaxed running 100 metres by 10 times.
Friday:	Jogging 30 minutes.
Saturday:	Race 5,000 metres.
Sunday:	Jogging 90 minutes.

One Week

Monday:	100-metre windsprints every 200 metres by 12 times.
Tuesday:	Easy fartlek running 60 minutes.
Wednesday:	Time trial 1,500 metres.
Thursday:	Fast relaxed running 100 metres by 10 times.
Friday:	Jogging 30 minutes.
Saturday:	Race 10,000 metres.
Sunday:	Jogging 90 minutes.

One Week

Monday:	45-metre windsprints every 100 metres by 20 times.
Tuesday:	Easy fartlek running 45 minutes.
Wednesday:	Time trial 1,500 metres.
Thursday:	Fast relaxed running 100 metres by 10 times.
Friday:	Jogging 30 minutes.

| Saturday: | Race 5,000 metres. |
| Sunday: | Jogging 60 minutes. |

One Week

Monday:	45-metre windsprints every 100 metres by 16 times.
Tuesday:	Time trial 800 metres.
Wednesday:	Fast relaxed running 100 metres by 6 times.
Thursday:	Jogging 30 minutes.
Friday:	Jogging 30 minutes.
Saturday:	**First important 10,000 race.**
Sunday:	/

Chapter 13: Marathon

If you are planning to run a marathon for a reasonable result, the first requirement is an application of intelligence. Give yourself plenty of time for development, take the long view. Some people are credited with running exceptionally fast marathons on as little as 20 miles (32 km) training a week but many fast times are far from authentic – run on downhill courses and with tail wind assistance between start and finish points many miles apart.

However, anyone without physical or health problems could walk 26 miles (42 km) if they had to. Many could walk and run the distance. But to run all the way without stopping and without undue stress and problems requires a reasonable weekly training mileage, possibly near 80-100 km a week for several months.

Instead of training haphazardly from day to day, it pays to set out a training schedule which takes into consideration your basic fitness and running background. Proven schedules used by other runners can be used for guidance but should never be rigidly followed. Use the intensity and volume that suits you. Study the guide for setting out your schedule to slot all the elements you need into the time you have before your target race.

The novice runner is advised to become initiated to training by tackling shorter distances first but this is not imperative. Condition by training for a period of time each day rather tha running set mileages. This usually gives better results and keeps the pressure off. The time spent running is far more important than the mileage covered.

Allow three days a week for long runs – what you consider long depends on your level of fitness – but the aim eventually should be 90 minutes on two days and about two hours or more on one day. That extra-long run could be increased every four or five weeks to take you near the actual time you would take to run the marathon distance.

The in-between days are used for runs up to 60 minutes over varying terrain to strengthen the legs and condition generally or for rest. If the legs start to get unduly tired, you must ignore the schedule and lighten the training for a few days until your legs have recovered and you can run again with reasonable comfort. Push when you feel tired and you could suffer muscle breakdown which will waste all your effort.

The best results come when you train to a comfortably tired state, knowing as you finish that the training could have been harder. Keep always in mind that you can never run too slowly but you can run too fast.

About three months of long aerobic running of this nature builds the desired minimum base. During the third month, add a day or two of easy fartlek to help to prepare for the faster training involved in the next phase. But keep that constant variation between long day and short day.

Throughout your running, think about your running technique and speed. Runs over hilly terrain or up steps help to develop leg strength and flexibility – a little often can work wonders. One method is to have a secondary training session each day; warm up and then bound a few easy hills, run some stadium steps or a steep hill or do a little hill springing on a gentle slope to work the ankles. You don't need a lot, just enough to make you feel the workout a little.

Once the conditioning period is over, four to six weeks can be used to concentrate on hill type training to add resistance to the leg muscles and develop muscle fibres, particularly the quick twitch. Two or three workouts a week of from fifteen to sixty minutes, depending on how you feel, are enough. Underdoing it is better than overdoing it.

The other days should see you on steady running, striding or easy fartlek according to how your legs feel. Try relaxed downhill striding on descents that are not too steep. The third phase requires some anaerobic running.

Usually, three days are enough and the other days should be relatively easy. If you do repetitions, the longer distances, such as six by 800 metres or three by 1,500 m are better because you are likely to have more muscular viscosity than athletes training for shorter distances and fast 200 m and 400 m reps could cause injury. Again, doing less is better than doing more and the tempo should always be governed by how you feel.

With the marathon five weeks away, you can ease your effort slightly but, just over four weeks out, a trial simulating actual race conditions can be run. Anything from 20 miles (32 km) to the full marathon distance works. It will give you a good indication of the result you can expect – you must allow for the fact that you will not be as truly fresh as you will be for the marathon itself – and it can help you to check your pace judgement because any mistake in the trial will be graphically remembered four weeks later. It will check your racing reactions to food and drink before and during the race.

The greatest benefit will come from the run itself in a sharp improvement in your racing fitness. Retain that by keeping all further training relatively easy and by resisting the temptation to run too much in the final week. It will be too late to add anything to your condition; it can only work against you. Make it a restful week – you've earned it.

Some Race-day Tips

Maintain normal balanced meals leading up to the marathon to keep your metabolism in balance. In the two days before the race, eat up to eight ounces of honey or sugars extra. Don't eat in the three hours before the start; make your breakfast light, preferably cereals, honey and toast with tea or coffee.

Don't wear new shoes. They should be comfortably broken in. When you put them on, force the heels hard into the backs of the shoes and lace firmly but not tightly to prevent foot movement within the shoes that could cause blisters.

Don't run too much before you start. Save your energy. Stretch and loosen a little and then use the early part of the run as your warm-up by holding yourself firmly in check whatever the runners around you are doing. Ignore them and run at the effort that suits you. The dividends will be paid later.

Try to relax. Don't lift the knees higher than necessary so that you save them for efficient use at the other end. Prepare electrolyte drinks for a hot day but make the mixtures weaker than directed and add some honey. Do **not** take salt tablets. Drink water and electrolyte drinks throughout the race. A cupful before you start helps. If you haven't got a proper drinking vessel, stop to drink so that you don't gulp air.

Keep your body wet. Squeeze sponges over your head, even dump a bucket of water over yourself as the best insurance against dehydration and high body temperatures.

Do not surge during the race and waste energy.
Do not use anti-perspirants.

Beginners Marathon

Four Weeks

Monday:	Jogging 30/45 minutes.
Tuesday:	Jogging 45/60 minutes.
Wednesday:	Jogging 30/45 minutes.
Thursday:	Jogging 45/60 minutes.
Friday:	Jogging 30 minutes.
Saturday:	Jogging 45 minutes.
Sunday:	Jogging 60 minutes.

Two Weeks

Monday:	Long aerobic runing 30/45 minutes.
Tuesday:	Jogging 60/75 minutes.
Wednesday:	Long aerobic runing 30/45 minutes.
Thursday:	Jogging 60/75 minutes.
Friday:	Jogging 30 minutes.
Saturday:	Long aerobic running 30/45 minutes.
Sunday:	Jogging 60/90 minutes.

Four Weeks

Monday:	Easy fartlek running 30/45 minutes.
Tuesday:	Long aerobic running 45/75 minutes.
Wednesday:	Easy fartlek running 30/45 minutes.
Thursday:	Long aerobic running 45/75 minutes.
Friday:	Relaxed striding 150 metres by 4/6 times.
Saturday:	Easy fartlek running 45/60 minutes.
Sunday:	Long aerobic running 60/120 minutes.

Four Weeks

Monday:	Hill springing/bounding, steep hill/steps running 30/45 minutes
Tuesday:	Long aerobic running 45/75 minutes.
Wednesday:	Easy fartlek running 30/45 minutes.
Thursday:	Hill springing/bounding, steep hill/steps running 30/45 minutes.
Friday:	Relaxed striding 200 metres by 4/6 times.
Saturday:	Hill springing/bounding, steep hill/steps running 30 minutes
Sunday:	Long aerobic running 60/120 minutes.

One Week

Monday:	Repetitions 800 metres by 2/4 times.
Tuesday:	Long aerobic running 45/75 minutes.
Wednesday:	Time trial 3,000 metres.
Thursday:	Long aerobic running 45/75 minutes.
Friday:	Relaxed striding 200 metres by 4/6 times.
Saturday:	Time trial 5,000 metres.
Sunday:	Long aerobic running 90/120 minutes.

One Week

Monday:	Repetitions 1,000 metres by 2/3 times.
Tuesday:	Long aerobic running 60/90 minutes.

Wednesday:	Time trial 3,000 metres.
Thursday:	Long aerobic running 60/75 minutes.
Friday:	Relaxed striding 200 metres by 4/6 times.
Saturday:	Time trial 10,000 metres.
Sunday:	Long aerobic running 90/120 minutes.

One Week

Monday:	Repetitions 1,500 metres by 2/3 times.
Tuesday:	Long aerobic running 60/90 minutes.
Wednesday:	Time trial 5,000 metres.
Thursday:	Long aerobic running 60/90 minutes.
Friday:	Relaxed striding 200 metres by 4/6 times.
Saturday:	Time trial 5,000 metres.
Sunday:	Long aerobic running 90/120 minutes.

One Week

Monday:	Repetitions 800 metres by 3/5 times.
Tuesday:	Long aerobic running 60/90 minutes.
Wednesday:	Time trial 3,000 metres.
Thursday:	Easy fartlek running 45 minutes.
Friday:	Relaxed striding 200 metres by 4/6 times.
Saturday:	Time trial 10,000 metres.
Sunday:	Long aerobic running 90/120 minutes.

One Week

Monday:	100-metre windsprints every 200 metres by 6/8 times.
Tuesday:	Jogging 60/90 minutes.
Wednesday:	Time trial 5,000 metres.
Thursday:	Jogging 60/90 minutes.
Friday:	P 100 metres by 6 times.
Saturday:	Time trial 3,000 metres.
Sunday:	Jogging 60/90 minutes.

One Week

Monday:	100-metre windsprints every 200 metres by 6 times.
Tuesday:	Jogging 60 minutes.
Wednesday:	Time trial 2,000 metres.
Thursday:	Jogging 45 minutes.
Friday:	Jogging 30 minutes.

Saturday:	Time trial 35 kms – **fast!**
Sunday:	Jogging 30/45 minutes.

One Week

Monday:	Jogging 45/60 minutes.
Tuesday:	Jogging 45/60 minutes.
Wednesday:	Relaxed striding 200 metres by 6 times.
Thursday:	Easy fartlek running 30 minutes.
Friday:	Jogging 30 minutes.
Saturday:	Time trial 3,000 metres.
Sunday:	Jogging 120 minutes.

One Week

Monday:	100-metre windsprints every 200 metres by 6/8 times.
Tuesday:	Jogging 60/90 minutes.
Wednesday:	Time trial 3,000 metres.
Thursday:	Jogging 60/90 minutes.
Friday:	Jogging 30 minutes.
Saturday:	Time trial 10,000 metres.
Sunday:	Jogging 90/120 minutes.

One Week

Monday:	100-metre windsprints every 200 metres by 6/8 times.
Tuesday:	Jogging 60/90 minutes.
Wednesday:	Time trial 5,000 metres.
Thursday:	Easy fartlek running 30/45 minutes.
Friday:	Jogging 30 minutes.
Saturday:	Time trial 3,000 metres.
Sunday:	Jogging 45/60 minutes.

One Week

Monday:	Fast relaxed running 100 metres by 6 times.
Tuesday:	Time trial 2,000 metres.
Wednesday:	Jogging 45 minutes.
Thursday:	Jogging 30 minutes.
Friday:	Jogging 30 minutes.
Saturday:	**Marathon race.**
Sunday:	Jog easily for at least one week.

Marathon

For as long a time as possible (12 weeks)

PHASE 1

Monday:	Long aerobic running 60 minutes.
Tuesday:	Long aerobic running 90 minutes.
Wednesday:	Long aerobic running 60 minutes.
Thursday:	Long aerobic running 90 minutes.
Friday:	Long aerobic running 60 minutes.
Saturday:	Long aerobic running 60 minutes.
Sunday:	Long aerobic running 120 minutes or more.

Four Weeks

PHASE 2 — 8 WEEKS OUT

Monday:	Hill springing/bounding, steep hill/steps running 45/60 minutes.
Tuesday:	Long aerobic running 90 minutes.
Wednesday:	Hill springing/bounding; steep hill/steps running 45/60 minutes.
Thursday:	Easy fartlek running 60 minutes.
Friday:	Relaxed striding 200 metres by 6 times.
Saturday:	Hill springing/bounding, steep hill/steps running 45/60 minutes.
Sunday:	Long aerobic running 120 minutes.

One Week

10. WEEKS

Monday:	Repetitions 800 metres by 6 times.
Tuesday:	Long aerobic running 90 minutes.
Wednesday:	Time trial 5,000 metres.
Thursday:	Long aerobic running 90 minutes.
Friday:	Relaxed striding 200 metres by 6 times.
Saturday:	Time trial 10,000 metres at 3/4 effort.
Sunday:	Long aerobic running 120 minutes or more.

One Week

Monday:	Repetitions 1,000 metres by 4 times.
Tuesday:	Long aerobic running 90 minutes.
Wednesday:	Time trial 5,000 metres.
Thursday:	Long aerobic running 90 minutes.
Friday:	Relaxed striding 200 metres by 6 times.
Saturday:	Time trial 10,000 metres at 3/4 effort.
Sunday:	Long aerobic running 120 minutes or more.

One Week

Monday:	Repetitions 1,500 metres by 3 times.
Tuesday:	Long aerobic running 90 minutes.
Wednesday:	Time trial 5,000 metres.
Thursday:	Long aerobic running 90 minutes.
Friday:	Relaxed striding 200 metres by 6 times.
Saturday:	Time trial 5,000 metres.
Sunday:	Long aerobic running 120 minutes or more.

One Week

Monday:	Repetitions 800 metres by 6 times.
Tuesday:	Long aerobic running 90 minutes.
Wednesday:	Time trial 3,000 metres.
Thursday:	Long aerobic running 90 minutes.
Friday:	Relaxed striding 200 metres by 6 times.
Saturday:	Time trial 10,000 metres.
Sunday:	Long aerobic running 120 minutes or more.

One Week

Monday:	100-metre windsprints every 200 metres by 10/12 times.
Tuesday:	Jogging 90 minutes.
Wednesday:	Time trial 5,000 metres.
Thursday:	Jogging 90 minutes.
Friday:	Fast relaxed running 100 metres by 6 times.
Saturday:	Time trial 5,000 metres.
Sunday:	Jogging 90 minutes.

One Week

Monday:	100-metre windsprints every 200 metres by 10/12 times.
Tuesday:	Jogging 90 minutes.
Wednesday:	Time trial 3,000 metres.
Thursday:	Jogging 60 minutes.
Friday:	Jogging 30 minutes.
Saturday:	Time trial 35 kms – **fast!**
Sunday:	Jogging 60 minutes.

One Week

Monday:	Jogging 60 minutes.
Tuesday:	Relaxed striding 200 metres by 6 times.

Wednesday:	Time trial 5,000 metres.
Thursday:	Jogging 90 minutes.
Friday:	Jogging 30 minutes.
Saturday:	Time trial 3,000 metres.
Sunday:	Jogging 120 minutes.

One Week

Monday:	100-metre windsprints every 200 metres by 10/12 times.
Tuesday:	Jogging 90 minutes.
Wednesday:	Time trial 3,000 metres.
Thursday:	Jogging 90 minutes.
Friday:	Jogging 30 minutes.
Saturday:	Time trial 10,000 metres.
Sunday:	Jogging 120 minutes.

One Week

Monday:	100-metre windsprints every 200 metres by 10 times.
Tuesday:	Jogging 90 minutes.
Wednesday:	Time trial 5,000 metres.
Thursday:	Easy fartlek running 45 minutes.
Friday:	Jogging 30 minutes.
Saturday:	Time trial 5,000 metres.
Sunday:	Jogging 60 minutes.

One Week

Monday:	Fast relaxed running 100 metres by 6 times.
Tuesday:	Time trial 2,000 metres.
Wednesday:	Jogging 45 minutes.
Thursday:	Jogging 30 minutes.
Friday:	Jogging 30 minutes.
Saturday:	**Marathon race.**
Sunday:	Jogging 60 minutes then jog easily for one week.

Chapter: 14 The Athlete and the Coach – the Vital Relationship

Motivation is the important factor in the relationship between the athlete and the coach and **hope** is the key word in motivation. We all have hopes. The coach, the athlete, everyone. But the goals on which hope is based have to be realistic. It's no good a coach telling an athlete he can run a four-minute mile when he knows damn well he's not going to do it.

You do not want to build up hopes unnecessarily. So we've got to use realism, otherwise both athlete and coach can be upset. The aim should be a minimum realisation rather than a maximum one. A coach should never tell an athlete he can perform better than a true evaluation of his current development shows.

I had this problem when I took a team to Europe which included one runner I had never trained but who had been trained by a coach who told him, more or less, that he could beat everyone.

The first race was an 800 m in White City and this guy, who had never run a big international race before, went out in front and led until he turned into the straight. He was a good runner but, when he ran into the straight, the whole pack went past him. Peter Snell, who I did train, won the race.

When I saw this runner after the race, he was walking off the track with his running shoes in his hands and his head down. I asked him where he was going and he said he was going back to the hotel.

"No you're not", I said, "just wait a while."

I had met the manager of the meet and his twenty-one-year-old secretary and I asked the young woman what she was doing that night.

"Nothing", she said. "Why?"

"See that guy", I said, "I'd like you to take him out to a night club tonight. Give him a good time and I'll pay for it."

I went back to the athlete and said, "See that girl over there? She's going to take you out for a nice evening."

I introduced them and I didn´t see him again until about 10 o'clock the next morning when he was racing out of the hotel.

"Where are you going?" I asked.

"I'm going out with that girl."

"Good on you", I said. And from then on, I never had any problems.

He'd got rid of his immediate dejection and he'd realised the world was full of very good runners - there weren't just a couple in New Zealand - and that when you get up against the best in the world you can't set yourself up to run it all from the front.
He ran very well for the rest of that tour, very well indeed.

Athletes need to be told why specific aspects of training are being used, both physiologically and mechanically. This is the best form of psychology and motivation to use. This is very important. The coach should appeal to an athlete's intelligence, explain clearly what every training session means and what they are trying to achieve.
    The athletes with the best motivation are those who are well informed, understand their training because it makes sense to them and have confidence in their coach. They can train according to their reactions without working to hypothetical figures, as some coaches insist on, and running into a distressed state.

When you are training athletes right through a programme for several months leading up to a big competition, there should be no need to tell them they can beat the opposition because they have gone through it all, understand it, have improved in training, have confidence in what is being done. If the win doesn't eventuate, they will know it wasn't through lack of trying.

Athletes need to enjoy their training. I know a lot don't. They don't enjoy going down to the track with a coach with a stopwatch making them do repetitions, even until they vomit or fall exhausted. That is not the way to train, even at the highest level. You have to hurt yourself a little but at the same time you must enjoy it.
    The training must be varied so the athlete is not doing the same thing over and over again.
    The potential of some athletes is not immediately apparent but improvement provides motivation and builds the coach's esteem. You cannot tell by looking at athletes what their prospects might be. Until they go through a systematic training programme, preferably for a number of seasons, their potential cannot always be judged. It calls for patience if an athlete wants to see what he can achieve as an international.

Incorrect training methods can cause stress and breakdown the relationship between athletes and coaches. If you use training methods that place a lot of stress on the athletes, particularly young ones, if you get imbalance in the training, you'll get that breakdown.
    Coaches need to be sensitive to the emotional factors which influence their athletes. They can have all sorts of differing emotional problems, they come from different homes, different environments and many other factors can affect their performance in training from day to day.

The coach, if he wants to get the best out of them, has to try to understand their differing points of view, any problems they may be facing at home and at work or school.

Coaches should welcome questions regarding training and other methods. There are coaches who work on training schedules that they don't fully understand themselves because they haven't grasped the physiological and mechanical fundamentals, so it follows that their athletes don't know either and when they ask questions about it, quite often both sides become upset because no one has the answers. I found this was particularly so with many American coaches.

The coach must develop a positive attitude in his athletes.

When I went to Denmark in 1971, to train its athletes for nine months, we had one athlete, Tom Hansen, who, we knew, could do well but he never succeeded when it came to big competitions. He just looked like a wet rag.

We knew he could run fast and I did everything I possibly could until we got him to the stage where he was a definite prospect to make the 1,500 at the Munich Olympics. Unfortunately for him, I had trained another guy who had already qualified and that really added the pressure on Tom to make it. And the more pressure we put on him, the worse he performed.

We went to Dublin for an Ireland v Denmark meet and Tom won the 1,500 but the conditions were so windy he couldn't get the time he required. He then had four days left.

As a life member of the Finnish Athletic Coaches Federation, I knew that Pekka Vassala, who had already qualified, was taking a group through to get more 1,500 qualifiers for Finland so I asked if Hansen could go over there and run with them.

He ran in Finland with no pressure on him. He was just one of the guys being pulled along by Vassala, he didn't have to take the lead or anything and he ran the qualifying time easily. He didn't have the background in conditioning training that I would have wanted but he did get to the Munich 1,500 final. The other Dane was knocked out in the semis.

Coaches quite often have athletes who they know can do well, who have every physical attribute but their nervousness and lack of confidence in themselves can cost them dearly.

Demand sincerity. I have always believed in this. It doesn't matter how good athletes are, they can have the best potential in the world but if they are not going to be sincere about training and sincere to their coach it is better that they should be told to go and take a jump at themselves. I never gave athletes a second chance; if they let me down once, I never let them put it over me again.

I demand sincerity. As a coach, your time is the most valuable thing you can give anyone; if that time is being wasted, you would be much better at home with your wife and family or making money for yourself. You don't have to be down at a track with athletes who are cheating on you.

If we knew how many minutes, months or years we had to live, we'd probably all be doing different things with our lives. So don't waste any part of that life on no-hopers. It's far too valuable.

I have known the situation in New Zealand where a coach has spent months with an athlete and, one day, he doesn't show for training. Next time you see him and ask what happened, he says casually, "Oh, I decided not to run any more."
You've spent all that time for nothing.
It may be all right for professional coaches but with amateur coaches, such as we have in New Zealand, that kind of insincerity can happen too often.

Athletes differ by nature – the confident and the unconfident, the soft and the hardy. I had two athletes who fitted that kind of comparison. One was a tough guy who won nearly every championship in New Zealand from 800 m to the six-mile of those days; the other had had problems with his family years before and seemed to like a lot of sympathy. If he hurt his leg, he would always be complaining about it and I would always ask him when he came in the door, "What the hell's wrong with you tonight?"

I eventually got him to the stage where, if he twisted his ankle, he wouldn't say a thing. He'd just keep running.

Some you have to pat on the back, some you have to kick in the backside. You've got to make them tougher, make them realise there is no easy way, it hurts everyone.
The coach-athletes relationship can be affected by more indirect influences.
    One is the coach-officials relationship. In Venezuela, they had Venezuelan coaches propped up by the federation. They got $18 million a year to run the track and field programme and, of course, in these Latin American countries, they get their brothers and sisters and cousins and every other relation in on the gravy train. I went to areas where the coach was getting a good salary but didn't know a thing he could usefully pass on to his athletes; no one was getting anywhere.

I found the wrong coaches in control through political influence, coaches in control who were good talkers but couldn't produce results. If they could have produced results, I wouldn't have been invited to go to help.

I always tell coaches in these situations that if they know what to do, they don't have to tell anyone. All they have to do is put their athletes on the Olympic dais. That tells everyone.

Then you get the coach v coach problem, a lack of co-operation between them which can upset athletes. In many countries, you will find coaches who are jealous of other coaches, who think their method of coaching is better than anyone else's. But they can't both be right. One is probably not adhering to the physiological and mechanical fundamentals and getting away from balance in training so, consequently, you get more upsets. And when you get coaches fighting, it usually brushes off on to the athletes and we have more problems.

In Finland, I encountered problems with athletes/officials relationships. The athletes were bypassing their coaches and going directly to the officials for money to go down to Majorca and the Canary Islands during the Finnish winter because they said they couldn't train in the snow. They were going down there all right but having a nice time and then coming back to Finland and running for money.

I had one athlete come back from Majorca and run seven 5,000 m races in ten days because when he won he got a trophy and also a brown envelope. The officials thought they were doing the right thing but that had to be stopped. I managed to get the control of the athletes placed under the coaches and they then didn't get the money unless they did what the coaches told them and they also had to back away from hard races for money before big international meets when they had to run for their country.

This has happened in many countries, where athletes have used the money for their own ends. They have performed badly when they had to run for their country but have run very well immediately afterwards when money was there to be won.

It's the coaches who develop the potential, it's the coaches who teach, it's the coaches who set up the national programmes which produce the champions which, in the long run turn the turnstiles.

Unless you have a national coaching federation or association which co-ordinates the coaching, you can never achieve the optimum results.

Some coaches can take the best potential in the country and destroy it; others can take much less promising material and craft it into champions.

It's important that coaches, athletes and officials understand the programme that's being set up, make sure it is co-ordinated throughout the country and fully appreciate the value in that programme of the coaching input.

The importance of coaches at international meets cannot be under-estimated. After Munich, I was invited to Finland to get an award from Finnish president Kekkonnen and the athletic federation head told me the three Scandinavian managers were having a celebration dinner together after the Olympics when the Norwegian remarked to the Finn, "How is it that your people did so well? You won several gold and bronze medals and you had no more runners than we did and the same number of officials – but you got all these medals and we didn't do very well."
The Swedish manager made the same comment.
The Finn said, "Well, we had the same number of athletes as you, but you had ten managers and one coach and we had one manager and ten coaches. That's the difference."

About seventy officials went with one hundred and forty athletes in the New Zealand team to Barcelona. I don't know how many coaches there were but there were only three for track and field.

The point so often missed is that coaches can often do the same job as a manager. They can fit easily into the dual role. But a manager cannot do the same job as a coach. The important thing is to have the people there who can help the athletes, not just people considered to have earned a trip away, who may even turn it into a holiday.

I have mentioned the importance of the respect and esteem of the athletes for their coach. A classic example was the late Mr Nakamura of Japan, who did so much to develop the mental and spiritual aspects of training. He was highly regarded by his athletes. That respect and esteem comes if coaches look after their athletes well, are straight and sincere with them and do everything they can to help them in every aspect of their lives.

Some athletes have said they have experienced a euphoria while running, a spiritual sensation of oneness, a communion with nature, the grass, trees, flowers, wild life and even God. These effects will occur if you let them and wish them to be there, if you are relaxed and taught to understand meditative exercising. The Japanese did that and many chose a form of environment which related to that. They would rather run in a park or along a forest trail than dodge traffic in the middle of a city's polluted air.
You do run better and you do feel better being close to nature like that. You train at an immeasurably higher rate and gain more benefit.

Let's consider some of the influences that touch athletes' performance.

Some athletes are prone to depression and then they blame the coach or team-mates or other runners. They try to under-rate others' efforts because they did not compete up to expectations. Maybe they expected too much. I think some of them direct their anger at themselves.

Take the case of Murray Halberg when he came back from the Melbourne Olympics 1956. He wasn't really strong enough at that time but he did get into the final of the 1,500 metres. But when he came home, he felt he had let everyone down because he did not win a medal so he took himself off down to the South Island's West Coast and we did not see him for a while. He was pointing his anger at himself and working it out of his system.

We must appreciate that sometimes, for reasons beyond control of the athlete or the coach, something can happen and the athlete doesn't perform up to the hoped-for best. The solution is to talk about it in a sensible way, analyse it and try to determine why the bid didn't succeed. This isn't looking for excuses but finding analytical reasons so that the same mistake isn't made again.

Indifference is a problem. An athlete can show little or no reaction to poor personal efforts and lack application. That's just the way some people are; they are more social runners than serious runners. They want to be there at the end and drink the beer, mingle with the bunch and go on the trips but they are not going to push themselves around too hard because they lack that application to do better. There is nothing wrong with them; they are out to enjoy life and are indifferent to the possibility that they might be champions. They may well enjoy their sport more than the elite.

Lack of confidence shows in some. They are always the underdogs to their training colleagues, running in the shadow of others. They compete with people they see as better than they are, develop an inferiority complex and this shows in their racing. They´re beaten even before they got out on the track.

Sometimes, we've got to make them realise that maybe it's because their background of training isn't sufficient, they haven't been at it long enough, they might lack the speed which means they're racing over the wrong distances. There are always ways to build up confidence but it needs to be approached carefully.

Elation is natural, through success, through personal improvement, even if the race hasn't been won, because they vindicated the faith of others or even just because they took part in an event. It's not an emotion to be squashed but encouraged.

Temporary disappointment, through a poor performance, through loss of training because of illness or injury, can lead athletes to be harsh on themselves. They attack themselves for having made a stupid blunder, perhaps feel they have let others or even their country down.

Some runners feel so good that halfway through a race they'll dash to the front, full of running, and set themselves up to be beaten at the end. Then they castigate themselves for lack of control. Or you get them walking about saying things like, "I left my run too late. If I'd gone earlier, I would have won." They're verging on making excuses but it´s a fact that runners do make stupid blunders from time to time, usually through lack of experience.

The important point is that they should analyse the performance objectively and precisely and learn from the experience, rather than hurling their running shoes around the dressing room and berating themselves. Every error or failure should be a learning experience.

From what I have observed of international runners who pull out of marathons or other events and don't perform anywhere near as well as when they're on tours and running for money, I'd say a lot of them don't feel any remorse, but there are many who, when they pull on the national colours, or even their club colours, are very conscious of an obligation to do well.

Some athletes display a complete, unquestioning confidence in their coaches but, often, they don't fully understand what they're about, they don't understand the fundamentals. They should question but they don't, accepting without questioning what the coach tells them. They're training unintelligently because they don't understand what they're doing when they go out to carry out a certain workload. They'll work to hypothetical training figures of distances and repetitions, whatever the coach tells them, without observing their own reaction.

They won't get the best out of themselves. Lacking confidence and knowledge, they need to be led. The good coach will build up their confidence, make them realise they've got to think for themselves and understand more clearly what they're about. They need morale boosters because sometimes they get nervous, they look at the opposition and get highly twitchy about them instead of forgetting the opposition and concentrating on getting the best out of themselves and then seeing what happens.

Murray Halberg, before he won the 1960 5,000 metres gold medal with a brilliant tactical performance, was a classical example. Crowded with the other eleven finalists in a small room before being led out to the track, he found he could not make eye contact with any of them. They all had their heads down and he realised he was sharing the confined space with eleven rivals who were more scared than he was.

You get self-centred types, often show-offs. They don't always make good team-mates. When I went to Finland, a runner called Kuha was getting quoted in the papers, appearing on the front of all the magazines. He was the top runner in Finland, where running is a big sport, particularly middle and distance running, and he was adulted like New Zealand's All Black captain. He was one of those who went down to Majorca to train and I think it went to his head a bit. When he got into the European championships and the Olympics, he failed dismally. He blew it all.

He didn't like to admit that my type of training was good, because I told the Finns to forget about Majorca and the Canary Islands as winter training bases. I said they could train in the winter in Finland.

I went out and found I could run for two hours in thirty-five below zero and it didn't hurt me, so I got the young Finns out with me. It meant I was cutting off their holidays.

Kuha spoke out against my type of training so I found a boy in a small town called Uslami in the middle of Finland and trained him for two years. He won the Finnish steeplechase championship in both years.

Kuha broke the world record when I first went there but this boy beat him both times so we rather proved that what we were doing was correct.

Prima donnas who think they're God's greatest gift to a team or a country do not usually make good team members. They don't mix as well as they should and help the others.

Then you get the hyper-anxious runners. Scared of losing, scared of what the coach will say if they let him down, worried about what the team or the school might have to say. Normally, this is because parents and friends expect too much. So they tire themselves out mentally and physically before a race even begins. They lose appetite and concentration and become bundles of nervous tension.

The demands of parents particularly affect younger runners. They may be the best athletes in their school but their parents expect them to be the best in the town and then the best in the country and they put so much pressure on the youngsters all the fun drains out of it. Often, those parents seek, through their children, compensation for their own lack of ability or achievement in sport.

Some people are scared of losing but competition is the best way to improve and, if you train with better athletes, both can gain. It beats training alone and coming out to race against the opposition only occasionally.

The news media can impose heavy stress by expecting too much and being over-critical when its expectations aren't met. Probably the worst sporting news media in the world is in Great Britain. I remember at the Rome Olympics picking up a British newspaper which carried four photos of British runners. They included Gordon Pirie and Mary Rand. Under each photo was the word, 'Gold' in big letters.

What happened was that Mary Rand did well but the others failed. The newspaper reprinted the photos and underneath each was the word 'Flop', again in big letters.

The point was that the athletes didn't say they were going to win medals. The newspaper did. But it didn't know what it was talking about.

From my own experience, I have found many sporting writers will talk to you but will already have made up their minds what they're going to write. What is printed isn't exactly what you said but is contorted into something controversial. This can upset some athletes.

Many runners go to bed the night before a race and run it twenty times in their minds. By the morning they are physically and mentally tired. They can't run at all. A coach has to recognise this flaw and overcome it. Don't let the anxious athlete go to bed too early; he should stay up and play cards, go to a movie, be with people who won't even talk about running and then go to bed when he or she feels tired.

Some runners resist coaching. They want the freedom of self-direction, believing they don't need a coach but know it all themselves.They may have wonderful talent and they will run the occasional good race but they're not going to perform at high levels as they could if they had objective direction.

Some runners want all the glory for themselves. In the 1964 Tokyo Olympics, the javelin was won by Nevalla, a Finn who had worked under Finland's very good javelin coach.

But when the athlete came home, he made it clear that it was he alone who did it. From then on, he more or less went his own way. The coach meantime had got hold of another athlete, Kinnonnen, and started training him. Inevitably Kinnonnen started beating Nevalla.

I had the same problem with one of my athletes but by the time he came to the Tokyo Olympics he had to come back to me to find out how to get back up there again.

Runners can resist foreplanning, rigid control and organisation, particularly those who are running for money. They won't plan to win races for their country but are more interested in their own aims, making money, and they resist any control or organisation of their programme. One thing I did in Finland was to eliminate that kind of thing, because they were getting several thousand dollars each to help them and wasting it as an investment in their country. They did have an obligation to repay the help they were getting and that meant they had to submit to planned programmes and some form of firm control.

Runners will avoid coaches but listen to lectures unobtrusively. Uuha Vartainnen was the head coach of Finland until about two years ago. He won the European 10,000 m title in around 27:33, covering the last 400 in about 53 s, and when I was there he was one of the Kuha group who didn't want to do my training.

But he took me out for dinner about three years ago and laughingly confessed that when I visited his home town of Oulu in 1967 to lecture in the course of my coaching contract in Finland, he considered he was too big a guy to be seen to go along to listen to me so he and a friend sat behind a partition in the hall so that they could hear me but I couldn't see them.

"Then", he said, "we went out and did your training. I look at it and laugh – but it worked."
He was not too big a man not to admit it.

Runners will try to assimilate knowledge from coaches and other athletes and then try to use parts of all methods, a kind of smorgasbord of ideas. I trained a runner years ago who was the cross-country and three miles champion. He was in Christchurch when he asked me to help him and came up to Auckland, where he should have won the six-mile championship in 1956. He didn't run well at all, although he finished second.

I couldn't work out why he wasn't improving as much as he should and discovered that he was doing my schedule in the afternoons and some other guy's schedule in the mornings.
My schedule called for about a hundred to one hundred and forty miles a week so he was piling on a major load. But his theory was that if he put both these schedules together he must get one hell of a good result. He should be twice as good.

You'll come across the argumentative runners, who question and challenge everything they are told about training.

"Oh, yes", they'll say, "but So-and-so trains differently to what you want us to do, so who says you're right?"
The answer is simply to tell them to go and do what they're told and led them make the choice.

This is different from asking questions and seeking explanations and reasons why schedules are set the way they are.

They'll try to use other authorities to refute a coach's teachings. They'll point to runners who trained along different lines and won championships. Question them and you'll probably find they didn't understand what the other athletes were doing in the first place or that they were possibly one-off successes for their particular coach.

Coaches are better without runners who are not going to have confidence in them and buckle down to doing what is prescribed to them. These runners are inclined to go from coach to coach and wind up getting nowhere because their training never has any consistent pattern or goal to it.

Let's consider the qualities of the top athletes:

They are sincere. They are intelligent; I've never seen an Olympic champion who wasn't intelligent. Kip Keino always impressed me as one of the most intelligent athletes I have met. He was totally dedicated and one of the reasons he succeeded was because he thought everything out carefully, ran all his races with intelligence, had control of himself.

They are dedicated. They have natural ability which suits their particular event.
They have coachability.
They have determination.
They are ambitious.
They have pride in themselves.
Put all those together in one athlete and you have a world beater.

And what are the qualities in the top coaches? Practical coaching experience for a start. An understanding of the physiology of athletics without trying to be an exercise physiologist. An understanding of psychological fundamentals without trying to be a psychologist. An understanding of mechanical fundamentals without trying to be a mechanic. The experts in physiology and mechanics can get off into too many tangents. I've yet to hear of one who trained an Olympic champion. But the top coach must understand the basics and adhere to them all the way through his programmes.

The ability to motivate. I was in Mexico with an American coach who carried a big book under his arm. He told me he had all his lectures in the book.

"Fine", I said, "but I've got it in my head."

That's the difference. Those people can't get up and motivate. They can't explain the important details even if they know because they don't spring readily to mind. If they've got to rifle through their notes for answers, they won't motivate.

It helps to be able to work out with athletes. You are young enough or fit enough to go with athletes during the conditioning phase and work with the slower ones, it is going to build their confidence in you. And while you're running with them, you are able to find out their potential more easily – if you're an experienced coach. Running with them gives a better indication of their strengths and weaknesses than standing by the road watching or waiting back at the start for them to finish.

A top coach is an affable, easy-going personality. He has the ability to joke with his athletes so that the enjoyment of each other's company is mutual. He has to be understanding and sympathetic.

The top coach doesn't mess around when he says that an athlete isn't going to make it. He tells him; there's no other way. He may be able to steer him towards an activity or a distance at which he'll do better but he has to be tactfully blunt. But he will recognise that everyone must improve. The margin might be greater in some than in others so the smart coach looks at basic speed as the governing factor and steers them to where that basic will work best.

A great many ultra runners turn to those distances because they cannot run fast enough to record a good marathon. So they find satisfaction in getting out there at an everlasting trot and running distances that make the rest of us boggle. It's good for them and it's something at which they can achieve personal goals, if nothing else.

Not all of us can run sub-four miles or sub-thirty ten kilometres – but we can find distances and events at which we can enjoy degrees of success, even if it's only personal satisfaction.

I recall a young Auckland girl who was an excellent 400 m runner but then she grew taller and got wider in the hips. She came to see me, sat down and burst into tears. Her coach had told her that she had to realise she would never be a champion and would be better to look at the social side of running. That really hurt her because she wanted to be a champion.

I told her we couldn't all be champions but she was welcome to come and join some lads I was training on their long runs and so on. So we trained her and put her in races and she did improve in strength. But she couldn't run 2:04 for 800 m; the best she could hope for was around 2:25.

So I explained that she had to face the fact the she would have a lot of trouble trying to get down to the kind of times that would make her a champion prospect or get her into an Auckland team.

Eventually, she said another coach had offered to help her. Okay, I said, knowing he was someone I once trained, so he took her under his wing. But when I last saw her running in a cross-country event, she was trailing around the back of the field.

All three of us had tried our best; her first coach and I had been straight with her and I imagine her third was no different but the main thing was that she could see herself improving, even if only slightly, and she would eventually find a level of fun running or social running at which she would enjoy herself.

She won't come last but she will never be in the first three either.

A coach can protect – or neglect – his athletes in many ways.

It should not be necessary with an experienced athlete, but a coach should have a look at all the gear his pupils run and train in, particularly the shoes. Some runners suffer from chafing – between the legs, under the arms, across the nipples – which can lead to infection, and the cause is usually the wrong clothing.

Shoes are the subject of a special chapter in this book. Diet is another factor which comes within the scope of the good coach. He needs to know that his pupils are getting the right elements, such as zinc for recovery from anaerobic effort. A lot of athletes lose time in training through influenza, coughs and colds because they don't build up their immune systems before winter by taking cod liver oil, vitamin A and C and so on. The immune system must be strong enough to resist infections when the whole body is under the stress of a tough training regime.

A coach must be careful during the transition from one stage of training to a harder phase, such as beginning full hill training, that the shift is gentle. The athlete who rushes madly into his hill work and finds it easy to accomplish runs into the risk that for the next few days he will have difficulty walking because he has used muscles not carefully conditioned for the extra stress.

The sore muscles will come in any case but if the athlete is eased into the new work the soreness will not hinder his programme and will quickly vanish.

For instance, before tackling hill training, athletes should jog lightly for a few mornings but include hills in the workout to begin conditioning the muscles for climbing under resistance.

Then the hill training programme, which is anaerobic to a degree, should also include some brief anaerobic wind-sprinting to prepare the body for the next fully anaerobic step in training. It does not need much but it does need some.

The whole purpose is to avoid shocking the muscles by suddenly piling a tough new workload onto them. It is a matter of building the foundation first for each new development to eliminate the risk of injuries. Certainly, athletes will get hurt, no matter how careful you are – a foot in a hole, an ankle twisted on a loose stone and so on – but you can eliminate much of the risk by the care you take in easing them into fresh and more difficult forms of exercise.

Occasionally, an athlete will develop a problem which doesn't respond to a coach's solution; at that stage, the coach or the athlete should seek another opinion, possibly from someone better versed in problem solving, a physiotherapist, a doctor, whatever the problem suggests.

The role of the coach should extend far beyond the athletes because a sound coaching structure is the key to national success. Without it, nothing worthwhile can be achieved but it is astonishing and dismaying to find how many countries ignore this vital truth.

Far too many don't have their officials in positions where they can wield the influence to have the athletic potential developed on a national basis. I am talking from my own experiences in Venezuela, Mexico and Turkey, among other countries, where you see wonderful athletes totally without development programmes which will bring out their full potential. The problem is to convince administrators that they must commit themselves to a five-year co-ordinated coaching programme, throughout the country, based on the correct physiological and mechanical fundamentals. They have to take a long view – for example, to think not of the next Olympic Games but the Games after that.

Unfortunately, most place their faith in a non-existent magic wand which, in one year, can begin to produce great Olympic champions. It doesn't work, not because they don't have the athletes but because you cannot develop a national programme that will produce spectacular results quickly. No human organism works that way.

In Turkey, a major glass works was prepared to back a running club to try to bring out the nation's track and field potential but the control lay with the Turkish Amateur Athletic Federation and, when I began to get a programme together to teach coaches and athletes to train systematically, the federation interfered and demanded that their athletes compete in certain events for which they were not prepared. They wanted instant results and would not accept that this would jeopardise the development of a good long-term programme which would eventually produce much better results.

I faced the same problem in Mexico and Venezuela – administrators in too much of a hurry to produce great champions. All these countries have the material but they lack the understanding of co-ordinated coaching plans and the need for a patient long-term developmental approach. The programme has to reach athletes wherever they are in the country and deliver the same controlled training system to them all.

While I was in Finland, I enjoyed the opposite result. With the full co-operation of the coaches and administrators, I worked on a five-year programme that eventually produced world-class athletes. But, soon after that, the people who supported this programme were pushed aside and many of those who had been responsible for the poor standard of Finnish middle and distance running before I got there were back in power.

Consequently, their programme has become unbalanced again and Finland has faded away again as a track and field power.

Administrators have to accept that, if they want results, they have to support a strong national coaching programme and spend money initially on that programme rather than on athletes. We have the same problem in New Zealand. We have many good coaches trying hard to set up a workable programme but much of the best potential is not being coached under this programme. We have, for instances, coaches supervising athletes in events for which they don't have the coaching credentials. It's a bit like John McEnroe trying to teach Maradona how to play soccer. It's obvious he's not going to get the optimum results.

Athletes, too, have to realise that their possibilities of success are limited by their basic speed in running. They must look at their natural attributes and realise that there are some events for which they are just not suited. In the 1990 Commonwealth Games, New Zealand fielded three 400-metre runners, only one of whom could break 47 seconds. The other two were just not fast enough and could never be. You can improve any runner's speed but you cannot make a basically slow person fast. Those two runners were in the wrong event and it is arguable that, prepared for a longer event, they might have had a good chance of succeeding.

Chapter 15: Food, Fats, Vitamins and Minerals

The saying that one man's food is another man's poison nits close to the mark in many instances. Many enjoy and benefit from food that others cannot stomach. Food likes and dislikes can be so strong that one individual cannot comfortably digest, let alone swallow, food that others find enjoyable.

Many of the world's great athletes have diets that widely differ, yet all of them are able to perform well on what and how they eat. So how do we arrive at what is going to be good for us?

Doctors say we must have balanced diets. But, in a modern society with abundant processed foods and little knowledge of the origins of our fruit and vegetables, it is unlikely that we can say confidently that we are following a diet properly balanced for all our nutritional needs.

We can go to the shops and buy fresh fruit and vegetables but, if they were grown in soil deficient in some of the trace elements humans need for a balanced diet, the fruit and vegetables will also be deficient. If all the selenium, zinc, chrome and cobalt we need has been removed from the ground in which the food is grown, obviously the plants will lack those elements and so will we. The quantities may be only small but they are all important to our metabolism.

I have never been a fan or an advocate of supplements but, unless you can be certain that the food you eat contains everything your body needs, I have to concede that it is wise to take multi-vitamin and mineral supplements. I'm not suggesting we should become pill-poppers ingesting mega doses of tablets but we should examine our diets closely and know the sources of our foods if we want to give our metabolism the chance to perform all its functions efficiently.

Many factors can affect the quality and freshness of foods, whether we come from the extremes such as north Finland's Arctic Circle and North Africa's tropics or from moderate climates. So much has been written about the need for analysing our diets and the values of minerals and vitamins, carbohydrates, fatty acids, proteins and so on that it is easy to become confused and seek the answer by raiding the shelves in the health food shops. That's an over-reaction, of course, but it would be wise to find out little more about the quality of the soils from which your food comes.

Some half a century ago when the pumice lands in the centre of the North Island of New Zealand were brought into production by the government, the developers put in the grass seed and the artificial fertilisers and then, when the grass was as high as the cows' bellies, added the stock, some of which immediately began to lose weight and even die. The soil was analysed and found to be deficient in just one trace element, cobalt. But that was enough to harm the cattle. The cobalt was added and the pumice lands now are some of the finest in the country.

Today, the average New Zealand farmer will analyse the soil of his farm to be certain the animals on which his livelihood depends are getting the right balance for their maximum production and development. Invariably, he will find that selenium and zinc are lacking. But in parts of California, some soils can have too much selenium. It's a pity the farmer doesn't always take the same interest in balancing the food he feeds his families.

Years ago, too, the average backyard in New Zealand contained a vegetable garden, in which most crops were grown organically. Today, you'll find instead lawns, maybe some fruit trees and a barbecue area. The vegetables people once grew now come from supermarkets and their origins are almost certain to be market gardens whose soil is laden with artificial fertiliser and light on essential trace elements.

Today, I always advise athletes to take a multi-vitamin supplement to counter that deficiency and to read enough to understand just what vitamins and minerals are all about.

Another problem is the increasing use of colourings, additives and preservatives in processed foods. This is nothing new. Dr. Curatin, one of the recognised health experts in the United States, told me in Champagne, Illinois, in the early seventies that he was concerned about the American nation's future because, with all the colourings, additives and preservatives they were putting in their food, they must be establishing a highly toxic state in their bodies which would expose them to all sorts of cancerous and arthritic problems.

"What do parents think", he asked, "when they give their children iceblocks which colour their tongues purple or green or red? Where do they think those toxic colouring substances are going?"

Since then, it has been found that some of those red dyes used to make food seem more attractive are carcinogenic and it's safe to suggest that many more additives have been developed since Dr Curatin raised the issue two decades ago.

Gary and Steven Null, in their book 'Poisons in Your Body' (Prentice Hall Press, 1977), disclosed that ninety percent of the colourings used by food manufacturers were synthetic and most of them were coal-tar derivatives. Even Florida oranges were dyed. So were dog foods, although dogs are colour-blind. The colourings were termed 'US certified artificial colour', which misled consumers to assume they were certified for safety. In fact, the term 'certified' merely meant they met certain government standards which allowed the presence of an established percentage of impurities, such as arsenic.

If you accept the Nulls' findings, you would never eat another chicken in the US. They are fed tranquilisers to calm them while they are forcefed and fattened in about half the time it took just after World War Two. The pasty white flesh they produce is quite bland so artificial dyes have been developed to colour it golden and the enzyme hyaluronidase is injected to add flavour. Because the enzyme would give of an acrid scent during cooking, it is masked with a seasoning mixture of herbs and garlic. Drugs, including arsenic, and antibiotics are included in the chickens' food to kill all bacteria, even beneficial bacteria. They eat it, you get it.

From the viewpoint of the person who wants to perform well as an athlete, the risk of filling the body with these toxic substances cannot be over-stated.

We discussed elsewhere in this book how the Africans' training and conditioning enable them to do so well in today's running scene but the food they eat and the sources of that food are other contributing factors. They mostly live nearer to nature than we do and they don't exhaust their soil by continued intensive cropping and grazing, which means most of the trace elements and minerals remain in the soil. Nor is their food processed as much as the food of the western world. So, while their food handling methods may not be as hygienic, they are probably enjoying much healthier, more nutritious diets than the rest of us and also developing a greater natural resistance to diseases.

We may get food in prettier packaging but it's also food from which a large proportion of the goodness has been extracted in the processing. We are fortunate in New Zealand that most of our beef is range-fed on land which is well-balanced in trace elements and minerals, so that the meat we get is high in quality and food value; in the US, the Nulls stated, animals are kept alive and fattened by the continuous administration of more than 2,700 drugs, all approved by the Food and Drug Administration.

It is a significant comment on the way of life in affluent countries that, some years ago, several bears in San Diego Zoo were killed by cancer. The cause was the processed food they were being given.

Scientist Linus Pauling, one of the few people to win the Nobel Prize twice, is the world's

finest expert on nutrition and even he agrees that it is a controversial rather than an exact science, which catches the average person somewhere between the dietitians who talk of the modern world's balanced natural diets and the health foodshop owners who maintain you need the help of every pill and powder on their shelves.

The American magazine 'Women's Sports', after a four-year study of nutrition, concluded that just about everyone needs to take vitamin supplements. You need them if you live in a smoggy city, if you train regularly in the heat, if you eat sugar, if you have an allergy, if you load on carbohydrates before a race, if you bruise easily, if you are about to compete.
The magazine said: "As any athlete knows, life is action. There is nothing static about the body. What sparks and controls that action – the beating of your heart, the steady fire of digestion, your breathing, your moving – are enzymes. Vitamins are a chemical part of your enzymes. Without vitamins, enzymes wouldn't work and neither would you.

"For instance, without thiamine (vitamin B1), the brain and nervous system collapse. Arms and legs lose their co-ordination. The eye muscles freeze into paralysis. The mind blackens into amnesia and coma. The heart stretches, swells – and stops."

Tough stuff but true. Let's consider, briefly, what vitamins mean form the viewpoint of athletic performance:

Vitamin A

The one vitamin on which you can overdose (but only on enormous daily doses), because the liver stores unused vitamin A, and also the one most people get too little of, because they don't eat enough fresh fruit and vegetables, the vitamin's prime source, and they do eat too much fast food, an awful source.
Vitamin A keeps the skin smooth, the vision sharp, the immune system strong and anti-stress mechanisms on the ball.

Dry, rough or flaky skin could indicate you need more A for first-rate cell replacement. Orange, yellow and green fruits and vegetables such as carrots, sweet potatoes, spinach, apricots and canteloupe, contain a substance called betacarotene, which is killed by over-cooking but changes to vitamin A in the body. One cup of cooked carrots contains more than 16,000 IU of vitamin A.

The most concentrated source is fish liver oil; and vitamin A supplements, virtually taste-less and odourless, are the best source of fish liver oil. A supplement of 10,000 IU a day is enough but you can take up to 30,000 a day without worry. And, if you take vitamin E with it, the body's ability to use vitamin A increases sixfold.

B-complex

Whatever gets on your nerves can be got off with the B-complex vitamins. You'd be a nervous wreck without them. Depression, irritability, poor concentration, insomnia, forgetfulness, confusion, anxiety and paranoia are all linked to some degree with B-complex vitamins, which go together as a family.

B1 (thiamine) helps the body to turn carbohydrates into glucose, which fuels the brain and the muscles. Any athlete who carbo loads before a race should take 5 milligrams of thiamine a day, which will turn all the pasta into energy.

Green leafy vegetables, whole grains, beans, nuts and seeds are thiamine-rich and also contain plenty of the other B vitamins, except B12.

B2 (riboflavin) helps the digestion of fats, is found in broccoli and asparagus, milk and cheese, almonds and liver. Any whole grain will do but wild rice is best.

At least 40 chemical reactions in the body depend on **B3 (niacin)**. The most important involves the red blood cells, which carry oxygen to all parts of the body. The last stage of their journey is through the capillaries, hair-thin blood vessels connecting to the tissues. The red blood cells line up in single file and march in, each kept apart from its neighbours by a negative electrical charge. Niacin keeps them charged and they keep the body charged with oxygen.

Like the rest of the B vitamins, **B12 (cobalamin)** helps to run the switchboard of the central nervous system, relaying messages between the body and the brain. Liver is the best B12 source but any animal product will do, although, interestingly, studies have shown that vegans (total vegetarians), who eat fermented foods such as tamari or tofu or large amounts of raw food, have B12 manufactured in their own intestinal tracts.

Folate, best found in green, leafy vegetables, particularly from the cabbage family, but also in wholewheat, brewers's yeast, oranges, beets, beans, meat and eggs, helps to form genes, the chemicals that blueprint every cell, including the oxygen-carrying red blood cells. Folate deficiency equals anaemia.

Pantothenic acid is needed if you train, compete or even play in cold water. Found in all foods, except canned and frozen foods and anything made with white flour, which may lose up to seventy-five per cent of pantothenic acid.

Choline and **inositol** are two B vitamins found in lecithin, a substance that is part of the cell walls of plants and animals. They make sure the cells absorb fat, no mean feat since fat is as vital a nutrient as protein or carbohydrate.

Vitamin C

So powerful that it detoxifies heroin, nicotine, alcohol and cancer-causing pollutants. One gram every two hours will cure the common cold. Taken daily, it will prevent cold. It's a natural antihistamine, so stops hay fever.

And it beats the heat. Increasing your C intake a week or so before an event in hot weather will increase your competitive edge. Fresh oranges are rich in vitamin C, as are all citrus fruits, and, surprisingly, so are potatoes, green peppers, parsley and broccoli. But not frozen or bottled juices; and potato chips have lost about 75 per cent of their vitamin C.

Bioflavinoids are vitamin C's close cousins. The white inner skin of citrus fruits and the white column inside a green pepper are packed with them and their great value is that they strenghten capillaries.

Vitamin E

Its sole function is to absorb calcium but, since calcium regulates muscle contraction, the heart couldn't beat without it. Little is acquired by eating. It comes from sunlight so, unless you spend most of your time indoors or cover every square inch of your skin when your are outside, there is little chance of a deficiency.
Improves glycogen storage, giving you more fuel for endurance sports. Improves the tone and strength of the heart muscle. Protects cells from oxidation, which suggests it could lengthen life.

Processed foods are vitamin E weaklings. Cornflakes have lost all but two per cent. Whole wheat bread has seven times more than white bread, brown rice six times more than white.

Vitamin E oil cleans up chapped lips, surgical incisions, burns (including sunburn), bedsores, warts, athlete's foot, poison ivy, any skin complaint.

Calcium

We carry about 1.3 kg of calcium around with us – more than any other mineral – most of it in the bones and teeth. But if we removed the remaining one-tenth of one per cent from our circulatory systems, our muscles wouldn't contract. The mechanism that regulates the level of that small but vital amount of calcium is so exact that, if the amount drops a microgram or two too low, calcium is immediately taken from the bones to cover the deficiency. A lack of calcium affects not only bones and teeth but nerves and muscles as well, which is why extra calcium will unknot muscle cramps.

Calcium, vital in checking osteoporosis, which hobbles millions of elderly, particularly women, should probably be given as a supplement from about age 25, when bone loss begins, according to expert Jennifer Jowsey. If calcium supplementation began then, she maintains, by the time the individual is 70, he or she may retain the bone mass and, therefore, the bone strength of a 40-year-old.

For the athlete, the important point here is the reduced risk of a stress fracture. Protein forces calcium out of the body, another argument for taking supplements. Best calcium sources are bone meal, cottage cheese, Swiss cheese, yoghurt, sardines and salmon, colard and turnip greens, tofu and, say macrobiotic enthusiasts, a green tea called Bancha they claim has more calcium than milk.

Milk as a source is question-marked because of its accompanying fats and calories and because many people have difficulty digesting it properly.

Dolomite: Is excellent (see Magnesium, below).

Phosphorus

Exists in every cell in your body and in every biochemical reaction. An equal partner with calcium, it keeps your skeleton sturdy, assists your heart beat, your digestion, your purification through the kidneys and the nervous system.

Everyone already gets too much and it needs to be as near as possible to a one-to-one ration with calcium – so get into those calcium supplements and watch the meat intake because meat has a phosphorous to calcium ratio of about 209 to 9.

Magnesium

If you toss and turn, turn to magnesium; it's a natural tranquiliser and also calms jumpy muscles and nerves. Enough magnesium and muscles relax; too little and they twitch and tremble.

Muscles (including the heart) and nerves depend on magnesium, which is also needed for the digestion of protein, fat and carbohydrates.

Good sources are whole grains, soybeans, nuts, green, leafy vegetables, fruits and blackstrap molasses but best of all is **dolomite**, a preparation of powdered dolomite limestone, which delivers magnesium **and** calcium in the exact proportions nature intended.

Potassium

Athletes who do not sweat do not need extra potassium. Those who do and take salt tablets need double doses. James Knochel, MD, a professor at the University of Texas Southwestern Medical School, found that fifty per cent of those hospitalised for heatstroke after intense exercise were potassium depleted. Many had taken salt tablets, which forced the potassium out of their bodies, and this, added to the potassium they were losing through sweating, produced a severe deficiency and all its symptoms – nausea, muscle weakness, cramps, irritability and, finally, total collapse.

The salt lost in sweat does not need to be replaced but the lost potassium does. Best sources are bananas, oranges, tomatoes, cabbage, celery, carrots, grapefruit, apples, beans and fish.

Sodium

You need about 2,000 mg of sodium a day – a typical salt-shaker diet delivers about 10,000 to 12,000 mg. The solution is to fill the salt shaker with natural spices and eat natural unprocessed foods, which provide a natural amount of sodium and taste better.

Salt in excess is thought to contribute to high blood pressure. For athletes training in hot weather, this is bad news.

Iron

Iron is used to fortify cereals, baked goods and other processed foods but the body absorbs less than one per cent of it because the only source of iron the body will absorb is vitamin C. A thousand mg with a meal will boost iron absorption tenfold. The iron in meat also aids the absorption of iron from other foods.

Processed foods often contain additives and preservatives which block iron absorption. Tannic acid from tea shifts iron out of the body and so does regular use of aspirin. All of which leads to a lack of iron being the most common nutritional deficiency, especially among women.

Studies have shown that people with normal blood levels of iron who added iron to their diets increased their work capacity four times, which should be significant for hard-training athletes. But be sparing. It is possible to overdose on iron. Vitamin C should be enough and maybe 20 mg of an iron supplement – but no more.

Chromium

Helps the body to use insulin, the hormone that regulates blood sugar (glucose). When you eat 120 pounds (54 kg) of sugar a year – as many people do even today – you need lots of insulin to burn the sugar and lots of chromium to help. The finest source is brewer's yeast and a chromium expert, the late Richard Doisy, recommended a supplement of two tablespoons a day.

Zinc

Almost nothing happens in the human body without zinc, which is a must for normal sexual maturation, speeds the healing of burns and all kinds of wounds, helps to stop the absorption of lead, protects against cadmium.

Oysters contain 100 times more zinc than any other food but other good sources are red meat, liver, wheat germ and nuts. Unless you pig out on oysters, a 20 mg a day supplement of zinc is recommended.

Selenium

Found in seafood, whole grains, organ meats and brewer's yeast, hailed as a nutritional cancer preventive and stroke stopper. In an area of Georgia and the Carolinas, which has less selenium per capita than anywhere else in the United States, the people have more strokes per capita than anywhere else. A must for normal bones and muscles and best found in beans, peas, spinach, bran, brussels sprout and blueberries.

Chapter 16: Team Training

Even in this enlightened age, many team players present themselves at the beginning of a season in the blind belief that 'dear old coach' is going to get them fit, teach them and polish the basics of their game, add the extra skills and play them competitively at one and the same time – successfully.

Making a silk purse from the pig's ear or trying to win a Grand Prix with a car that's been sitting on the roadside for six months might be simpler.

So what do we get? We get, on the eve of the season, a crash course in running – and, if there are hills around the ground, the crashes come heavily – in sprinting, in basic game techniques. All crowded into viciously vigorous sessions which tend to produce, in the majority, exactly the wrong kind of physical condition – a sweat-achieved artificial or superficial fitness (measured in terms of aching muscles), which can lead to early serious injuries, to mid-season staleness or, at best, a mediocre all-season effort in which true fitness is always a wish away.

Fortunately, the trend is slowly away from this masochistic approach to the enjoyment of sport. You don't now see quite so many oddly-garbed footballers trudging their summer stomachs along the streets, gasping in the gathering dusk which kindly obscures their apoplectic expressions, over-dressed in a desperate rush to get the surplus weight off. You don't see quite so many of those half-hearted sprint sessions on the training paddock – half-hearted because the players can't sustain the pressure they are forced to submit themselves to just to get reasonably ready for their first game of the season.

In the past, though, it wasn't too bad. Any other team you were likely to meet early in the season could be expected to be in the same semi-prepared state, so it all evened out.

You could safely gamble that when you kicked the ball out of the field of play or delayed a movement to give yourself and your team-mates a breather, the other side was just as relieved and you could all stand about with your hands on your knees, gulping for oxygen in a great spirit of companionable suffering.

The secret was, if you had the strength left, to kick the ball as far as possible into the grandstand or the next paddock and hope that whoever went to fetch it took his time.

In the sphere of amateur sport, played – theoretically – for fun, this may not seem a situation of much concern. But when the circumstances apply to the gilded heights of professional or international football, even in lesser degree, we're looking at a disaster scene of human endeavour. And even the amateur game, through rising overheads and sponsorship demands, has a thickening veneer of seriousness about it these days.

A lot of coaches will have had this experience: You're earning maybe $ 50,000 – $ 60,000 a year coaching your college team and your college is looking to you for results. So you scour the country for the best available players. You pay them high recruiting money, scholarships, cars and other perquisites. They're a big investment with big reputations. You get them out on the field at the beginning of the season and you begin working them hard, as you're entitled to do.

Before you can say, Snap, some of them are sitting on the sideline with pulled hamstrings or torn tendons. And they're likely to be still sitting there, eating up college funds – and **your** reputation – for much of the season for which you acquired them.

Here in New Zealand, the pinnacle of a rugby footballer's career is to make the national team, the All Blacks, and play against the rest of the world's rugby nations. And, even while this book was being written, All Blacks were on a short tour of Australia and South Africa and players were being rested, even replaced, because of injuries. On an earlier tour to Ireland, two players experienced serious muscle injuries during their first training session in Ireland and were unavailable for selection for at least the first two games. Yet they had gone to Ireland as soon as the New Zealand rugby season ended and were, in theory, playing fit. The records show there has not been a tour yet which has not produced its crop of avoidable, unnecessary muscle and tendon breakdown.

More recently, New Zealand has been fielding international cricket teams which are constantly in difficulties because of injured players who either see the tour out as extra baggage or are desperately replaced.

If the injury is to a hamstring or groin muscle, the player is not likely to recover fully for the rest of the season. He is always going to have to nurse his problem, which makes him a less effective player than he should be. In professional spheres, he is an investment that is not paying off; in an oversea touring team, he is a next-to-useless passenger.

The sudden strickening injury is the worst end-result of unpreparedness. Just as bad is the player who is never really fit to maintain the necessary pace and pressure of the game. He is exposing himself, more than he needs, to damage of the kind that's inevitable in an physical contact sport and he's also letting his team down.

When I was in the United States talking to fooball coaches, I quickly realised that a lot of the fault rested with them. Even some of the megabucks men did not understand the simplest physiology of exercise and, consequently, were not presenting their extensive stables of players with balanced programmes which would steer them over and beyond these injury areas.

They were working still on the theories of German interval training which say that, as long as you are doing anaerobic training (exercising at a level which creates an oxygen debt), you can increase your ability to exercise anaerobically. We have known for a long that this is physiologically incorrect. You can build your oxygen debt capacity to 15 to 20 litres and that's the maximum. If you try to go on with continued hard anaerobic exercise, the result is certain to be a lowering of the body's ability. Incredibly, coaches and athletes go on trying – and failing. It is a locked-in tradition that players come in from their summer vacations, go into their high-pressure training programmes and, very quickly, are running series of windsprints. These are strictly anaerobic and they are not ready to use them to improve their fitness level. Just why, I'll explain shortly.

Footballers will argue that football is sprint, sprint, sprint and I won't argue with them. But I will argue that the training for it is not just sprint, sprint, sprint. My athletes could sprint but they never did until they developed a high oxygen uptake level which would allow them to sprint easily; until they had developed and exercised their muscles to withstand the stress and strain of sprinting. Footballers have to do this, too – and it's even more important when you think that a runner sprints flat out once in a race and a footballer may be called on to sprint innumerable times in the course of a match.

Maybe they can get through a succession of 12 hard windsprints before they suffer a neuro-muscular breakdown and their muscles will no longer contract. They should be able to do 30. If they can't, what hope have they when the 30th demand for a sprint comes near the end of a close and critical match?

Many of the coaches I spoke to could not comprehend this at first. It was as if I was talking a foreign language when I told them to get their players out, loosen them up, jog them around, build up their oxygen uptake levels, exercise their muscular systems, stretch their tendons and muscles – all thoroughly and all long before they thought about sprinting – if they wanted to avoid injuries, if they wanted to get the full potential from their players, if they wanted to see ball-handling skills employed to the maximum.

These crippling early season injuries occur because powerful strong muscles are developed without a preliminary full stretching and extending of muscles and sinews. So what happens? The players go out for a game or an extra hard training session on tactics and suddenly, for the first time, are called on to stretch out fully. A tendon pops, the muscles round a tendon pull – curtains for that guy for weeks, maybe, as far as his potential is concerned, for the rest of the season.

The best psychology is to make the athlete aware of the physical and mechanical reactions to what he is doing. This means, of course, that the coach has to be aware first. Any athlete sent out to do something taxing without being given a reason for it is unlikely to put his heart and soul into it. Not knowing the purpose of training is a virtual guarantee the footballer will begin skipping sessions, especially those he is left to do on his own.

Players who know exactly why they're supposed to be doing certain things but also know, when the competitions come, that they haven't done them, also know they cannot win, no matter what their coach tells them on the day, however much he puts into his pep talk. But the guy who knows why he is doing things – and does them – doesn't need any psychological boosting. He knows he's ready.

Too many coaches give team talks moments before a game begins, when players are hyped up and edgy and their minds are already out on the field. The best thing to do is to leave them alone. Don't bail them up in the dressing room and hammer them with words as they line up to run out. Have a team talk on tactics two nights before the game and don't mention the subject again. Make it work on the Thursday night because it won't on the Saturday afternoon.

A rugby team in New Zealand some years ago enjoyed remarkable success in major competition. But it always played the first half of its games without great flair, even sluggishly, and didn't really spark until the second half. For the first half, the players always seemed inhibited, as if they could not trust their own undoubted talents and superiority. I believe a reason is that, immediately before a game, they were subjected to too much brain-washing from their coach, too much last-minute psychological conditioning, which put a block on their natural freedom, initiative and fitness and the immediate expression of those assets.

It could be argued that the team's run of successes proved the coach's theories but these were all experienced, gifted players and we are left to wonder what they might have done if they had been treated as I suggest – given their tactics two nights before the game and then left to relax and prepare in the knowledge of their own fitness and expertise.

Chapter 17: Evaluating Your Training

Whether you are a gridiron end, a rugby football lock forward, a soccer striker, a baseball outfield or a cricketer, you're an athlete with the same physiological problems and the same mechanical behaviour as the world champion miler or sprinter.

Coaching plans can sometimes be made to appear infallible on paper, with a continuous and mathematical development taking place. But, invariably, coaches and athletes working this way lack practical knowledge of exercise evaluation and the intensities that can be applied in exercising. Many become obsessed with particular aspects of training and are inclined to emphasise one at the expense of the others – endless windsprints, for example, or non-stop rucking drills.

I have seen coaches using psychology on their charges, telling them they can't lose, that they're in peak form, when, in fact, they haven't completed a balanced schedule and physically are not prepared and ready for competition. I have known coaches to be more concerned with techniques than basic fitness in the belief that superior skills will overcome physical lacks and beat the side that's balanced the other way. So they produce players perfectly skilled in ball handling yet unable to carry the ball competitively for the duration of the game. Those guys are sitting ducks for the players who may drop every second pass but are fit enough to catch, every time, opponents who have got the ball.

I have also known athletes who train hard by running big mileages but don't concern themselves with improving their style of running and so don't gain the full benefit from their long training hours. Or they run large mileages but don't develop their speed or their capacity to exercise aerobically, which is a key factor in most sports.

Years of disappointing results can follow when athletes and coaches are guessing instead of carefully balancing their schedules, gaining the best advice available and giving play to every phase of physiological development. It amounts to this: Training for any sport is like putting a jigsaw puzzle together. Every piece is necessary if the picture is to be completed and every piece fits into place only in relation to all the other pieces.

As I have said, many coaches and athletes are inclined to follow training methods that proved successful years before and are not keeping up with the evolution of sport. Not that I believe there should be revolutionary changes – only gradual ones as we learn more of the extremes under which the human constitution can exercise and continue to improve; as we gain understanding of the ages at which athletes are best able to apply development techniques and intense training schedules.

Many look for quick methods of developing potential and invariably end up using disproportionate amounts of anaerobic running compared with aerobic running. This may not have mattered before we discovered the differences but, now that we do know, I consider those people the real menaces to sport because they continually overlook the problems now known to be associated with the use of excessive anaerobic training. They are responsible for retarding the development of the best potential of the athletes they are handling.

Anaerobic running and exercise are necessary – but their value and use should be clearly understood before they can be used successfully.

These are the things I have had to explain on many visits to the United States and many other places in the world, too: To make coaches realise they had to motivate their players and appeal to their intelligence to keep conditioning out of season, during vactions, all the time, if they want to be real successes.

Happily, I've found this motivation comes easy once you get across the benefits to be gained from what is a comparatively easy programme. Out of season, they might not work as hard as they would under the eyes of their coaches but they'll do more than they would have done before motivation and every little bit helps.

Even the guy who is half-hearted is going ahead physically of the guy who spreads his shoulder blades on a sunny beach and leaves them there all day, considering that by being out in the sun and fresh air he's keeping himself healthy. He would be if he also used the beach and fresh air for light running.

The professional player in American gridiron or Canadian ice hockey or basketball stands to be a wealthy man. He doesn't have to be a world-beater to make a lot of money. Young men can do well for themselves in college football; a lot is going for them there.

In New Zealand, the arrival of professional rugby has opened the door to serious riches for the top players.

So there are many incentives to train seriously, quite apart from doing what the coach tells them in training sessions. Just the feeling of going into a playing season fitter than ever before and, therefore, better able to absorb the techniques and put them into practice on the field is going to give a player a boost.

Many gridiron men are already great runners and hurdlers and, while you don't have to reach their equivalent levels in track and field you have to consider that the only way you can hope to compete with them in gridiron is to do at least some of the conditioning they do.

One suggestion I have made to many coaches: Build a ramp with a coconut matting cover, maybe 30 or 40 yards/metres long, and have the players spring up this every day. This is an easy on-the-spot adaptation of the hill-springing our athletes do to stretch their muscles before they get into speed work. A session just long enough to get the legs feeling tired pays remarkable bonuses.

Another: Running up steps strengthens the lifting muscles to improve knee lift, increases leg speed and stretches stride length. The hamstring group of muscles benefits as muscles are stretched and strengthened.

These are relatively gentle exercises which rapidly build a basis for tougher training later. We'll be talking more about them. The point is that it's a lot cheaper to put up a wooden ramp or utilise the grandstand steps at the side of the ground than to pay some player big fees and then never get to play him anyway because of inept or inadequate conditioning or inept instruction by the coach on conditioning.

Unlike rugby or soccer, in which a man plays all the game, gridiron teams keep taking players on and off, interchanging them so that they get breathing spells right out of the game. That's fine but coaches must still realise that fitness comes mainly through a higher oxygen uptake and, even if a man is going to be on the field only briefly, his powers of concentration and co-ordination are increased by that higher level. The effects of extra oxygen and better-toned blood on the central nervous system sharpen reflexes, enable the player to employ his skills better.

We've proved this many times with golfers who couldn't improve their scores, even if they improved their technique. We got them on a programme of jogging fifteen minutes a day and they lowered their handicaps by up to ten strokes because of their improved physical condition, sharpened reflexes and increased co-ordination and concentration. The biggest difference shows near the end of a round when, instead of being tired, the player is as fresh as when he began.

A coach, given time and understanding, can develop champions from athletes of reasonable talent. Champions are developed, not born, although some have greater natural ability than others. But all talents have to be developed before their full potential is seen – and many athletes have undeveloped talents far greater than they imagine.

Coaches and athletes must have a clear picture in their minds of the development they're aiming for and those individual targets must be kept in view during every training session and every progressive section of training. Each phase must be carefully evaluated and its effects on the athlete's body understood. Each stage is completed before the next begins. You've got to learn to walk before you begin to run – you've got to equip yourself to take punishment before you begin to inflict it on yourself.

Chapter 18 Training Terms

We'll keep this chapter short because it's only to explain the meanings of some of the terms we've used so far and will use later. And we want it as simple as possible. Our aim isn't to turn you into physiological whizkids – just better athletes.

Aerobic training

means running within your capacity to use oxygen. Everyone, according to his or her physical condition, is able to assimilate, from the air, transport and use a limited amount of oxygen every minute. This limit can be increased through exercise. Your limit in using oxygen this way is called your maximum **steady state** or **aerobic threshhold**.

Anaerobic training

means that you are exercising without sufficient oxygen; beyond your maximum Steady State. This is possible through chemical changes in your body's metabolism and is the uneconomic way of exercising because great oxygen debts can be incurred which quickly produce waste products, such as lactic acid, and in turn, result in neuro muscular breakdown. In short, tired muscles that refuse to function. With proper training, you can develop the ability to incur an oxygen debt of approximately 15 litres to 20 litres, when exercising anaerobically.

Muscular conditioning

Muscular strength is the ability to exert a single explosive force against an object.

Because football is a contact sport, it is necessary to condition your muscular system generally to develop strong supple muscles capable of acting quickly and withstanding the hard contacts made during play.

The muscles you concentrate on depend on the type of football you play and the position you play in but it has to be of benefit to all players to go through a general strengthening programme of weights training. This is something that, initially at least, should be done under the guidance of an experienced coach and should always be done regularly.
   These observations by Professor M Howell, of Canada, relating to the weights training for strength experiments of Mueller and Hettinger, two internationally recognised weights training experts, are of value to anyone not fully understanding the fundamentals of weights training:

1. The maximum training effect is achieved by using only 40 to 50 per cent of the maximum strength in voluntary isometric muscle contractions.

2. No increases or decreases in strength are observed when only 20 to 30 per cent of muscle strength is used. This percentage of muscle exertion would appear to approximate the areas of normal daily activity, during which mere repetitions of the same sub-maximal effort cause no change in muscle strength.

3. Gradual losses in muscle strength occur when less than 20 per cent of muscle strength is used.

4. It is unnecessary to train to the point of complete muscular fatigue to stimulate increased muscle strength.

5. Maintaining a maximum isometric contraction for one or two seconds is sufficient to provide a training stimulus. When the contraction involves only two-thirds of the maximum strength, it should be maintained for between four and six seconds and so on. On the other hand, muscle contractions of very short duration have no effect.

6. It is found that the maximum increase in muscle strength is obtained with one training stimulus a day.

7. Several maximum contractions one after the other (say, 12 contractions in a one-second rhythm) do not increase the strength any faster than only one contraction.

8. It seems, therefore, that the muscle, after one training stimulus during any one day, is unresponsive to any further stimulus on the same day. When training sessions are held only every second day, the increase in strength is about 80 per cent; with two training sessions a week, the increase is about 60 per cent; and when training sessions are held only once a week, the increase is only about 40 per cent of the improvement in strength gained through the daily regime. One training stimulus every 14 days produces no change at all in muscle strength.

9. The effect in trainability is shown as increases in muscle strength week by week in percentage of the training value. The average gain in strength a week is found to be approximately 1.79 per cent. About 10 per cent of all subjects show no or a very small training effect during these training periods but, also , about 12 per cent show a very good trainability, with a strength increase of more than 3 per cent a week.

10. There is a difference in the rate of increase in strength in different muscle groups in the same subject. When these muscle groups are analysed in relation to their use in daily activity, it is found that those showing only slight increases in strength a week are those used most strenuously in day-to-day activities.

11. An atrophied muscle group, when trained, may show a rate of increase in strength five to six times as great as when we begin with an untrained normal muscle in a condition of normal strength.

12. The speed of increases in strength during a training session – in the same subject and the same muscle groups – may be quite different in different training periods; especially, for example, the different effects in increasing muscle strength by different training methods.

Muscular endurance is the quality which enables muscles to maintain contractions in conditions of fatigue; or the ability to continue work and postpone and tolerate fatigue. Therefore, you need muscular endurance as well as muscular strength.

Fourteen and fifteen-year-old youngsters can – and do – break world swimming records. They are not as strong in the sense that they can lift big weights above their heads but they have considerable strength because they use isokinetic weight programmes and other resistance work. And hours and hours of aerobic swimming give them fine muscular endurance, fine capillarisation that allows for the maximum use of oxygen. They are, of course, aided in carrying through a huge volume of training by buoyancy which reduces the gravitational pull on their bodies.

Youngsters of this age could not break records on the running track because here the gravitational pull would make the same degree of exercise highly anaerobic.
 Murray Halberg, 1960 Olympic 5,000 metres champion and holder of several world middle distance records, had one virtually useless arm – paralysed during surgery after a football accident – weighed nothing and had little muscular strength. But he used aerobic running to put himself into a virtually tireless state which enabled him, in racing, to exert an incredible anaerobic effort for considerable distances.

As a footballer, you need muscular strength as well as muscular endurance. You get the endurance by using muscle groups continually for long periods. Running for long periods and hill training give you that endurance in the legs but other muscle groups which also need this development must be tuned by weights training. So, during the conditioning period, you need two or three sessions of weights training every week, as shown shortly.

Here again, you must work to a systematic and progressive schedule. As the muscle fibres are activated by the resistance they encounter, they become thicker and more efficient and are able to withstand greater workloads.

Here is a schedule that can be used for guidance in relation to your current fitness level and working to your individual strength and capacity to exercise. In these exercises, a set is a period of exertion in which a number of repetitions are done without setting the weights down. A set can be any number of repetitions.

In your first workout, you should perform only one set of each exercise; in the second workout, two sets; in the third, three sets.

Obviously, it isn't possible to set a standard starting poundage because individual strengths vary widely. As a guide, it is wise to begin with weights you can comfortably raise ten times in succession.

As a general rule, aim to do eight to ten exercises in each workout. It is a good idea to alternate the exercises between upper-body and lower-body muscle groups to spread them evenly throughout the session. The following are examples of what you can do:

1. Two-arm barbell military press. Approximate starting poundage 50, 55, 60 lb (23, 25, 27 kg). Three sets, 3 to 5 reps. Concentrate on fast explosive-type presses rather than slow deliberate movements.

2. Biceps curl. Approx. starting weights 40, 45, 50 lb (18, 20, 23 kg). Three sets of 10 reps.

3. Full squat with barbell on shoulders. Approximate starting weights 70, 80, 90 lbs (32, 36 41 kg). Three sets of 10-12 reps. Concentrate on keeping back straight, head up and a fairly fast drive up with the weight. Go down far enough so that the thighs are parallel with the ground. Squats can be performed flat-footed, or with the heels on a 2 or 3-inch (5 cm to 8 cm) block, or you can go up on to the toes each time to get really good results with a double effect.

4. Jump squats with dumbbells held at sides. Approximately starting weights 20, 25, 30 lb a piece. Three sets of 15 reps.

5. Two-arm dumbbell prone press on bench. Approx. starting weight 15, 20, 25 lb a piece. Three sets of 8 to 10 reps. Concentrate on a fast type of press.

6. Sit ups. Start without weights. Three sets of 10 to 15 reps. Begin by lying flat on the floor; later use an inclined board with straps; then add a 2 lb (1 kg) weight behind the neck.

7. Two-arm barbell clean and jerk. Approx. starting weights 80, 90, 100 lb (35, 41, 45 kg). Three sets of 2 to 4 reps. This exercise is for overall strength, co-ordination and timing, using most muscles in the body.

8. Chin ups. Two or three sets of what you're capable of. Palms of hands facing away, repeat with palms facing towards as separate exercise.

9. Finger flips off a wall, three sets of 10 to 15 reps. Use the fingers only and lock the arms.

10. Finger push-ups off the floor, three sets of 10 to 15 reps, start on finger-tips and push up with back straight.

Increases in the weight when you're performing three sets could be, for example, 5 or 10 lb (2 or 4 kg) from the first set to the second and another 5 or 10 lb from the second to the third. This would give you, for example, sets at 90, 95 and 100 or at 90, 100 an 110. According to reactions and progress, weights can be increased each week by 5 or 10 lb. Use the same poundage for one week of three sessions or at least three workouts, If you are training three days a week, make them alternate days with a rest between, not three in a row and then a lay-off.
Rest for about a minute between sets and three minutes between exercises.

Keep a record of your training, listing starting weights, number of reps and sets and be careful to note upward progression.

Weight training could be done three days a week until about two weeks before the season begins. Then reduce to two sessions a week until you begin playing and then back to a session a week, early in the week, throughout the playing season.

What we've done here is lay out the fundamentals. In conjunction with a weight training coach, you need to look at your basic weakness and your individual needs and work on those. I know some football clubs have weights training equipment or have linked up with gymnasiums but I believe every club should develop a small gym or weights room. From the viewpoint of team success and individual physical fitness, it would be a better way to invest club funds than constructing better and more luxurious bar facilities for members, supporters and free-loaders. What are you playing football for: To keep fit and enjoy the outward expressions of fitness? Or to gain yourself entry to a fancy all-hours boozer?

Not every one of you will be able to get at proper weights but there are plenty of things you can do to compromise.

Knowing that it will pay you to strengthen every muscle you've got, here is one very simple exercise: Get a yard of loose metal and put it where you can shovel it across to another site one day and shovel it back again the next. You are going to use, and develop, all your muscles just shovelling metal.

You can get a piece of pipe and fix a bag of sand on each end. Sand or gravel is pretty easy to find most places.

Or you can get spring-resistant expanding exercisers – they are excellent for anyone who wants to move muscles fast.

In other words, you don't need a lot of expensive equipment. If you know what you're trying to do and you've got the will to do it, you will find the way.

Developing Speed

There are three running exercises you must consider to improve knee lift, improve ankle flexibility and power and to learn to run 'tall' by keeping up on the toes and, in effect, lifting the body off the pelvis.

Improvement in sprinting speed can be achieved best by developing the running techniques of the athlete. The fastest runners or movers are those who co-ordinate their movements best; so, obviously, to get top speed on the football field this is what you've got to aim for.

Here is a typical sprint workout:

Warm up for about 15 minutes by running easily for 7, doing two or three stride-outs over 60 metres, suppling and stretching with exercises until your body feels loose and then, with 3-minute intervals between runs, go twice through the following exercises over 100 metres:

High knees

Keeping the upper body as relaxed as possible, move the legs as fast as you can, with a high knee-lifting action. The forward momentum should be slow. Keep up on your toes throughout the exercise. **Straight back legs.**

Bounding

By running with a bounding action and a good knee lift, concentrate on working the ankles hard. Drive hard with each stride. **Up a slope is more effective.**

Running tall

Concentrate on keeping high up on the toes and lifting the body upwards while you're running.

Now combine all three of these actions while running fast. High knees, using your ankles for driving forward and running tall.

Cool down with a 15-minute jog.

Chapter: 19 Shoes and Feet

Broken metatarsals are caused by badly fitting and badly laced shoes which do not allow them to function without stress. Joints, sinews and the legs generally are all adversely affected by the wrong shoes and lacing.

Today's footballer wears half-boots and no longer gets the ankle support that earlier boots provided. The half-boots enables him to run faster because they permit free flexing of the ankles but a big man who doesn't condition his ankles for strength puts tremendous stress on them when, for instance, he tries to sidestep with traction. For him particularly, the hill springing and stretching exercises with blocks underneath the toes become vital.

Even walking about the house on the sides of the feet – doing a little often – is good conditioning.

When you try shoes for size, try them properly. Put the heel in and push the foot back as far as possible. You must make sure the toes do not touch the end of the shoe. And, when you stand up, you must feel that you're right on top of the shoes. The back of the shoe should not bite on the tendons and the joint on the inside of the foot should not be touching the shoe.

This applies to both training and playing shoes. There is no sense in getting the right shoes for training and then playing in shoes that aren't right. Or vice versa.

When you lace the shoes, place the laces so that when they are tightened they don't pull down on the sinews and metatarsals on top of the foot. Bring the laces from front to back without crossing them diagonally across the foot; they must cross over the top from the hole on one side to the hole directly opposite on the other side.

A simple matter such as incorrect lacing can prevent the foot from functioning freely and lead to damage.

Watch shoe wear closely because excessive wear leads to stress right through the leg to the hip and to bone wear.

Leg Problems

People who run on the balls of their feet and cannot get their hells down are much more liable to injury than natural heel runners. Many run this way and, during aerobic running, their centre of gravity doesn't get over the leading leg far enough; the foot begins to lose forward momentum and a strain is thrown on the metatarsals.

The cause of toe running is usually tight tendons. You can beat the problem by running on grass or sand, where there is some give and traction.

Knee Problems

Knee trouble arises during conditioning work when the upper front leg muscles and sinews are too tight and stressed. These quadriceps must be strengthened by uphill running or by doing squats.

As explained earlier, ill-fitting or worn shoes can be a source of ankle, knee or hip troubles by throwing stress on different parts of the legs. Check your shoes every week. If you are running correctly, the main wear should be on the outside of the heel, the outside of the forepart and slightly on the toes. Wear in these areas is a good indicator that you are running with balance. The wear should be even on both shoes; if it is not, it could be because of tight arm or shoulder muscles, badly fitting shoes or even a spinal defect that makes you run lopsidedly. This is not entirely dangerous but it adds a reason for keeping your shoes in good order.

Achilles Tendon Problems

Achilles tendon trouble is usually caused during resistance work when you could be trying to build powerful muscles without doing enough suppling and stretching exercises. The importance of the full extension of muscles and sinews must be understood. A man working with weights never gets full extensions on his legs until he goes out and sprints – and at that point he's just not ready for it.

Hamstring Problems

Hamstring trouble is caused by leg-speed running if muscles and sinews aren't stretched – yet another reason for using the full range of calisthenics for the full range of movement. An imbalance in muscle development in the legs is another common cause of hamstring breakdown in footballers. They concentrate on developing their quadriceps but neglect the hamstrings then, when they apply full power, the hamstrings are unable to take the strain.

Pulled muscles are simply a breakdown of the sheathing round muscles fibres and tearing of the fibres themselves. The causes are usually poor warming up or poor conditioning. It can happen even if everything is done properly because of the stress of using these muscles for long periods and a breaking down of muscle tissues. Even the athlete who takes every precaution can experience this trouble under the most perfect conditions.

When it happens, you can put your finger accurately on the spot. There will be internal bleeding there and you must stop it. Ice or cold water is most effective. Treat it this way for three days before you begin massage. By then, scar tissue will have formed around the affected area and the massage will help to get rid of the excess blood around the tissue and to stimulate food supplies to the injury area.

Incidentally, in all cases of injury, go to a qualified physician rather than play around. You could make the damage worse. Even with stresses of the knee and ankle joints, see an expert.

Shin splints are membrane ruptures between the muscle and the bone and often arise because of the jarring of downhill running or overstriding. You can counter overstriding by building up the front of your shoes a little and you should always be careful when running down hills.

Water therapy, cold packs and **heat treatment** can help this injury. Water therapy is invaluable for leg injuries generally. Even shin splints, which tend to be the most difficult to overcome, will respond. Just get into a tepid pool with a kickboard – and kick.

Injuries to joints and bone wear are invariably caused by poor buffers and jarring on hard surfaces. Without plenty of soft rubber between you and the ground, the shock of each stride is felt over a wider area of the body and problems arise in unexpected places. You need padding which gives you a recoil from the ground.

Shoes which achieve this may not be cheap to buy but they will prove cheap in the long term because the damage is difficult to eliminate, particularly in the big man. Consider the loss of training and playing time and the possible effect on your career as a player – and get good shoes.

But be warned against the hype surrounding some of the modern high-cost running shoes with their built-in aids to better running. It is a fact that most runners have no experience of pronation or supination until they start running in these hitech shoes. Another fact is that some of these shoes lack the essential sole flexibility which allows the feet to function properly.

All this advice gets back to one thing: It is better to prevent than it is to cure. Consider at the outset what you are going to do in your sport, try to understand the stresses involved and estimate the weaknesses you might have to contend with and the work to alleviate the problems you can foresee before you begin any kind of training programme. Cushion yourself against shock and injury from the beginning.

This applies generally to the footballer, whatever position he is going to play in. He must work to strengthen those parts of his body he knows are going to be used most against the stresses he knows he is going to be exposed to most.

Chapter 20: Foods and Fats

A vast amount has been written about diets and special foods for athletes. Most of what has been written has been meaningless in terms of improving levels of competition. Herbert A de Vries, of the University of Southern California, summarised it in his 'Physiology of Exercise': "There is no scientific evidence at the present time to indicate that athletic performance can be improved by modifying a basically sound diet ... the best diet for one athlete will seldom be the best diet for all athletes."

Most footballers eat balanced meals which give them the necessary vitamins, minerals and calories but it is quite possible to suffer from various deficiencies even when you think your diet is properly balanced. If training is progressing and the results are disappointing, it would pay to have a look at your diet and also take a blood test to check for deficiencies or a low blood count.

Athletes in all sports can be deficient in iron, calcium and other minerals and here is where they need medical advice.

During the hard training periods, you should make sure of a good intake of proteins so that muscle tissue can be developed.

Athletes' diets often vary from one to another, particularly between nations, yet they all can still derive from their food intake whatever their individual metabolism requires. The wise course is to eat the foods you feel like eating, as long as they are fresh and wholesome, rather than making drastic changes to foods you might not enjoy as much. If you cannot get the wholesome food you need, then take multi-vitamin tablets, even though some of you may be sceptical of their value. Vitamin supplements, in my experience, can definitely be valuable.

During aerobic exercise, the body uses for energy about 48 per cent carbohydrates, 48 per cent fat acids and 4 per cent protein. In anaerobic exercise, the ratio changes to about 60 per cent carbohydrates; 25 per cent fat acids and 15 per cent protein. It is apparent thath the extra energy for competition comes from carbohydrates, therefore, for pre-game meals, you should have mainly carbohydrates, such as honey sandwiches, baked beans, etc., and be sure the meal has time to digest by eating at least three hours before you compete.

Apart from the effect of nervous tension on the digestive system, a distended stomach restricts the downward movement of the diaphragm during inhalation and can also encroach on heart action, restricting the blood flow through the heart. The first effect results in 'cutting the wind' and the second in reduced endurance.

In the two days before competition, when training should be light, the taking of extra glucose or fructose can help in building up the body's glycogen content. During anaerobic exercise the blood sugars are burned up about 19 times faster than during aerobic training so it is important to rebuild this level as high as possible before you take the field. The intake of up to 200 grams or half a pound of glucose or fructose during the two days before you play is sufficient. No more.

It is unwise to eat sugar within three hours of a game. The liver has to process this into glycogen and while it is doing that it will not release the glycogen it holds. Glucose, however, is all right.

Taking calcium gluconate before a game and during the training week is helpful because muscle contractions require calcium ions and, unless you provide enough, you can experience cramps and nervous reactions, such as edgy, jumpy muscles which play up at night and cost you valuable sleep.

Drinking alcohol within 12 hours of a game prevents the red cells from combining with oxygen with maximum efficiency, because the alcohol is absorbed by the red cells. Carbonated drinks have the same effect so you're wise if you avoid them as well.

During a game or just before it, any of the specially prepared drinks that can be bought from the pharmacies are better than merely sucking an orange. These drinks have been developed to replace salts and minerals lost through perspiration. They are extremely valuable on hot days when your perspiration level is extreme.

I get a lot of questions about the value of food supplements. Sportspeople have been brainwashed about their value as pre-game meals. I wouldn't consider them ideal for this but anyone who is doing a lot of heavy work, who is having heavy workloads put on him or her, needs a lot of protein and therefore could be helped by food supplements. But they don't agree with everyone and, if they don't, forget them. There is no value in upsetting your digestive system.

I believe the best tactic is to build up your blood sugar level the day before you compete and eat sparingly on the day of competition, which rules food supplements out as a pre-game meal.

The hearty lunch was once a traditional pre-game meal in New Zealand. For years, footballers hacked into massive steaks an hour or three before playing, in the belief they were piling in extras reserves of strength and energy that would come pouring out during the game. Possibly, some still believe in this complete rubbish.

Morehouse and Miller ('Physiology of Exercise' authors), of the University of California, have traced the advocacy of large meat meals for the replenishment of 'muscle substance', supposedly lost during severe muscular work, back to the Greeks of the 5th Century BC. The evidence now is that champions range from pure vegetarians to raw meat eaters.

So my basic diet is simple: If you like it, eat it; if you don't, it's not really going to do you all that much good. The body reacts to and is made from whatever enters the mouth and that is the test.

De Vries reduced his dietary advice to these fundamentals:

1. Distribute the consumption of food over three regularly-spaced meals. To gain weight or prevent weight loss, an evening snack can be added.

2. Eliminate as much as possible foods which furnish only calories without contributing their share of vitamins and minerals (candy, cakes, carbonated beverages, etc.) and substitute fruit and fruit juices for desserts and snacks.

3. Eliminate coffee, tea and alcohol, which usurp more nutritious foods and can cause undesirable pharmacological effects, such as decreased muscular efficiency. (I would add here that there is today a strong school of thought that says one or two alcoholic drinks a day can be of long-term benefit.)

4. Avoid fatty foods; they slow paristalsis and, therefore gastric emptying.

5. Eat two servings daily of fresh fruit (one to be citrus fruits or tomatoes).

6. Eat vegetables daily, including leafy, green vegetables (salads) and roots and tubers (turnips, beet, potatoes, etc.).

7. Eat at least three slices of whole-grain bread daily.

8. Eat enough butter or fortified margarine to supplement the bread.

9. Drink at least three glasses of milk daily.
   Watch yor salt intake. In small doses, it is immediately eliminated from the body through sweat and urine; in large doses, it is contained in the body tissues and blood stream, resulting in a state of hyperchloremia.
   Research has disclosed that the Indians, the Eskimos and the people of interior China, none of whom ate salt, were perfectly healthy; proof that salt is **not** necessary for life. In small doses, it is a stimulant, like coffee, tobacco, alcohol and morphine. But, like them, it can become concentrated in the blood and body tissues and, like them, its sudden discontinuation can cause violent upsets in the nervous equilibrium. Stirring up the adrenalin with stimulants makes you feel better but it is an effect of exhilaration that only emphasises the underlying fatigue.

We are not condemning the social drink; we are warning against too much. We carry no brief at all for the sportsperson whose fitness only conditions him to be a better drinker.

Chapter 21: The Value of a Good Preparation

The programme we have set out here is basically the same wherever you play in a team, whatever game your team plays. You should all work along the same lines, within the limits of your ability, building up the distance running and hill work, because you all need strength, you all need muscular endurance and you all need good oxygen uptake levels.

When we are training for athletics, we don't introduce the specialty exercises until we get into the last 10 weeks of a training programme. Until then, the 800-metre runner does much the same conditioning work as the marathoner.

Once you've got the good endurance and speed and developed your aerobic capacity to exercise, you have built the nucleus of your specialty programme, whatever it is, by establishing the foundations on which you co-ordinate your specialist's skills and by accustoming your body to do what you expect it to do on the day of competition.

If you're going to a rugby five-eighth or a quarterback, you have to learn to move your body a yard before anyone else moves. You're going to be a quick, short, sharp, repetitive sprinter; if you can really burst for 10 or 20 metres, you're going to get through.

Years ago, when I was training for rugby, we would stand facing a wall, our backs to a mark some 15 metres away. The coach would blow a whistle and we'd turn and sprint for the mark. Then we'd walk back and, at some stage, the coach would whistle and, zip, we'd spin and sprint back again. We would do this perhaps 20, 30 or 40 times. We needed to be fit to handle this workload but, if we were fit, the exercise really sharpened us. We were fast and we were anaerobically exercised with excellent reflexes.

We would give our backs good sprint training, making them really run, sprinting through markers like a slalom to get them sidestepping and weaving their bodies correctly. This is what speed training and co-ordination is all about.

A rugby forward needs a lot of windsprints, even more than any of the backs. He is going to be doing them continually in a game so he must prepare for them by doing them hard and often in training, working on them for between four and six weeks at least. Forwards in rugby are usually big men, topping six feet and 15 stone (2 meters and 95 kg), but they've also got to be fast men to play the modern game. The days of the lumbering giant who put a lot of weight into the scrums and lineout mauls and spent the rest of the day catching up with the ball when it went out of play are over. Today's forward has to be fast enough to show up on the wing and score tries.

New Zealand, although it has been at the top of the rugby world most of the time in the past half-century, consistently suffered from a lack of real speed. This was marked when they played British. British players had such good leg speed they didn't need to break through New Zealand defenders; they just ran around them by using that vital first metre of quick movement.

The difference is no longer significant. One of our greatest post-war forwards, the late Kel Tremain, proved the point every time he played over many years but most coaches didn't get it. Kel trained every day out of season to a programme I suggested at his request and the result was that he was always up where the ball was or was going to be and he was still going strongly at the end of a game when others were down on their knees. He scored a lot of tries in the fourth quarters of matches because he prepared himself to play hard for 80 minutes.

Stan and Colin Meads were the same. They were farmers and they ran all the time on their farm work to get fit and stay fit for football. It was generally accepted that the average New Zealander was basically slow but we know now that this is not true. Today's All Blacks have proved that we can turn out footballers as quick as any when we condition and train them for speed.

This applies for any field game – gridiron, hockey, soccer, Australian rules, netball. These games are not looking for all-in wrestlers but big strong players who can run an endless series of sprints for the length of the game.

We've all seen the player who handles the ball, passes it on and then drops out of the play; and we've all seen the player who handles, passes and immediately repositions to get back into the play. The properly conditioned one is easy to identify.

In summary: No one can train hard and compete well at the same time; no one can fail to train and expect to play well; but everyone who does the basic preparation honestly in the off-season goes into the season at a peak of physical fitness and can then reduce trainining to hold that peak – and play right up to the limit of his or her ability.

Players who use the early part of the playing season as the getting-fit period in the belief that they'll be at peak when the important games come along later are fooling themselves as well as risking throwing away those early games. They will never reach the peaks of which they may be capable. Nor, therefore, will the teams they represent.

This, on a national or international level, is unforgiveable.

Chapter 22: Warming up and Cooling down
Two Musts

In discussing training schedules and sessions, we have been careful to emphasise adequate warm-ups. They are just as important when you are going out to play. You must guard against cold muscles, get the whole system ticking along at the right pace so that you can comfortably and effectively get into the game from the first whistle.

Getting changed and spending a few minutes shuffling around or running on the spot in the dressing room while your coach confuses you with last-minute instructions and exhortations is not adequate.

The warm-up has two functions: To increase the pulse rate and blood circulation; and to warm muscles and reduce their viscosity so they will function better. To achieve both these objectives, you have to run on the spot or jog at reasonable aerobic effort for about five minutes and your body should be kept warm. A track suit over the playing gear, for instance.

The warm-up should include suppling and stretching exercises to relax the muscles and stretch the sinews. Some short sharp windsprints are desirable. The team should be taken outside and pushed through two or three 30 to 50-metre windsprints and then left to run or jog quietly until the game is called. This gets the players into the 'second wind' stage and keeps them there. Remember that the average fit athlete has enough oxygen for a 133-metre sprint and the 'second wind' stage, as it was once called, is not reached until the body begins to work to cope with the demand fo anaerobic exercise. This usually takes about 15 minutes and it is a most-essential safeguard against straining tendons and pulling muscles. It is not to be achieved in the first 15 minutes of the match you are playing.

Playing seasons are tending to become longer and players, especially the elite, are being called on to compete in extremes of both hot and cold weather. This means, that, in winter sports, they can be affected by heat so they must develop the arterioles in the skin to enable the blood to be pumped adequately out to skin level to keep the temperature down and reduce the drain on working muscles. You can use a sauna to condition for this or deliberately train in the heat in the early season – long steady runs will very quickly develop this surface arteriole condition.

If you prefer saunas, do not use them near actual competition. A Thursday sauna is all right but a Friday sauna would be unwise because it could dehydrate you too much and remove too many salts and minerals which cannot be replaced in time by normal eating and drinking.

Now you are conditioned, you have used your fitness to absorb the finer points of technique, you are warmed up so get going. Get out there and win and enjoy the process.

Take these two words with you into your competitive season:
fresh and **sharp**. Always go into a game fresh and sharp so never do training during the week which is too exacting. You have trained to compete, not to keep on training.

Fettfreies Körpergewicht (kg) bestimmt auf Basis anthropometrischer Meßdaten

Körpergröße rechte und linke Kniebreite x rechte und linke Handgelenkbreite

	170	180	190	200	210	220	230	240	250	260	270
140	35.5	36.9	38.5	40.0	41.3	42.6	43.9	45.3	46.5	47.7	49.1
141	35.9	37.1	38.9	40.4	41.7	43.0	44.4	45.7	47.0	48.2	49.6
142	36.3	37.5	39.3	40.8	42.2	43.4	44.9	46.2	47.5	48.7	50.1
143	36.6	37.9	39.7	41.2	42.6	43.9	45.4	46.7	48.0	49.2	50.6
144	37.0	38.3	40.1	41.6	43.0	44.4	45.8	47.2	48.5	49.7	51.2
145	37.4	38.7	40.5	42.1	43.5	44.9	46.3	47.6	49.0	50.3	51.7
146	37.7	39.2	40.9	42.5	43.9	45.3	46.8	48.1	49.5	50.8	52.2
147	38.1	39.6	41.3	42.9	44.3	45.8	47.2	48.6	50.0	51.3	52.8
148	38.5	40.0	41.7	43.5	44.8	46.2	47.7	49.1	50.5	51.9	53.3
149	38.8	40.4	42.1	43.7	45.2	46.7	48.2	49.6	51.0	52.4	53.8
150	39.2	40.8	42.5	44.1	45.6	47.1	48.6	50.1	51.5	52.9	54.4
151	39.6	41.2	42.9	44.5	56.0	47.6	49.1	50.5	52.0	53.4	54.9
152	40.4	41.6	43.3	44.9	46.5	48.1	49.6	51.0	52.5	53.9	55.4
153	40.3	42.0	43.7	45.4	46.9	48.6	50.1	51.5	53.0	54.5	56.0
154	40.7	42.4	44.1	45.8	47.4	49.0	50.6	52.0	53.5	55.0	56.5
155	41.1	42.8	44.5	46.2	47.8	49.5	51.1	52.5	54.0	55.5	57.0
156	41.5	43.2	44.9	46.6	48.3	49.9	51.5	53.0	54.6	56.1	57.6
157	41.8	43.6	45.4	47.0	48.7	50.4	52.0	53.5	55.1	56.6	58.1
158	42.2	44.0	45.8	47.5	49.2	50.8	52.5	45.0	55.6	57.1	58.7
159	42.6	44.4	46.2	47.9	49.6	51.3	52.9	54.5	56.1	57.7	59.2
160	43.0	44.8	46.6	48.3	50.0	51.7	53.4	55.0	56.6	58.2	59.8
161	43.4	45.2	47.0	48.7	50.5	52.2	53.8	55.5	57.1	58.7	60.3
162	43.8	45.6	47.4	49.2	50.9	52.6	54.3	56.0	57.6	59.3	60.9
163	44.2	46.0	47.8	49.6	51.4	53.1	54.8	56.5	58.1	59.8	61.4
164	44.6	46.4	48.2	50.0	51.8	53.5	55.3	57.8	58.7	60.3	62.0
165	45.0	46.8	48.7	50.5	52.2	54.0	55.8	57.5	59.2	60.8	62.5
166	45.3	47.2	49.1	50.9	52.7	54.5	56.2	58.0	59.7	61.4	63.0
167	45.7	47.6	49.5	51.3	53.2	54.9	56.7	58.5	60.2	61.9	63.6
168	46.1	48.0	49.9	51.8	53.6	55.4	57.2	59.0	60.7	62.4	64.1
169	46.5	48.4	50.3	52.2	54.1	55.9	57.7	59.5	61.2	62.9	64.7
170	46.9	48.9	50.8	52.7	54.5	56.4	58.2	60.0	61.7	63.5	65.2
171	47.3	49.3	51.2	53.1	55.0	56.8	59.7	60.5	62.2	64.0	65.8
172	47.7	49.7	51.6	53.5	55.4	57.3	59.1	61.0	62.8	64.8	66.3
173	48.1	50.1	52.1	54.0	55.9	57.8	59.6	61.5	63.3	65.1	66.9
174	48.5	50.5	52.5	54.4	56.4	58.3	60.1	62.0	63.8	65.6	67.4
175	48.9	50.9	52.9	54.9	56.8	58.7	60.6	62.5	64.3	66.2	68.0
176	49.3	51.3	53.3	55.3	57.3	59.2	61.1	63.0	64.9	66.7	68.5
177	49.7	51.7	53.8	55.8	57.7	59.7	61.6	63.5	65.4	67.2	69.1
178	50.1	52.2	54.2	56.2	58.2	60.2	62.1	64.0	65.9	67.8	69.6
179	50.5	52.6	54.6	56.7	58.7	60.7	62.6	64.5	66.4	68.3	70.3
180	50.9	53.0	55.1	57.1	59.1	61.1	63.1	65.0	67.0	68.9	70.7
181	51.3	53.4	55.5	57.6	59.6	61.6	63.6	65.6	67.5	69.4	71.3
182	51.7	53.8	56.0	58.0	60.1	62.1	64.1	66.6	68.6	70.5	72.4
183	52.1	54.3	56.4	58.5	60.6	62.6	64.6	66.6	68.6	70.5	72.4
184	52.5	54.7	56.8	58.9	61.0	63.1	65.1	67.1	69.1	71.1	73.0
185	52.9	55.1	57.2	59.3	61.5	63.6	65.6	67.6	69.6	71.6	73.5
186	53.5	55.5	57.7	59.5	62.0	64.1	66.1	68.2	70.2	72.2	74.1
187	53.7	56.0	58.1	60.3	62.4	64.5	66.6	68.7	70.7	72.7	74.7
188	54.1	56.4	58.6	60.8	62.9	65.0	67.1	69.2	71.2	73.3	75.3
189	54.5	56.8	59.0	61.2	63.4	65.5	67.6	69.7	71.8	73.5	75.8
190	55.0	57.2	59.5	61.7	63.9	66.0	68.2	70.3	72.3	74.4	75.4
191	55.4	57.7	59.9	62.2	64.4	66.5	68.7	70.8	72.9	74.9	77.0
192	55.8	58.1	60.3	62.6	64.8	67.0	69.2	71.3	73.4	75.5	77.5
193	56.2	58.5	60.8	63.1	65.3	67.5	69.7	71.8	74.0	76.0	78.1

Körpergröße	rechte und linke Kniebreite x rechte und linke Handgelenkbreite										
	170	180	190	200	210	220	230	240	250	260	270
194	56.6	59.0	61.2	63.6	65.8	68.0	70.2	72.4	74.5	76.6	78.7
195	57.0	59.4	61.7	64.0	66.3	68.5	70.3	72.9	75.0	77.2	79.3
196	57.4	59.8	62.1	64.5	66.8	69.0	71.3	73.5	75.6	77.7	79.9
197	57.9	60.3	62.6	65.0	67.3	69.5	71.8	74.0	76.1	78.3	80.5
198	58.3	60.7	63.0	65.5	67.8	70.0	72.4	74.6	77.7	78.8	81.1
199	58.7	61.1	63.5	65.9	68.3	70.5	72.9	75.2	78.2	79.4	81.6
200	59.2	61.6	63.9	66.4	68.8	71.1	73.5	75.7	77.8	80.0	82.2
201	59.6	62.0	64.4	66.9	69.3	71.6	74.0	76.3	78.3	80.5	82.8

Sauerstoffaufnahme in Litern pro Minute

Fettfreies Körpergewicht (kg)	In 15 min gelaufene Meter - Männer														
	1200	1300	1400	1500	1600	1700	1800	1900	2000	2100	2200	2300	2400	2500	2600
45	0.89	0.96	1.04	1.11	1.19	1.26	1.33	1.41	1.48	1.53	1.58	1.63	1.69	1.74	1.79
46	0.91	0.96	1.06	1.14	1.21	1.29	1.36	1.44	1.52	1.57	1.61	1.67	1.72	1.78	1.83
47	0.93	1.01	1.08	1.16	1.24	1.32	1.39	1.47	1.55	1.60	1.65	1.71	1.76	1.81	1.87
48	0.95	1.03	1.11	1.19	1.27	1.34	1.42	1.50	1.58	1.64	1.69	1.74	1.80	1.85	1.91
49	0.97	1.05	1.13	1.21	1.29	1.37	1.45	1.53	1.62	1.67	1.72	1.78	1.84	1.89	1.95
50	0.99	1.07	1.15	1.24	1.32	1.40	1.48	1.57	1.65	1.70	1.76	1.82	1.87	1.93	1.99
51	1.01	1.09	1.18	1.26	1.34	1.43	1.51	1.60	1.68	1.74	1.79	1.85	1.91	1.97	2.03
52	1.03	1.11	1.20	1.29	1.37	1.46	1.54	1.63	1.71	1.77	1.83	1.89	1.95	2.01	2.07
53	1.05	1.13	1.22	1.31	1.40	1.48	1.57	1.66	1.75	1.81	1.86	1.92	1.99	2.05	2.11
54	1.07	1.16	1.25	1.33	1.42	1.51	1.60	1.69	1.78	1.84	1.90	1.96	2.02	2.09	2.15
55	1.09	1.18	1.27	1.36	1.45	1.54	1.63	1.72	1.81	1.88	1.93	2.00	2.06	2.12	2.19
56	1.11	1.20	1.29	1.38	1.48	1.57	1.66	1.75	1.85	1.91	1.97	2.03	2.10	2.16	2.23
57	1.13	1.22	1.31	1.41	1.50	1.60	1.69	1.79	1.88	1.95	2.00	2.07	2.14	2.20	2.27
58	1.15	1.24	1.34	1.43	1.53	1.63	1.72	1.82	1.91	1.98	2.04	2.11	2.18	2.24	2.31
59	1.17	1.26	1.36	1.46	1.56	1.65	1.75	1.85	1.95	2.01	2.07	2.14	2.21	2.28	2.35
60	1.19	1.29	1.38	1.48	1.58	1.68	1.78	1.88	1.98	2.05	2.11	2.18	2.25	2.32	2.39
61	1.21	1.31	1.41	1.51	1.61	1.71	1.81	1.91	2.01	2.08	2.14	2.22	2.29	2.36	2.43
62	1.23	1.33	1.43	1.53	1.64	1.74	1.84	1.94	2.05	2.11	2.18	2.25	2.33	2.40	2.47
63	1.24	1.35	1.45	1.56	1.66	1.77	1.87	1.97	2.08	2.15	2.21	2.29	2.36	2.43	2.51
64	1.26	1.37	1.48	1.58	1.69	1.79	1.90	2.01	2.11	2.18	2.23	2.32	2.40	2.47	2.55
65	1.28	1.39	1.50	1.61	1.71	1.82	1.93	2.04	2.14	2.22	2.28	2.36	2.44	2.51	2.59
66	1.30	1.41	1.52	1.63	1.74	1.85	1.96	2.07	2.18	2.25	2.32	2.40	2.48	2.55	2.63
67	1.32	1.44	1.55	1.66	1.77	1.88	1.99	2.10	2.21	2.29	2.35	2.43	2.51	2.59	2.66
68	1.34	1.46	1.57	1.68	1.79	1.91	2.02	2.13	2.24	2.32	2.39	2.47	2.55	2.63	2.70
69	1.36	1.48	1.59	1.71	1.82	1.93	2.05	2.16	2.28	2.35	2.42	2.51	2.59	2.67	2.74
70	1.38	1.50	1.62	1.73	1.85	1.96	2.08	2.19	2.31	2.39	2.46	2.54	2.63	2.70	2.78
71	1.40	1.52	1.64	1.76	1.87	1.99	2.11	2.23	2.34	2.42	2.49	2.58	2.66	2.74	2.82
72	1.42	1.54	1.66	1.78	1.90	2.02	2.14	2.26	2.38	2.46	2.53	2.62	2.70	2.78	2.86
73	1.44	1.56	1.68	1.81	1.93	2.05	2.17	2.29	2.41	2.49	2.57	2.65	2.74	2.82	2.90
74	1.46	1.59	1.71	1.83	1.95	2.08	2.20	2.32	2.44	2.53	2.60	2.69	2.78	2.86	2.94
75	1.48	1.61	1.73	1.86	1.98	2.10	2.23	2.35	2.48	2.56	2.64	2.73	2.81	2.90	2.98
76	1.50	1.63	1.75	1.88	2.01	2.13	2.26	2.41	2.51	2.59	2.67	2.76	2.85	2.94	3.02
77	1.52	1.65	1.78	1.91	2.03	2.16	2.29	2.41	2.54	2.63	2.71	2.80	2.89	2.98	3.06
78	1.54	1.67	1.80	1.93	2.06	2.19	2.32	2.45	2.57	2.66	2.74	2.83	2.93	3.01	3.10
79	1.56	1.69	1.82	1.95	2.09	2.22	2.35	2.48	2.61	2.70	2.78	2.87	2.96	3.05	3.14
80	1.58	1.72	1.85	1.98	2.11	2.24	2.38	2.51	2.64	2.73	2.81	2.91	3.00	3.09	3.18
81	1.60	1.74	1.87	2.00	2.14	2.27	2.41	2.54	2.67	2.76	2.85	2.94	3.04	3.13	3.22
82	1.62	1.76	1.89	2.03	2.16	2.30	2.44	2.57	2.71	2.80	2.88	2.98	3.08	3.17	3.26
83	1.64	1.78	1.92	2.05	2.19	2.33	2.47	2.60	2.74	2.83	2.92	3.02	3.11	3.21	3.30
84	1.66	1.80	1.94	2.08	2.22	2.36	2.50	2.63	2.77	2.87	2.95	3.05	3.15	3.25	3.34
85	1.68	1.82	1.96	2.10	2.24	2.38	2.53	2.67	2.81	2.90	2.99	3.09	3.19	3.29	3.38
86	1.70	1.84	1.99	2.13	2.27	2.41	2.56	2.70	2.84	2.94	3.02	3.13	3.23	3.32	3.42
87	1.72	1.87	2.01	2.15	2.30	2.44	2.58	2.73	2.87	2.97	3.06	3.16	3.27	3.36	3.46
88	1.74	1.89	2.03	2.18	2.32	2.47	2.61	2.76	2.91	3.00	3.09	3.20	3.30	3.40	3.50
89	1.76	1.91	2.06	2.20	2.35	2.50	2.64	2.79	2.94	3.04	3.13	3.23	3.34	3.44	3.54
90	1.78	1.93	2.08	2.23	2.38	2.52	2.67	2.82	2.97	3.07	3.16	3.27	3.38	3.48	3.58
91	1.80	1.95	2.10	2.25	2.40	2.52	2.70	2.85	3.00	3.11	3.20	3.31	3.42	3.52	3.62
92	1.82	1.97	2.12	2.28	2.43	2.58	2.73	2.89	3.04	3.14	3.23	3.34	3.45	3.56	3.66
93	1.84	1.99	2.15	2.30	2.46	2.61	2.76	2.92	3.07	3.17	3.27	3.38	3.49	3.60	3.70
94	1.86	2.02	2.17	2.33	2.48	2.64	2.79	2.95	3.10	3.21	3.30	3.42	3.53	3.63	3.74
95	1.88	2.04	2.19	2.35	2.51	2.67	2.82	2.98	3.14	3.24	3.34	3.45	3.57	3.67	3.78
96	1.90	2.06	2.22	2.38	2.54	2.69	2.85	3.01	3.17	3.28	3.38	3.49	3.60	3.71	3.82
97	1.92	2.08	2.24	2.40	2.56	2.72	2.88	3.04	3.20	3.31	3.41	3.53	3.64	3.67	3.86
98	1.94	2.10	2.26	2.43	2.59	2.75	2.91	3.07	3.24	3.35	3.45	3.56	3.68	3.79	3.90

Fettfreies Körpergewicht (kg)	In 15 min gelaufene Meter - Männer													
	1200	1300	1400	1500	1600	1700	1800	1900	2000	2100	2200	2300	2400	2500	2600
99	1.96	2.12	2.29	2.45	2.61	2.78	2.95	3.11	3.27	3.38	3.48	3.60	3.72	3.83	3.94
100	1.98	2.15	2.31	2.48	2.64	2.81	2.97	3.14	3.30	3.41	3.52	3.64	3.75	3.87	3.98
101	2.00	2.17	2.33	2.50	2.67	2.83	3.00	3.17	3.34	3.45	3.55	3.67	3.79	3.98	4.02
102	2.02	2.19	2.36	2.53	2.69	2.86	3.03	3.20	3.37	3.48	3.59	3.71	3.83	3.94	4.06
103	2.04	2.21	2.38	2.55	2.72	2.89	3.06	3.23	3.40	3.52	3.62	3.79	3.87	3.98	4.10
104	2.06	2.23	2.40	2.58	2.76	2.92	3.09	3.26	3.43	3.55	3.66	3.78	3.90	4.02	4.14
105	2.08	2.25	2.43	2.60	2.77	2.95	3.12	3.29	3.47	3.58	3.69	3.82	3.94	4.06	4.18
106	2.10	2.27	2.45	2.62	2.80	2.97	3.15	3.33	3.50	3.62	3.73	3.85	3.98	4.10	4.22
107	2.12	2.30	2.47	2.65	2.83	3.00	3.18	3.36	3.53	3.65	3.76	3.89	4.02	4.14	4.26
108	2.14	2.32	2.50	2.67	2.85	3.03	3.21	3.39	3.57	3.69	3.80	3.93	4.05	4.18	4.30
109	2.16	2.34	2.52	2.70	2.88	3.06	3.24	3.42	3.60	3.72	3.83	3.96	4.09	4.21	4.34
110	2.18	2.36	2.54	2.72	2.91	3.09	3.27	3.45	3.63	3.76	3.87	4.00	4.13	4.25	4.38
111	2.20	2.38	2.56	2.75	2.93	3.12	3.30	3.48	3.67	3.79	3.90	4.04	4.17	4.29	4.42
112	2.22	2.40	2.59	2.77	2.96	3.14	3.33	3.51	3.70	3.82	3.94	4.07	4.21	4.33	4.46
113	2.24	2.42	2.61	2.80	2.98	3.17	3.36	3.55	3.73	3.86	3.97	4.11	4.24	4.37	4.50
114	2.26	2.45	2.63	2.82	3.01	3.20	3.39	3.58	3.76	3.89	4.01	4.14	4.28	4.41	4.54
115	2.28	2.47	2.66	2.85	3.03	3.23	3.42	3.61	3.80	3.93	4.04	4.18	4.32	4.45	4.58
116	2.30	2.49	2.68	2.87	3.06	3.26	3.45	3.64	3.83	3.96	4.08	4.22	4.36	4.49	4.62
117	2.32	2.51	2.70	2.90	3.09	3.28	3.48	3.67	3.86	4.00	4.11	4.25	4.39	4.52	4.66
118	2.34	2.53	2.73	2.92	3.12	3.31	3.51	3.70	3.90	4.06	4.15	4.29	4.43	4.56	4.70
119	2.36	2.55	2.75	2.95	3.14	3.34	3.54	3.73	3.93	4.06	4.18	4.33	4.47	4.60	4.74
120	2.38	2.58	2.77	2.97	3.17	3.37	3.57	3.77	3.96	4.10	4.22	4.36	4.51	4.64	4.78
121	2.40	2.60	2.80	3.00	3.20	3.40	3.60	3.80	4.00	4.13	4.26	4.40	4.54	4.68	4.82
122	2.42	2.62	2.82	3.02	3.22	3.42	3.63	3.83	4.03	4.17	4.29	4.44	4.58	4.72	4.86
123	2.44	2.64	2.84	3.05	3.25	3.45	3.66	3.86	4.06	4.20	4.33	4.47	4.62	4.76	4.90
124	2.46	2.66	2.87	3.07	3.28	3.48	3.69	3.89	4.10	4.23	4.36	4.51	4.66	4.80	4.94
125	2.48	2.68	2.89	3.10	3.30	3.51	3.72	3.92	4.13	4.27	4.40	4.55	4.69	4.83	4.98
126	2.49	2.70	2.68	3.12	3.33	3.54	3.75	3.95	4.16	4.30	4.43	4.58	4.73	4.87	5.02
127	2.51	2.73	2.94	3.15	3.36	3.56	3.78	3.99	4.19	4.34	4.47	4.62	4.77	4.91	5.06
128													4.81	4.96	5.10
129													4.84	4.99	5.14
130													4.88	5.03	5.18
131													4.92	5.07	5.22
132													4.96	5.10	5.26
133													4.99	5.14	5.30
134													5.03	5.18	5.33
135													5.07	5.22	5.37
136													5.11	5.26	5.41
137													5.14	5.30	5.45
138													5.18	5.34	5.49
139													5.22	5.38	5.53
140													5.26	5.41	5.57

In 15 min gelaufene Meter - Männer

gewicht (kg)	2700	2800	2900	3000	3100	3200	3300	3400	3500	3600	3700	3800	3900	4000	4100
45	1.84	1.89	1.94	1.99	2.04	2.09	2.15	2.20	2.25	2.30	2.35	2.40	2.45	2.50	2.55
46	1.88	1.93	1.99	2.04	2.09	2.14	2.19	2.24	2.30	2.35	2.40	2.45	2.51	2.56	2.61
47	1.92	1.97	2.03	2.08	2.13	2.19	2.24	2.29	2.35	2.40	2.45	2.51	2.56	2.61	2.67
48	1.96	2.02	2.07	2.13	2.18	2.23	2.29	2.34	2.40	2.45	2.51	2.56	2.62	2.67	2.72
49	2.00	2.06	2.11	2.17	2.22	2.28	2.34	2.39	2.45	2.50	2.56	2.61	2.67	2.72	2.78
50	2.04	2.10	2.16	2.21	2.27	2.33	2.38	2.44	2.50	2.55	2.61	2.67	2.72	2.78	2.84
51	2.09	2.14	2.20	2.26	2.32	2.37	2.43	2.49	2.55	2.61	2.66	2.72	2.78	2.84	2.89
52	2.13	2.18	2.24	2.30	2.36	2.42	2.48	2.54	2.60	2.66	2.72	2.77	2.83	2.89	2.95
53	2.17	2.23	2.29	2.35	2.41	2.47	2.53	2.59	2.65	2.71	2.77	2.83	2.89	2.95	3.01
54	2.21	2.27	2.33	2.39	2.45	2.51	2.58	2.64	2.70	2.76	2.82	2.88	2.94	3.00	3.06
55	2.25	2.31	2.37	2.44	2.58	2.55	2.62	2.69	2.75	2.81	2.87	2.93	3.00	3.06	3.12
56	2.29	2.35	2.42	2.48	2.54	2.61	2.67	2.73	2.80	2.86	2.92	2.99	3.05	3.11	3.18
57	2.33	2.40	2.46	2.53	2.59	2.65	2.72	2.78	2.85	2.91	2.98	3.04	3.11	3.17	3.24
58	2.37	2.44	2.50	2.57	2.63	2.70	2.77	2.83	2.90	2.96	3.03	3.10	3.16	3.23	3.29
59	2.41	2.48	2.55	2.61	2.68	2.75	2.81	2.88	2.95	3.02	3.08	3.15	3.22	3.28	3.35
60	2.45	2.52	2.59	2.66	2.73	2.79	2.86	2.93	3.00	3.07	3.13	3.20	3.27	3.34	3.41
61	2.50	2.56	2.63	2.70	2.77	2.84	2.91	2.98	3.05	3.12	3.19	3.26	3.32	3.39	3.46
62	2.54	2.61	2.68	2.75	2.82	2.89	2.96	3.03	3.10	3.17	3.24	3.31	3.38	3.45	3.52
63	2.58	2.65	2.72	2.79	2.86	2.93	3.01	3.08	3.15	3.22	3.29	3.36	3.43	3.50	3.58
64	2.62	2.69	2.765	2.74	2.91	2.98	3.05	3.13	3.20	3.27	3.34	3.42	3.49	3.56	3.63
65	2.66	2.73	2.81	2.88	2.95	3.03	3.10	3.17	3.25	3.32	3.40	3.47	3.54	3.62	3.69
66	2.70	2.77	2.85	2.92	3.00	3.07	3.15	3.22	3.30	3.37	3.45	3.52	3.60	3.67	3.75
67	2.74	2.82	2.89	2.97	3.04	3.12	3.20	3.27	3.35	3.42	3.50	3.58	3.65	3.73	3.80
68	2.78	2.86	2.94	3.01	3.09	3.17	3.24	3.32	3.40	3.48	3.55	3.63	3.71	3.78	3.86
69	2.82	2.90	2.98	3.06	3.14	3.21	3.29	3.37	3.45	3.53	3.60	3.68	3.76	3.84	3.92
70	2.86	2.94	3.02	3.10	3.18	3.26	3.34	3.42	3.50	3.58	3.66	3.74	3.82	3.89	3.97
71	2.91	2.98	3.07	3.15	3.23	3.31	3.39	3.47	3.55	3.63	3.71	3.79	3.87	3.95	4.03
72	2.95	3.03	3.11	3.19	3.27	3.35	3.44	3.52	3.60	3.68	3.76	3.84	3.93	4.01	4.09
73	2.99	3.07	3.15	3.24	3.32	3.40	3.48	3.57	3.65	3.73	3.81	3.90	3.98	4.06	4.15
74	3.03	3.11	3.20	3.28	3.36	3.45	3.53	3.61	3.70	3.78	3.87	3.95	4.03	4.12	4.20
75	3.07	3.15	3.24	3.32	3.41	3.49	3.58	3.66	3.75	3.83	3.92	4.00	4.09	4.17	4.26
76	3.11	3.20	3.28	3.37	3.45	3.54	3.63	3.71	3.80	3.89	3.97	4.06	4.14	4.23	4.32
77	3.15	3.24	3.33	3.41	3.50	3.59	3.67	3.76	3.85	3.94	4.02	4.11	4.20	4.28	4.37
78	3.19	3.28	3.37	3.46	3.54	3.63	3.72	3.81	3.90	3.99	4.08	4.16	4.25	4.34	4.43
79	3.23	3.32	3.41	3.50	3.59	3.68	3.77	3.86	3.93	4.04	4.13	4.22	4.31	4.40	4.49
80	3.27	3.36	3.46	3.55	3.64	3.73	3.82	3.91	4.00	4.09	4.18	4.27	4.36	4.45	4.54
81	3.32	3.41	3.50	3.59	3.68	3.77	3.87	3.96	4.05	4.14	4.23	4.32	4.42	4.51	4.60
82	3.36	3.45	3.54	3.63	3.73	3.82	3.91	4.01	4.10	4.19	4.28	4.38	4.47	4.56	4.66
83	3.40	3.49	3.58	3.68	3.77	3.87	3.96	4.05	4.15	4.24	4.34	4.43	4.53	4.62	4.71
84	3.44	3.53	3.63	3.72	3.82	3.91	4.01	4.10	4.20	4.29	4.39	4.48	4.58	4.67	4.77
85	3.48	3.57	3.67	3.77	3.86	3.96	4.06	4.15	4.25	4.35	4.44	4.54	4.64	4.73	4.83
86	3.52	3.62	3.71	3.81	3.91	4.01	4.10	4.20	4.30	4.40	4.49	4.59	4.69	4.79	4.88
87	3.56	3.66	3.76	3.86	3.95	4.05	4.15	4.25	4.35	4.45	4.55	4.65	4.74	4.84	4.94
88	3.60	3.70	3.80	3.90	4.00	4.10	4.20	4.30	4.40	4.50	4.60	4.70	4.80	4.90	5.00
89	3.64	3.74	3.84	3.95	4.05	4.15	4.25	4.35	4.45	4.55	4.65	4.75	4.85	4.95	5.05
90	3.68	3.78	3.89	3.99	4.09	4.19	4.30	4.40	4.50	4.60	4.70	4.81	4.91	5.01	5.11
91	3.73	3.83	3.93	4.03	4.14	4.24	4.34	4.45	4.55	4.65	4.76	4.86	4.96	5.06	5.17
92	3.77	3.87	3.97	4.08	4.18	4.29	4.39	4.49	4.60	4.70	4.81	4.91	5.02	5.12	5.23
93	3.81	3.91	4.02	4.12	4.23	4.33	4.44	4.54	4.65	4.76	4.86	4.97	5.07	5.18	5.28
94	3.85	3.95	4.06	4.17	4.27	4.38	4.49	4.59	4.70	4.81	4.91	5.02	5.13	5.23	5.34
95	3.89	4.00	4.10	4.21	4.32	4.43	4.54	4.64	4.75	4.86	4.96	5.07	5.18	5.29	5.40
96	3.95	4.04	4.15	4.26	4.36	4.47	4.58	4.69	4.80	4.91	5.02	5.13	5.24	5.34	5.45
97	3.97	4.08	4.19	4.30	4.41	4.52	4.63	4.74	4.85	4.96	5.07	5.18	5.29	5.40	5.51
98	4.01	4.12	4.23	4.35	4.45	4.57	4.68	4.79	4.90	5.01	5.12	5.23	5.43	5.45	5.57

Fettfreies Körpergewicht (kg)	In 15 min gelaufene Meter – Männer														
	2700	2800	2900	3000	3100	3200	3300	3400	3500	3600	3700	3800	3900	4000	4100
99	4.05	4.16	4.28	4.39	4.50	4.61	4.73	4.84	4.95	5.06	5.17	5.29	5.40	5.51	5.62
100	4.09	4.21	4.32	4.43	4.55	4.66	4.77	4.89	5.00	5.11	5.23	5.34	5.45	5.57	5.68
101	4.13	4.25	4.36	4.48	4.59	4.71	4.82	4.93	5.05	5.17	5.28	5.39	5.51	5.62	5.74
102	4.18	4.29	4.41	4.52	4.64	4.75	4.87	4.98	5.10	5.22	5.33	5.45	5.56	5.68	5.79
103	4.22	4.33	4.45	4.57	4.68	4.80	4.92	5.03	5.15	5.27	5.38	5.50	5.62	5.73	5.85
104	4.26	4.37	4.49	4.61	4.73	4.85	4.97	5.08	5.20	5.32	5.44	5.55	5.67	5.79	5.91
105	4.30	4.42	4.54	4.66	4.77	4.89	5.01	5.13	5.25	5.37	5.49	5.61	5.73	5.84	5.96
106	4.34	4.46	4.58	4.70	4.82	4.94	5.06	5.18	5.30	5.42	5.54	5.66	5.78	5.90	
107	4.38	4.50	4.62	4.74	4.86	4.99	5.11	5.23	5.35	5.47	5.59	5.71	5.84	5.96	
108	4.42	4.54	4.67	4.79	4.91	5.03	5.16	5.22	5.40	5.52	5.64	5.77	5.89		
109	4.46	4.58	4.71	4.83	4.96	5.08	5.20	5.33	5.45	5.57	5.70	5.82	5.95		
110	4.50	4.63	4.75	4.88	5.00	5.13	5.25	5.38	5.50	5.63	5.75	5.87	6.00		
111	4.54	4.67	4.80	4.92	5.05	5.17	5.30	5.42	5.55	5.68	5.80	5.93			
112	4.59	4.71	4.84	4.97	5.09	5.22	5.35	5.47	5.60	5.73	5.85	5.98			
113	4.63	4.75	4.88	5.01	5.15	5.27	5.40	5.52	5.65	5.78	5.91				
114	4.67	4.80	4.93	5.06	5.18	5.31	5.44	5.57	5.70	5.83	5.96				
115	4.71	4.84	4.97	5.10	5.23	5.36	5.49	5.62	5.75	5.88	6.00				
116	4.75	4.88	4.01	5.14	5.27	5.41	5.54	5.67	5.80	5.93					
117	4.79	4.92	5.06	5.19	5.32	5.45	5.59	5.72	5.85	5.98					
118	4.83	4.96	5.10	5.23	5.37	5.50	5.63	5.77	5.90						
119	4.87	5.01	5.14	5.28	5.41	5.55	5.68	5.82	5.95						
120	4.91	5.05	5.32	5.46	5.59	5.73	5.86	6.00							
121	4.95	5.09	5.23	5.37	5.50	5.64	5.78	5.91							
122	5.00	5.13	5.27	5.41	5.55	5.69	5.83	5.96							
123	5.04	5.17	5.31	5.45	5.59	5.73	5.87	6.00							
124	5.08	5.22	5.36	5.50	5.64	5.78	5.92								
125	5.12	5.26	5.40	5.54	5.68	5.83	5.97								
126	5.16	5.30	5.44	5.59	5.73	5.87									
127	5.20	5.34	5.49	5.63	5.77	5.92									
128	5.24	5.39	5.53	5.68	5.82	5.97									
129	5.28	5.43	5.57	5.72	5.87										
130	5.32	5.47	5.62	5.77	5.91										
131	5.36	5.51	5.56	5.81	5.96										
132	5.41	5.55	5.70	5.85	6.00										
133	5.45	5.60	5.75	5.90											
134	5.49	5.64	5.79	5.94											
135	5.53	5.68	5.83	5.99											
136	5.57	5.72	5.88												
137	5.61	5.76	5.92												
138	5.65	5.81	5.96												
139	5.69	5.85	6.01												
140	5.73	5.89													

Fettfreies Körpergewicht (kg)	In 15 min gelaufene Meter – Männer														
	4200	4300	4400	4500	4600	4700	4800	4900	5000	5100	5200	5300	5400	5500	5600
45	2.60	2.65	2.71	2.76	2.81	2.86	2.91	2.96	3.01	3.06	3.11	3.17	3.22	3.27	3.32
46	2.66	2.71	2.77	2.82	2.87	2.97	2.98	3.03	3.08	3.13	3.18	3.24	3.29	3.34	3.39
47	2.72	2.77	2.83	2.88	2.93	2.99	3.04	3.09	3.14	3.20	3.25	3.31	3.36	3.41	3.47
48	2.78	2.83	2.89	2.94	3.00	3.05	3.10	3.16	3.21	3.27	3.32	3.38	3.43	3.49	3.54
49	2.84	2.89	2.95	3.00	3.06	3.11	3.17	3.22	3.28	3.34	3.39	3.45	3.50	3.56	3.61
50	2.89	2.95	3.01	3.06	3.12	3.18	3.23	3.29	3.35	3.40	3.46	3.52	3.57	3.63	3.69
51	2.95	3.01	3.07	3.13	3.18	3.24	3.30	3.36	3.41	3.47	3.53	3.59	3.65	3.70	3.76
52	3.01	3.07	3.13	3.19	3.25	3.30	3.36	3.42	3.48	3.54	3.60	3.66	3.72	3.78	3.84
53	3.07	3.13	3.19	3.25	3.31	3.37	3.43	3.49	3.55	3.61	3.67	3.73	3.79	3.85	3.91
54	3.13	3.19	3.25	3.31	3.37	3.43	3.49	3.55	3.61	3.68	3.74	3.80	3.86	3.92	3.98
55	3.18	3.25	3.31	3.37	3.43	3.50	3.56	3.62	3.68	3.75	3.81	3.87	3.93	3.99	4.06
56	3.24	3.31	3.37	3.43	3.50	3.56	3.62	3.69	3.75	3.81	3.88	3.94	4.00	4.07	4.13
57	3.30	3.36	3.43	3.49	3.56	3.62	3.69	3.76	3.82	3.88	3.95	4.01	4.08	4.14	4.20
58	3.36	3.42	3.49	3.56	3.62	3.69	3.75	3.82	3.88	3.95	4.01	4.08	4.15	4.21	4.28
59	3.42	3.48	3.55	3.62	3.68	3.75	3.82	3.88	3.95	4.02	4.08	4.15	4.22	4.28	4.35
60	3.47	3.54	3.61	3.68	3.75	3.81	3.88	3.95	4.02	4.09	4.15	4.22	4.29	4.36	4.41
61	3.53	3.60	3.67	3.74	3.81	3.88	3.95	4.02	4.08	4.15	4.22	4.29	4.36	4.43	4.50
62	3.59	3.66	3.73	3.80	3.87	3.94	4.01	4.08	4.15	4.22	4.29	4.36	4.43	4.50	4.57
63	3.65	3.72	3.79	3.86	3.93	4.00	4.08	4.15	4.22	4.29	4.36	4.43	4.51	4.58	4.63
64	3.71	3.78	3.85	3.92	4.00	4.07	4.14	4.21	4.28	4.36	4.43	4.50	4.58	4.65	4.72
65	3.76	3.84	3.91	3.99	4.06	4.13	4.21	4.28	4.35	4.43	4.50	4.57	4.65	4.72	4.80
66	3.82	3.90	3.97	4.05	4.12	4.20	4.27	4.35	4.42	4.50	4.57	4.64	4.72	4.79	4.87
67	3.88	3.96	4.03	4.11	4.18	4.26	4.34	4.41	4.49	4.56	4.64	4.72	4.79	4.87	4.94
68	3.94	4.01	4.09	4.17	4.25	4.32	4.40	4.48	4.55	4.63	4.71	4.79	4.86	4.94	5.02
69	4.00	4.07	4.15	4.23	4.31	4.39	4.47	4.54	4.62	4.70	4.78	4.86	4.93	5.01	5.09
70	4.05	4.13	4.21	4.29	4.37	4.45	4.53	4.61	4.69	4.77	4.85	4.93	5.01	5.08	5.16
71	4.11	4.19	4.27	4.35	4.38	4.51	4.60	4.67	4.75	4.84	4.92	5.00	5.08	5.16	5.24
72	4.17	4.25	4.33	4.42	4.50	4.58	4.66	4.74	4.82	4.90	4.99	5.07	5.15	5.23	5.31
73	4.23	4.31	4.39	4.48	4.56	4.64	4.72	4.81	4.89	4.97	5.05	5.14	5.22	5.30	5.39
74	4.29	4.37	4.45	4.54	4.62	4.71	4.79	4.87	4.95	5.05	5.12	5.21	5.29	5.38	5.46
75	4.34	4.43	4.51	4.60	4.68	4.77	4.85	4.94	5.02	5.11	5.19	5.28	5.36	5.45	5.53
76	4.40	4.49	4.57	4.66	4.75	4.83	4.92	5.00	5.09	5.18	5.26	5.35	5.44	5.52	5.61
77	4.46	4.55	4.63	4.72	4.81	4.90	4.98	5.07	5.16	5.25	5.33	5.42	5.51	5.59	5.68
78	4.52	4.61	4.69	4.78	4.87	4.96	5.05	5.14	5.22	5.31	5.40	5.49	5.58	5.67	5.76
79	4.58	4.66	4.75	4.84	4.93	5.02	5.11	5.20	5.29	5.38	5.47	5.56	5.65	5.74	5.83
80	4.63	4.72	4.82	4.91	5.00	5.09	5.18	5.27	5.36	5.45	5.54	5.63	5.72	5.81	5.90
81	4.69	4.78	4.88	4.97	5.06	5.15	5.24	5.33	5.42	5.52	5.61	5.70	5.79	5.88	5.98
82	4.75	4.84	4.94	5.03	5.12	5.21	5.31	5.40	5.49	5.59	5.68	5.77	5.87	5.96	
83	4.81	4.90	5.00	5.09	5.18	5.28	5.37	5.47	5.56	5.65	5.75	5.84	5.94		
84	4.87	4.96	5.06	5.15	5.25	5.34	5.44	5.53	5.62	5.72	5.82	5.91	6.00		
85	4.92	5.02	5.12	5.21	5.31	5.41	5.50	5.60	5.69	5.79	5.89	5.98			
86	4.98	5.08	5.18	5.27	5.37	5.47	5.57	5.66	5.76	5.86	5.96				
87	5.04	5.14	5.24	5.34	5.43	5.53	5.63	5.73	5.83	5.93					
88	5.10	5.20	5.30	5.40	5.50	5.60	5.70	5.80	5.89	6.00					
89	5.16	5.26	5.36	5.46	5.56	5.66	5.76	5.86	5.96	5.40					
90	5.21	5.31	5.42	5.52	5.62	5.72	5.83	5.93							
91	5.27	5.37	5.48	5.58	5.68	5.79	5.89	5.99							
92	5.33	5.43	5.54	5.64	5.75	5.85	5.96								
93	5.39	5.49	5.60	5.70	5.81	5.91									
94	5.45	5.55	5.66	5.77	5.87	5.98									
95	5.50	5.61	5.72	5.83	5.93										
96	5.56	576	5.78	5.89	6.00										
97	5.62	5.73	5.84	5.95											
98	5.68	5.79	5.90	6.00											

Fettfreies Körpergewicht (kg)	1000	1100	1200	1300	1400	1500	1600	1700	1800	1900	2000	2100	2200	2300	2400	2500	2600
					In 12 min gelaufene Meter - Frauen												
40	0.82	0.90	0.99	1.07	1.15	1.24	1.32	1.37	1.43	1.49	1.54	1.60	1.66	1.71	1.77	1.83	1.88
41	0.84	0.92	1.01	1.09	1.17	1.27	1.35	1.41	1.47	1.52	1.58	1.64	1.70	1.76	1.81	1.87	1.93
42	0.86	0.94	1.04	1.12	1.20	1.30	1.38	1.44	1.50	1.56	1.62	1.68	1.74	1.80	1.86	1.92	1.98
43	0.88	0.97	1.06	1.15	1.23	1.33	1.41	1.48	1.54	1.60	1.66	1.72	1.78	1.84	1.90	1.96	2.03
44	0.90	0.99	1.09	1.17	1.26	1.36	1.45	1.51	1.57	1.64	1.70	1.76	1.82	1.89	1.95	2.01	2.07
45	0.92	1.01	1.11	1.20	1.29	1.39	1.48	1.55	1.61	1.67	1.74	1.80	1.86	1.93	1.99	2.06	2.12
46	0.94	1.03	1.14	1.23	1.32	1.42	1.51	1.58	1.65	1.71	1.78	1.84	1.91	1.97	2.04	2.10	2.17
47	0.96	1.06	1.16	1.25	1.35	1.45	1.55	1.62	1.68	1.75	1.81	1.88	1.95	2.01	2.08	2.15	2.21
48	0.98	1.08	1.19	1.28	1.38	1.48	1.58	1.65	1.72	1.79	1.85	1.92	1.99	2.06	2.13	2.19	2.26
49	1.00	1.10	1.21	1.31	1.40	1.51	1.61	1.68	1.75	1.82	1.89	1.96	2.03	2.10	2.17	2.24	2.31
50	1.02	1.12	1.23	1.33	1.43	1.55	1.65	1.72	1.79	1.86	1.93	2.00	2.07	2.14	2.21	2.29	2.36
51	1.05	1.15	1.26	1.36	1.43	1.58	1.68	1.75	1.83	1.90	1.97	2.04	2.11	2.19	2.26	2.33	2.40
52	1.07	1.17	1.29	1.39	1.49	1.61	1.71	1.79	1.86	1.93	2.01	2.08	2.16	2.23	2.30	2.38	2.45
53	1.09	1.19	1.31	1.41	1.52	1.64	1.74	1.82	1.90	1.97	2.05	2.12	2.20	2.27	2.35	2.42	2.50
54	1.11	1.21	1.33	1.44	1.55	1.67	1.78	1.86	1.93	2.01	2.09	2.16	2.24	2.32	2.39	2.47	2.54
55	1.13	1.24	1.36	1.47	1.58	1.70	1.81	1.89	1.97	2.05	2.12	2.20	2.28	2.36	2.44	2.51	2.59
56	1.15	1.26	1.38	1.50	1.61	1.73	1.84	1.93	2.00	2.08	2.16	2.24	2.32	2.40	2.48	2.56	2.64
57	1.17	1.28	1.41	1.52	1.63	1.76	1.88	1.96	2.04	2.12	2.20	2.28	2.36	2.44	2.53	2.61	2.69
58	1.19	1.30	1.43	1.55	1.66	1.79	1.91	1.99	2.08	2.16	2.24	2.32	2.40	2.49	2.57	2.65	2.73
59	1.21	1.33	1.46	1.58	1.69	1.82	1.94	2.03	2.11	2.20	2.28	2.36	2.45	2.53	2.61	2.70	2.78
60	1.23	1.35	1.48	1.60	1.72	1.86	1.98	2.06	2.15	2.23	2.32	2.40	2.49	2.57	2.66	2.74	2.83
61	1.25	1.37	1.51	1.63	1.75	1.89	2.01	2.10	2.18	2.27	2.36	2.44	2.53	2.62	2.70	2.79	2.88
62	1.27	1.39	1.53	1.66	1.78	1.92	2.04	2.13	2.22	2.31	2.40	2.48	2.57	2.66	2.75	2.83	2.92
63	1.29	1.42	1.56	1.68	1.81	1.95	2.07	2.17	2.26	2.34	2.43	2.52	2.61	2.70	2.79	2.88	2.97
64	1.31	1.44	1.58	1.71	1.84	1.98	2.11	2.20	2.29	2.38	2.47	2.56	2.65	2.75	2.84	2.93	3.02
65	1.33	1.46	1.61	1.74	1.87	2.01	2.14	2.24	2.33	2.42	2.51	2.60	2.70	2.79	2.88	2.97	3.06
66	1.35	1.48	1.63	1.76	1.89	2.04	2.17	2.27	2.36	2.46	2.55	2.64	2.74	2.83	2.92	3.02	3.11
67	1.37	1.51	1.66	1.79	1.92	2.07	2.21	2.30	2.40	2.49	2.59	2.68	2.78	2.87	2.97	3.06	3.16
68	1.40	1.53	1.68	1.82	1.95	2.10	2.24	2.34	2.44	2.53	2.63	2.72	2.82	2.92	3.01	3.11	3.21
69	1.42	1.55	1.71	1.84	1.98	2.13	2.27	2.37	2.47	2.57	2.67	2.76	2.86	2.96	3.06	3.16	3.25
70	1.44	1.57	1.73	1.87	2.01	2.17	2.31	2.41	2.51	2.61	2.71	2.80	2.90	3.00	3.10	3.20	3.30
71	1.46	1.60	1.76	1.90	2.04	2.20	2.34	2.44	2.54	2.64	2.74	2.84	2.95	3.05	3.15	3.25	3.35
72	1.48	1.62	1.78	1.92	2.07	2.23	2.37	2.48	2.58	2.68	2.78	2.89	2.99	3.09	3.19	3.29	3.39
73	1.50	1.64	1.81	1.95	2.10	2.26	2.40	2.51	2.61	2.72	2.82	2.93	3.03	3.13	3.24	3.34	3.44
74	1.52	1.67	1.83	1.98	2.12	2.29	2.44	2.55	2.65	2.76	2.86	2.97	3.07	3.17	3.28	3.38	3.49
75	1.54	1.69	1.86	2.00	2.15	2.32	2.47	2.58	2.69	2.79	2.90	3.01	3.11	3.22	3.32	3.43	3.54
76	1.56	1.71	1.88	2.03	2.18	2.35	2.50	2.61	2.72	2.83	2.94	3.05	3.15	3.26	3.37	3.48	3.58
77	1.58	1.73	1.91	2.06	2.21	2.38	2.54	2.65	2.76	2.87	2.98	3.09	3.19	3.30	3.41	3.52	3.63
78	1.60	1.76	1.93	2.08	2.24	2.41	2.57	2.68	2.79	2.90	3.02	3.13	3.24	3.35	3.46	3.57	3.68
79	1.62	1.78	1.95	2.11	2.27	2.44	2.60	2.72	2.83	2.94	3.05	3.17	3.28	3.39	3.50	3.61	3.73
80	1.64	1.80	1.98	2.14	2.30	2.48	2.64	2.75	2.87	2.98	3.09	3.21	3.32	3.43	3.55	3.66	3.77
81	1.66	1.82	2.00	2.16	2.33	2.51	2.67	2.79	2.90	3.02	3.13	3.25	3.36	3.48	3.59	3.70	3.82
82	1.68	1.85	2.03	2.19	2.35	2.54	2.70	2.82	2.94	3.05	3.17	3.29	3.40	3.52	3.63	3.72	3.87
83	1.70	1.87	2.05	2.22	2.38	2.57	2.73	2.86	2.97	3.09	3.21	3.33	3.44	3.56	3.68	3.76	3.91
84	1.72	1.89	2.08	2.25	2.41	2.60	2.77	2.89	3.01	3.13	3.25	3.37	3.49	3.60	3.72	3.81	3.96
85	1.75	1.91	2.10	2.27	2.44	2.63	2.80	2.92	3.05	3.17	3.29	3.41	3.53	3.65	3.77	3.85	4.01
86	1.77	1.94	2.13	2.30	2.47	2.66	2.83	2.96	3.08	3.20	3.32	3.45	3.57	3.69	3.81	3.90	4.06
87	1.78	1.96	2.15	2.33	2.50	2.69	2.87	2.99	3.12	3.24	3.36	3.49	3.61	3.73	3.86	3.94	4.10
88	1.81	1.98	2.18	2.35	2.53	2.72	2.90	3.03	3.15	3.28	3.40	3.53	3.65	3.78	3.90	3.99	4.15
89	1.83	2.00	2.20	2.38	2.56	2.75	2.93	3.06	3.19	3.31	3.44	3.57	3.69	3.82	3.95	4.04	4.20
90	1.85	2.03	2.23	2.41	2.58	2.79	2.97	3.10	3.23	3.35	3.48	3.61	3.73	3.86	3.99	4.08	4.24
91	1.87	2.05	2.25	2.43	2.61	2.82	3.00	3.13	3.26	3.39	3.52	3.65	3.78	3.91	4.03	4.13	4.29
92	1.89	2.07	2.28	2.46	2.64	2.85	3.03	3.17	3.30	3.43	3.56	3.69	3.82	3.95	4.08	4.17	4.34
93	1.91	2.09	2.30	2.49	2.67	2.88	3.06	3.20	3.33	3.46	3.60	3.73	3.86	3.99	4.12	4.22	4.39

Fettfreies Körpergewicht (kg) — In 12 min gelaufene Meter - Frauen

(kg)	1000	1100	1200	1300	1400	1500	1600	1700	1800	1900	2000	2100	2200	2300	2400	2500	2600
94	1.93	2.12	2.33	2.51	2.70	2.91	3.10	3.24	3.37	3.50	3.63	3.77	3.90	4.03	4.17	4.26	4.43
95	1.95	2.14	2.35	2.54	2.73	2.94	3.13	3.27	3.40	3.54	3.67	3.81	3.94	4.08	4.21	4.31	4.48
96	1.97	2.16	2.38	2.57	2.76	2.97	3.16	3.30	3.44	3.58	3.71	3.85	3.98	4.12	4.26	4.35	4.53
97	1.99	2.18	2.40	2.59	2.79	3.00	3.20	3.34	3.48	3.61	3.75	3.89	4.03	4.16	4.30	4.40	4.58
98	2.02	2.21	2.43	2.62	2.81	3.03	3.23	3.37	3.51	3.65	3.79	3.93	4.07	4.21	4.35	4.44	4.62
99	2.03	2.23	2.45	2.65	2.84	3.06	3.26	3.41	3.55	3.69	3.83	3.97	4.11	4.25	4.39	4.49	4.67
100	2.05	2.25	2.48	2.67	2.87	3.10	3.30	3.44	3.58	3.73	3.87	4.01	415	4.29	4.43	4.54	4.72
101	2.07	2.27	2.50	2.70	2.90	3.13	3.33	3.48	3.62	3.76	3.91	4.05	4.19	4.33	4.48	4.58	4.76
102	2.10	2.30	2.53	2.73	2.93	3.16	3.36	3.51	3.66	3.80	3.94	4.09	4.23	4.38	4.52	4.63	4.81
103	2.12	2.32	2.55	2.75	2.96	3.19	3.39	3.55	3.69	3.84	3.98	4.13	4.27	4.42	4.57	4.67	4.86
104	2.14	2.34	2.58	2.78	2.99	3.22	3.43	3.58	3.73	3.87	4.02	4.17	4.32	4.46	4.61	4.72	4.91
105	2.16	2.36	2.60	2.81	3.02	3.25	3.46	3.61	3.76	3.91	4.06	4.21	4.36	4.51	4.66	4.76	4.95
106	2.18	2.39	2.62	2.83	3.04	3.28	3.49	3.65	3.80	3.95	4.10	4.25	4.40	4.55	4.70	4.81	5.00
107	2.20	2.41	2.65	2.86	3.07	3.31	3.53	3.68	3.84	3.99	4.14	4.29	4.44	4.59	4.74	4.85	5.05
108	2.22	2.43	2.67	2.89	3.10	3.34	3.56	3.72	3.87	4.02	4.18	4.33	4.48	4.64	4.79	4.90	5.09
109	2.24	2.46	2.70	2.92	3.13	3.38	3.59	3.75	3.91	4.06	4.22	4.37	4.52	4.68	4.83	4.94	5.14
110	2.26	2.48	2.72	2.94	3.16	3.41	3.63	3.79	3.94	4.10	4.25	4.41	4.57	4.72	4.88	4.99	5.19
111	2.28	2.50	2.75	2.97	3.19	3.44	3.66	3.82	3.98	4.14	4.29	4.45	4.61	4.76	4.92	5.03	5.24
112	2.30	2.52	2.77	3.00	3.22	3.47	3.69	3-86	4.01	4.17	4.33	4.49	4.65	4.81	4.97	5.08	5.28
113	2.32	2.55	2.80	3.02	3.25	3.50	3.72	3.89	4.05	4.21	4.37	4.53	4.69	4.85	5.01	5.13	5.33
114	2.34	2.57	2.82	3.05	3.27	3.53	3.76	3.92	4.09	4.25	4.41	4.57	4.73	4.89	5.06	5.17	5.38
115	2.36	2.59	2.85	3.08	3.30	3.56	3.79	3.96	4.12	4.28	4.45	4.61	4.77	4.94	5.10	5.22	5.43
116	2.38	2.61	2.87	3.10	3.33	3.59	3.82	3.99	4.16	4.32	4.49	4.65	4.81	4.98	5.14	5.26	5.47
117	2.40	2.64	2.90	3.13	3.36	3.62	3.86	4.03	4.19	4.36	4.53	4.69	4.86	5.02	5.19	5.31	5.52
118	2.42	2.66	2.92	3.16	3.39	3.65	3.89	4.06	4.23	4.40	4.56	4.73	4.90	5.07	5.23	5.35	5.57
119	2.45	2.68	2.95	3.18	3.42	3.69	3.92	4.10	4.27	4.43	4.60	4.77	4.94	5.11	5.28	5.40	5.61
120	2.47	2.70	2.97	3.21	3.45	372	3.96	4.13	4.30	4.47	4.64	4.81	4.98	5.15	5.32	5.44	5.66
121	2.49	2.73	3.00	3.24	3.48	3.75	3.99	4.17	4.34	4.51	4.68	4.85	5.02	5.19	5.37	5.49	5.71
122	2.51	2.75	3.02	3.26	3.50	3.78	4.02	4.20	4.37	4.55	4.72	4.89	5.06	5.24	5.41	5.53	5.76
123	2.53	2.77	3.05	3.29	3.53	3.81	4.05	4.23	4.41	4.58	4.76	4.93	5.11	5.28	5.45	5.58	5.80
124	2.55	2.79	3.07	3.32	3.56	3.84	4.09	4.27	4.45	4.62	4.80	4.97	5.15	5.32	5.50	5.62	5.85
125	2.57	2.82	3.10	3.34	3.59	3.87	4.12	4.30	4.48	4.66	4.84	5.01	5.19	5.37	5.54	5.67	5.90
126	2.59	2.84	3.12	3.37	3.62	3.90	4.15	4.34	4.52	4.69	4.87	5.05	5.23	5.41	5.59	5.72	5.94
127	2.61	2.86	3.15	3.40	3.65	3.93	4.19	4.37	4.55	4.73	4.91	5.09	5.27	5.45	5.63	5.76	5.99

Fettfreies Körpergewicht (kg)	In 12 min gelaufene Meter - Frauen															
	2700	2800	2900	3000	3100	3200	3300	3400	3500	3600	3700	3800	3900	4000	4100	4200	4300
40	1.94	2.00	2.05	2.11	2.17	2.22	2.28	2.34	2.39	2.45	2.51	2.56	2.62	2.68	2.73	2.79	2.85
41	1.99	2.05	2.11	2.16	2.22	2.28	2.34	2.40	2.45	2.51	2.57	2.63	2.69	2.74	2.80	2.86	2.93
42	2.04	2.10	2.16	2.22	2.28	2.34	2.39	2.45	2.51	2.57	2.63	2.69	2.75	2.81	2.87	2.93	2.99
43	2.09	2.15	2.21	2.27	2.33	2.39	2.45	2.51	2.57	2.63	2.70	2.76	2.82	2.88	2.94	3.00	3.06
44	2.14	2.20	2.26	2.32	2.38	2.45	2.51	2.57	2.63	2.70	2.76	2.82	2.88	2.95	3.01	3.07	3.13
45	2.18	2.25	2.31	2.38	2.44	2.50	2.57	2.63	2.69	2.76	2.82	2.88	2.95	3.01	3.08	3.14	3.20
46	2.23	2.30	2.36	2.43	2.49	2.56	2.62	2.69	2.75	2.82	2.88	2.95	3.01	3.08	3.14	3.21	3.27
47	2.28	2.65	2.41	2.48	2.55	2.61	2.68	2.75	2.81	2.88	2.95	3.01	3.08	3.15	3.21	3.28	3.35
48	2.33	2.40	2.47	2.53	2.60	2.67	2.74	2.81	2.87	2.94	3.01	3.08	3.15	3.21	3.28	3.35	3.42
49	2.38	2.45	2.52	2.59	2.66	2.73	2.79	2.86	2.93	3.00	3.07	3.14	3.21	3.28	3.35	3.42	3.49
50	2.43	2.50	2.57	2.64	2.71	2.78	2.85	2.92	2.99	3.06	3.14	3.21	3.28	3.35	3.42	3.49	3.56
51	2.48	2.55	2.62	2.69	2.76	2.84	2.91	2.98	3.05	3.13	3.20	3.27	3.34	3.41	3.49	3.56	3.63
52	2.52	2.60	2.57	2.75	2.82	2.89	2.97	3.04	3.11	3.19	3.26	3.33	3.41	3.48	3.56	3.63	3.70
53	2.57	2.65	2.72	2.80	2.87	2.95	3.02	3.10	3.17	3.25	3.32	3.40	3.47	3.55	3.62	3.70	3.77
54	2.62	2.70	2.77	2.85	2.93	3.00	3.08	3.16	3.23	3.31	3.39	3.46	3.54	3.62	3.69	3.77	3.85
55	2.67	2.75	2.83	2.90	2.98	3.06	3.14	3.22	3.29	3.37	3.45	3.53	3.61	3.68	3.76	3.84	3.92
56	2.72	2.80	2.88	2.96	3.04	3.12	3.19	3.27	3.35	3.43	3.51	3.59	3.67	3.75	3.83	3.91	3.99
57	2.77	2.85	2.93	3.01	3.09	3.17	3.25	3.33	3.41	3.49	3.57	3.66	3.74	3.82	3.90	3.98	4.06
58	2.82	2.90	2.98	3.06	3.14	3.23	3.31	3.39	3.47	3.56	3.64	3.72	3.80	3.88	3.97	4.05	4.13
59	2.86	2.95	3.03	3.12	3.20	3.28	3.37	3.45	3.53	3.62	3.70	3.78	3.87	3.95	4.03	4.12	4.20
60	2.91	3.00	3.08	3.17	3.25	3.34	3.42	3.51	3.59	3.68	3.76	3.85	3.93	4.02	4.10	4.19	4.27
61	2.96	3.05	3.13	3.22	3.31	3.39	3.48	3.57	3.65	3.74	3.83	3.91	4.00	4.09	4.17	4.26	4.34
62	3.01	3.10	3.19	3.27	3.36	3.45	3.54	3.63	3.71	3.80	3.89	3.98	4.06	4.15	4.24	4.33	4.42
63	3.05	3.15	3.24	3.33	3.42	3.51	3.59	3.68	3.77	3.86	3.95	4.04	4.13	4.22	4.31	4.40	4.49
64	3.11	3.20	3.29	3.38	3.47	3.56	3.65	3.74	3.83	3.92	4.01	4.11	4.20	4.29	4.38	4.47	4.56
65	3.16	3.25	3.34	3.43	3.52	3.62	3.71	3.80	3.89	3.99	4.08	4.17	4.26	4.35	4.45	4.54	4.63
66	3.21	3.30	3.38	3.49	3.58	3.67	3.77	3.86	3.95	4.05	4.14	4.23	4.33	4.42	4.51	4.61	4.70
67	3.25	3.35	3.44	3.54	3.63	3.73	3.82	3.92	4.01	4.11	4.20	4.30	4.39	4.49	4.58	4.68	4.77
68	3.30	3.40	3.49	3.59	3.69	3.78	3.88	3.98	4.07	4.17	4.27	4.36	4.46	4.55	4.65	4.75	4.84
69	3.35	3.45	3.55	3.64	3.74	3.84	3.94	4.03	4.13	4.23	4.33	4.43	4.52	4.62	4.72	4.82	4.91
70	3.40	3.50	3.60	3.70	3.80	3.90	3.99	4.09	4.19	4.29	4.39	4.49	4.59	4.69	4.79	4.89	4.99
71	3.45	3.55	3.65	3.75	3.85	3.95	4.05	4.15	4.25	4.35	4.45	4.55	4.66	4.76	4.86	4.96	5.06
72	3.50	3.60	3.70	3.80	3.90	4.01	4.11	4.21	4.31	4.42	4.52	4.62	4.72	4.82	4.92	5.03	5.13
73	3.55	3.65	3.75	3.86	3.96	4.06	4.17	4.27	4.37	4.48	4.58	4.68	4.79	4.89	4.99	5.10	5.20
74	3.59	3.70	3.80	3.91	4.01	4.12	4.22	4.33	4.43	4.54	4.64	4.75	4.85	4.96	5.06	5.17	5.27
75	3.64	3.75	3.86	3.96	4.07	4.17	4.28	4.39	4.49	4.60	4.71	4.81	4.92	5.02	5.13	5.24	5.34
76	3.69	3.80	3.91	4.01	4.12	4.23	4.34	4.44	4.55	4.66	4.77	4.88	4.98	5.09	5.20	5.31	5.41
77	3.74	3.85	3.96	4.07	4.18	4.29	4.39	4.50	4.61	4.72	4.83	4.94	5.05	5.16	5.27	5.38	5.49
78	3.79	3.90	4.01	4.12	4.23	4.34	4.45	4.56	4.67	4.78	4.89	5.00	5.11	5.22	5.34	5.45	5.56
79	3.84	3.95	4.06	4.17	4.28	4.40	4.51	4.62	4.73	4.82	4.96	5.07	5.18	5.29	5.40	5.52	5.63
80	3.89	4.00	4.11	4.23	4.34	4.45	4.57	4.68	4.79	4.91	5.02	5.13	5.25	5.36	5.47	5.59	5.70
81	3.93	4.05	4.16	4.28	4.39	4.51	4.62	4.74	4.85	4.97	5.08	5.20	5.31	5.43	5.54	5.66	5.77
82	3.98	4.10	4.28	4.33	4.45	4.56	4.68	4.80	4.91	5.03	5.14	5.26	5.38	5.49	5.61		
83	4.03	4.15	4.27	4.38	4.50	4.62	4.74	4.85	4.97	5.09	5.21	5.33	5.44	5.56	5.68		
84	4.08	4.20	4.32	4.44	4.56	4.68	4.79	4.91	5.03	5.15	5.27	5.39	5.51	5.63	5.75		
85	4.13	4.25	4.37	4.49	4.61	4.73	4.85	4.97	5.09	5.21	5.33	5.45	5.57	5.69	5.81		
86	4.18	4.30	4.42	4.54	4.66	4.79	4.91	5.03	5.15	5.27	5.40	5.52	5.64	5.76	5.88		
87	4.23	4.35	4.47	4.60	4.72	4.84	4.97	5.09	5.21	5.34	5.46	5.58	5.71	5.83	5.59		
88	4.28	4.40	4.52	4.65	4.77	4.90	5.02	5.15	5.27	5.40	5.52	5.65	5.77	5.90	6.02		
89	4.32	4.45	4.58	4.70	4.83	4.95	5.08	5.21	5.33	5.46	5.58	5.71	5.84	5.96	6.09		
90	4.37	4.50	4.63	4.76	4.88	5.01	5.14	5.26	5.39	5.52	5.65	5.77	5.90	6.03	6.16		
91	4.42	4.55	4.68	4.81	4.94	5.07	5.19	5.32	5.45	5.58	5.71	5.84	5.97	6.10	6.23		
92	4.47	4.60	4.73	4.86	4.99	5.12	5.25	5.38	5.51	5.64	5.77	5.90	6.03	6.16	6.29		
93	4.52	4.65	4.78	4.91	5.04	5.18	5.31	5.44	5.57	5.70	5.84	5.97	6.10	6.23	6.36		

Fettfreies Körpergewicht (kg) — In 12 min gelaufene Meter – Frauen

gewicht (kg)	2700	2800	2900	3000	3100	3200	3300	3400	3500	3600	3700	3800	3900	4000	4100	4200	4300
94	4.57	4.70	4.83	4.97	5.13	5.23	5.37	5.50	5.63	5.77	5.90	6.03	6.17	6.30	6.43		
95	4.62	4.75	4.88	5.02	5.15	5.29	5.42	5.56	5.69	5.83	5.96	6.10	6.23	6.36	6.50		
96	4.66	4.80	4.94	5.07	5.21	5.34	5.48	5.62	5.75	5.89	6.02	6.16	6.30	6.43	6.57		
97	4.71	4.85	4.99	5.13	5.26	5.40	5.54	5.67	5.81	5.95	6.09	6.22	6.36	6.50	6.64		
98	4.76	4.90	5.04	5.18	5.32	5.46	5.59	5.73	5.87	6.01	6.15	6.29	6.43	6.57	6.71		
99	4.81	4.95	5.09	5.23	5.37	5.51	5.65	5.79	5.93	6.07	6.21	6.35	6.49	6.63	6.77		
100	4.86	5.00	5.14	5.28	5.43	5.57	5.71	5.85	5.99	6.13	6.28	6.42	6.56	6.70	6.84		
101	4.91	5.05	5.34	5.34	5.48	5.62	5.77	5.91	6.05	6.20	6.34	6.48	6.62	6.77	6.91		
102	4.96	5.10	5.24	5.39	5.53	5.68	5.82	5.97	6.11	6.26	6.40	6.55	6.69	6.83	6.98		
103	5.00	5.15	5.30	5.44	5.59	5.73	5.88	6.03	6.17	6.32	6.46	6.61	6.76	6.90	7.05		
104	5.05	5.20	5.35	5.50	5.64	5.79	5.95	6.08	6.23	6.38	6.53	6.67	6.82	6.97	7.12		
105	5.10	5.25	5.40	5.55	5.70	5.85	5.99	6.14	6.29	6.44	6.59	6.74	6.89	7.04	7.18		
106	5.15	5.30	5.45	5.60	5.57	5.90	6.05	6.20	6.35	6.50	6.65	6.80	6.95	7.10	7.25		
107	5.20	5.35	5.50	5.65	5.81	5.96	6.11	6.26	6.41	6.56	6.71	6.87	7.02	7.17	7.32		
108	5.25	5.40	5.55	5.71	5.86	6.01	6.17	6.32	6.47	6.63	6.78	6.93	7.08	7.24	7.39		
109	5.30	5.45	5.61	5.76	5.91	6.07	6.22	6.38	6.53	6.69	6.84	6.99	7.15	7.30	7.46		
110	5.35	5.50	5.66	5.81	5.97	6.12	6.28	6.44	6.59	6.75	6.90	7.06	7.22	7.37	7.53		
111	5.39	5.55	5.71	5.87	6.02	6.18	6.34	6.49	6.65	6.81	6.97	7.12	7.28	7.44	7.60		
112	5.44	5.60	5.76	5.92	6.08	6.24	6.39	6.55	6.71	6.87	7.03	7.19	7.35	7.50	7.66		
113	5.49	5.65	5.81	5.97	6.13	6.29	6.45	6.61	6.77	6.93	7.09	7.25	7.41	7.57	7.72		
114	5.54	5.70	5.86	6.02	6.19	6.35	6.51	6.67	6.83	6.99	7.15	7.32	7.48	7.64	7.80		
115	5.59	5.75	5.91	6.08	6.24	6.40	6.57	6.73	6.89	7.05	7.22	7.38	7.54	7.71	7.87		
116	5.64	5.80	5.97	6.13	6.29	6.46	6.62	6.79	6.95	7.12	7.28	7.44	7.61	7.77	7.94		
117	5.69	5.85	6.02	6.18	6.35	6.51	6.68	6.85	7.01	7.18	7.34	7.51	7.67	7.84	8.01		
118	5.73	5.90	6.07	6.24	6.40	6.57	6.72	6.90	7.07	7.24	7.41	7.57	7.74	7.91	8.07		
119	5.78	5.95	6.12	6.29	6.46	6.63	6.79	6.96	7.13	7.30	7.47	7.64	7.81	7.97	8.14		
120	5.83	6.00	6.17	6.34	6.51	6.68	6.85	7.02	7.19	7.36	7.53	7.70	7.87	8.04	8.21		
121	5.88	6.05	6.22	6.39	6.57	6.74	6.91	7.08	7.25	7.42	7.59	7.77	7.94	8.11	8.28		
122	5.93	6.10	6.27	6.45	6.62	6.79	6.97	7.14	7.31	7.48	7.66	7.83	8.00	8.18	8.35		
123	5.98	6.15	6.33	6.50	6.67	6.85	7.02	7.20	7.37	7.55	7.72	7.89	8.07	8.24	8.42		
124	6.03	6.20	6.38	6.55	6.73	6.90	7.08	7.26	7.43	7.61	7.78	7.96	8.13	8.31	8.49		
125	6.08	6.25	6.43	6.61	6.78	6.96	7.14	7.31	7.49	7.67	7.85	8.02	8.20	8.38	8.55		
126	6.12	6.30	6.48	6.66	6.84	7.02	7.19	7.37	7.55	7.73	7.91	8.09	8.27	8.44	8.62		
127	6.17	6.35	6.53	6.71	6.89	7.07	7.25	7.43	7.61	7.79	7.97	8.15	8.33	8.51	8.69		

Einstufungstabellen

| 800 Meter – Männer | | | | | | | | | | | |
	16-17	18-19	20-29	30-34	35-39	40-44	45-49	50-54	55-59	60-64	65-69	ab 70
A	1.55	1.51	1.48	1.50	1.53	1.58	2.05	2.12	2.20	2.30	2.40	2.52
B	1.58	1.54	1.51	1.53	1.56	2.01	2.08	2.15	2.23	2.34	2.44	2.56
C	2.01	1.57	1.54	1.56	1.59	2.04	2.12	2.19	2.27	2.38	2.48	3.00
D	2.04	2.00	1.57	1.59	2.02	2.07	2.15	2.22	2.30	2.42	2.52	3.04
E	2.07	2.03	2.00	2.02	2.05	2.10	2.19	2.29	2.37	2.50	3.00	3.12
F	2.10	2.06	2.03	2.05	2.08	2.13	2.22	2.29	2.37	2.50	3.00	3.12
G	2.13	2.09	2.06	2.08	2.11	2.16	2.26	2.33	2.41	2.54	3.04	3.16
H	2.16	2.12	1.09	2.11	2.14	2.19	2.29	2.36	2.44	2.58	3.08	3.20
I	2.19	2.15	2.12	2.14	2.17	2.22	2.33	2.40	2.48	3.02	3.12	3.24
J	2.22	2.18	2.15	2.17	2.20	2.25	2.36	2.43	2.51	3.06	3.16	3.28
K	2.25	2.21	2.18	2.20	2.23	2.28	2.40	2.47	2.55	3.10	3.20	3.32
L	2.28	2.24	2.21	2.23	2.26	2.31	2.43	2.50	2.58	3.14	3.24	3.36
M	2.31	2.27	2.24	2.26	2.29	2.34	2.47	2.54	3.02	3.18	3.28	3.40
N	2.34	2.30	2.27	2.29	2.32	2.37	2.50	2.57	3.05	3.22	3.32	3.44
O	2.37	2.33	2.30	2.32	2.35	2.40	2.54	3.01	3.09	3.26	3.36	3.48
P	2.40	2.36	2.33	2.35	2.38	2.43	2.57	3.04	3.12	3.30	3.40	3.52
Q	2.43	2.39	2.36	2.38	2.41	2.46	3.01	3.08	3.16	3.34	3.44	3.56
R	2.46	2.42	2.39	2.41	2.44	2.49	3.04	3.11	3.19	3.38	3.48	4.00
S	2.49	2.45	2.42	2.44	2.47	2.52	3.08	3.05	3.23	3.42	3.52	4.04
T	2.52	2.48	2.45	2.47	2.50	2.55	3.11	3.18	3.26	3.46	3.56	4.08
U	2.55	2.51	2.48	2.50	2.52	2.58	3.15	3.22	3.30	3.50	4.00	4.12
V	2.58	2.54	2.51	2.53	2.56	3.01	3.18	3.25	3.33	3.54	4.04	4.16
W	3.01	2.57	2.54	2.56	2.59	3.04	3.22	3.29	3.37	3.58	4.08	4.20
X	3.04	3.00	2.57	2.59	3.02	3.07	3.25	3.32	3.40	4.02	4.12	4.24
Y	3.07	3.03	3.00	3.02	3.05	3.10	3.29	3.36	3.44	4.06	4.16	4.28
Z	3.10	3.06	3.03	3.05	3.08	3.13	3.32	3.39	3.47	4.10	4.20	4.32

| 1000 Meter – Männer | | | | | | | | | | | |
	16-17	18-19	20-29	30-34	35-39	40-44	45-49	50-54	55-59	60-64	65-69	ab 70
A	2.28	2.24	2.18	2.20	2.26	2.33	2.42	2.52	3.03	3.15	3.28	3.43
B	2.32	2.28	2.22	2.24	2.30	2.37	2.46	2.56	3.07	3.19	3.32	3.48
C	2.36	2.32	2.26	2.28	2.34	2.41	2.50	3.00	3.12	3.24	3.37	3.53
D	2.40	2.36	2.29	2.31	2.37	2.44	2.54	3.04	3.16	3.28	3.41	3.58
E	2.44	2.40	2.33	2.35	2.41	2.48	2.58	3.08	3.21	3.33	3.46	4.03
F	2.48	2.44	2.37	2.39	2.45	2.52	3.02	3.12	3.25	3.37	3.50	4.08
G	2.52	2.48	2.41	2.43	2.49	2.56	3.06	3.16	3.30	3.42	3.55	4.13
H	2.56	2.52	2.45	2.47	2.53	3.00	3.10	3.20	3.34	3.46	3.59	4.18
I	3.00	2.56	2.48	2.50	2.56	3.03	3.14	3.24	3.39	3.51	4.04	4.23
J	3.04	3.00	2.52	2.54	3.00	3.07	3.18	3.28	3.43	3.55	4.08	4.28
K	3.08	3.04	2.56	2.58	3.04	3.11	3.22	3.32	3.48	4.00	4.13	4.33
L	3.12	3.08	3.00	3.02	3.08	3.15	3.26	3.36	3.52	4.04	4.17	4.38
M	3.16	3.12	3.04	3.06	3.12	3.19	3.30	3.40	3.57	4.09	4.22	4.43
N	3.20	3.16	3.07	3.09	3.15	3.22	3.34	3.44	4.01	4.13	4.26	4.48
O	3.24	3.20	3.11	3.13	3.19	3.26	3.38	3.48	4.06	4.18	4.31	4.53
P	3.28	3.24	3.15	3.17	3.23	3.30	3.42	3.52	4.10	4.22	4.35	4.58
Q	3.32	3.28	3.19	3.21	3.27	3.34	3.46	3.56	4.15	4.27	4.40	5.03
R	3.36	3.32	3.23	3.25	3.31	3.38	3.50	4.00	4.19	4.31	4.44	5.00
S	3.40	3.36	3.26	3.28	3.34	3.41	3.54	4.04	4.24	4.36	4.49	5.13
T	3.44	3.40	3.30	3.32	3.38	3.45	3.58	4.08	4.28	4.40	4.53	5.18
U	3.48	3.44	3.34	3.36	3.42	3.49	4.02	4.12	4.33	4.45	4.58	5.23
V	3.52	3.48	3.38	3.40	3.46	3.53	4.06	4.16	4.37	4.49	5.02	5.28
W	3.56	3.52	3.42	3.44	3.50	3.57	4.10	4.20	4.42	4.54	5.07	5.33
X	4.00	3.56	3.45	3.47	3.53	4.00	4.14	4.24	4.46	4.58	5.11	5.38
Y	4.04	4.00	3.49	3.51	3.57	4.04	4.18	4.28	4.51	5.03	5.16	5.43
Z	4.08	4.04	3.53	3.55	4.01	4.08	4.22	4.32	4.55	5.07	5.20	5.48

1500 Meter – Männer

	16-17	18-19	20-24	25-29	30-34	35-39	40-44	45-49	50-54	55-59	60-64	65-69	ab 70
A	4.00	3.52	3.46	3.44	3.48	3.54	4.05	4.20	4.36	4.54	5.15	5.37	6.03
B	4.06	3.58	3.52	3.50	3.54	4.00	4.11	4.26	4.42	5.01	5.22	5.44	6.11
C	4.12	4.04	3.58	3.56	4.00	4.06	4.17	4.32	4.48	5.08	5.29	5.51	6.19
D	4.18	4.10	4.04	4.02	4.06	4.12	4.23	4.38	4.54	5.15	5.36	5.58	6.27
E	4.24	4.16	4.10	4.08	4.12	4.18	4.29	4.44	5.00	5.22	5.43	6.05	6.35
F	4.30	4.22	4.16	4.14	4.18	4.24	4.35	4.50	5.06	5.29	5.50	6.12	6.43
G	4.36	4.28	4.22	4.20	4.24	4.30	4.41	4.56	5.12	5.36	5.57	6.19	6.51
H	4.42	4.34	4.28	4.26	4.30	4.36	4.47	5.02	5.18	5.43	6.04	6.26	6.59
I	4.48	4.40	4.34	4.32	4.36	4.42	4.53	5.08	5.24	5.50	6.11	6.33	7.07
J	4.54	4.46	4.40	4.38	4.42	4.48	4.59	5.14	5.30	5.57	6.18	6.40	7.15
K	5.00	4.52	4.46	4.44	4.48	4.54	5.05	5.20	5.36	6.04	6.25	6.47	7.23
L	5.06	4.58	4.52	4.50	4.54	5.00	5.11	5.26	5.42	6.11	6.32	6.54	7.31
M	5.12	5.04	4.58	4.56	5.00	5.06	5.17	5.32	5.48	6.18	6.39	7.01	7.39
N	5.18	5.10	5.04	5.02	5.06	5.12	5.23	5.38	5.54	6.25	6.46	7.08	7.47
O	5.24	5.16	5.10	5.08	5.12	5.18	5.29	5.44	6.00	6.32	6.53	7.15	7.55
P	5.30	5.22	5.16	5.14	5.18	5.24	5.35	5.50	6.06	6.39	7.00	7.22	8.03
Q	5.36	5.28	5.22	5.20	5.24	5.30	5.44	5.56	6.12	6.46	7.07	7.29	8.11
R	5.42	5.34	5.28	5.26	5.30	5.36	5.47	6.02	6.18	6.53	7.14	7.36	8.19
S	5.48	5.40	5.34	5.32	5.36	5.42	5.53	6.08	6.24	7.00	7.21	7.43	8.27
T	5.54	5.46	5.40	5.38	5.42	5.48	5.59	6.14	6.30	7.07	7.28	7.50	8.35
U	6.00	5.52	5.46	5.44	5.48	5.54	6.05	6.20	6.36	7.14	7.35	7.57	8.43
V	6.06	5.58	5.52	5.50	5.54	6.00	6.11	6.26	6.42	7.31	7.42	8.04	8.51
W	6.12	6.04	5.58	5.56	6.00	6.06	6.17	6.32	6.48	7.28	7.49	8.11	8.59
X	6.18	6.10	6.04	6.02	6.06	6.12	6.23	6.38	6.54	7.35	7.56	8.18	9.07
Y	6.24	6.16	6.10	6.08	6.12	6.18	6.29	6.44	7.00	7.42	8.03	8.25	9.15
Z	6.30	6.22	6.16	6.14	6.18	6.24	6.35	6.50	7.06	7.49	8.10	8.32	9.23

2000 Meter – Männer

	16-17	18-19	20-24	25-29	30-34	35-39	40-44	45-49	50-54	55-59	60-64	65-69	ab 70
A	5.34	5.21	5.08	5.04	5.10	5.21	5.34	5.54	6.16	6.40	7.08	7.38	8.14
B	5.42	5.29	5.16	5.12	5.18	5.29	5.43	6.03	6.25	6.50	7.19	7.49	8.25
C	5.50	5.37	5.24	5.20	5.26	5.37	5.52	6.12	6.34	7.00	7.30	8.00	8.36
D	5.58	5.45	5.32	5.28	5.34	5.45	6.01	6.21	6.43	7.10	7.41	8.11	8.47
E	6.06	5.53	5.40	5.36	5.42	5.53	6.10	6.30	6.52	7.20	7.52	8.22	8.58
F	6.14	6.01	5.48	5.44	5.50	6.01	6.19	6.39	7.01	7.30	8.03	8.33	9.09
G	6.22	6.09	5.56	5.52	5.58	6.09	6.28	6.48	7.10	7.40	8.14	8.44	9.00
H	6.30	6.17	6.04	6.00	6.06	6.17	6.37	6.57	7.19	7.50	8.25	8.55	9.31
I	6.38	6.25	6.12	6.08	6.14	6.25	6.46	7.06	7.28	8.00	8.36	9.06	9.42
J	6.46	6.33	6.20	6.16	6.22	6.33	6.55	7.15	7.37	8.10	8.47	9.17	9.53
K	6.54	6.41	6.28	6.24	6.30	6.41	7.04	7.24	7.46	8.20	8.58	9.28	10.04
L	7.02	6.49	6.36	6.32	6.38	6.49	7.13	7.33	7.55	8.30	9.09	9.39	10.15
M	7.10	6.57	6.44	6.40	6.46	6.57	7.22	7.42	8.04	8.40	9.20	9.50	10.26
N	7.18	7.05	6.52	6.48	6.54	7.05	7.31	7.51	8.13	8.50	9.31	10.01	10.37
O	7.26	7.13	7.00	6.56	7.02	7.13	7.40	8.00	8.22	9.00	9.42	10.12	10.48
P	7.34	7.21	7.08	7.04	7.10	7.21	7.49	8.09	8.31	9.10	9.53	10.23	10.59
Q	7.42	7.29	7.16	7.12	7.18	7.29	7.50	8.18	8.40	9.20	10.04	10.34	11.10
R	7.50	7.37	7.24	7.20	7.26	7.37	8.07	8.27	8.49	9.30	10.15	10.45	11.21
S	7.58	7.45	7.32	7.28	7.34	7.45	8.16	8.36	8.58	9.40	10.26	10.56	11.32
T	8.06	7.53	7.40	7.36	7.42	7.53	8.25	8.45	9.07	9.50	10.37	11.07	11.43
U	8.14	8.01	7.48	7.44	7.50	8.01	8.34	8.54	9.16	10.00	10.48	11.18	11.54
V	8.22	8.09	7.56	7.52	7.58	8.09	8.43	9.03	9.25	10.10	10.59	11.29	12.05
W	8.30	8.17	8.04	8.00	8.06	8.17	8.52	9.12	9.34	10.20	11.10	11.40	12.16
X	8.38	8.25	8.12	8.08	8.14	8.25	9.01	9.21	9.43	10.30	11.21	11.51	12.27
Y	8.46	8.33	8.20	8.16	8.22	8.33	9.10	9.30	9.52	10.40	11.32	12.02	12.38
Z	8.54	8.41	8.28	8.24	8.30	8.41	9.19	9.39	10.01	10.50	11.43	12.13	12.49

3000 Meter – Männer

	16-17	18-19	20-24	25-29	30-34	35-39	40-44	45-49	50-54	55-59	60-64	65-69	ab 70
A	8.45	8.25	8.05	7.55	7.55	8.20	8.50	9.20	9.57	10.39	11.24	12.12	13.09
B	8.57	8.37	8.17	8.07	8.07	8.32	9.03	9.34	10.11	10.54	11.40	12.29	13.27
C	9.09	8.49	8.29	8.19	8.19	8.44	9.16	9.48	10.25	11.09	11.56	12.46	13.45
D	9.21	9.01	8.41	8.31	8.31	8.56	9.29	10.02	10.39	11.24	12.12	13.03	14.03
E	9.33	9.13	8.53	8.43	8.43	9.08	9.42	10.16	10.53	11.39	12.28	13.20	14.21
F	9.45	9.25	9.05	8.55	8.55	9.20	9.55	10.30	11.07	11.54	12.44	13.37	14.39
G	9.57	9.37	9.17	9.07	9.07	9.32	10.08	10.44	11.21	12.09	13.00	13.54	14.57
H	10.09	9.49	9.29	9.19	9.19	9.44	10.21	10.58	11.35	12.24	13.16	14.11	15.15
I	10.21	10.01	9.41	9.31	9.31	9.56	10.34	11.12	11.49	12.39	13.32	14.28	15.33
J	10.33	10.13	9.53	9.43	9.43	10.08	10.47	11.26	12.03	12.54	13.48	14.45	15.51
K	10.45	10.25	10.05	9.55	9.55	10.20	11.00	11.40	12.17	13.09	14.04	15.02	16.09
L	10.57	10.37	10.17	10.07	10.07	10.32	11.13	11.54	12.31	13.24	14.20	15.19	16.27
M	11.09	10.49	10.29	10.19	10.19	10.44	11.26	12.08	12.45	13.39	14.36	15.36	16.45
N	11.21	11.01	10.41	10.31	10.31	10.56	11.39	12.22	12.59	13.54	14.52	15.53	17.03
O	11.33	11.13	10.53	10.43	10.43	11.08	11.52	12.36	13.13	14.09	15.08	16.10	17.21
P	11.45	11.25	11.05	10.55	10.55	11.20	12.05	12.50	13.27	14.24	15.24	16.27	17.39
Q	11.57	11.37	11.17	11.07	11.07	11.32	12.18	13.04	13.41	14.39	15.40	16.44	17.57
R	12.09	11.49	11.29	11.19	11.19	11.44	12.31	13.18	13.55	14.54	15.56	17.01	18.15
S	12.21	12.01	11.41	11.31	11.31	11.56	12.44	13.32	14.09	15.09	16.12	17.18	18.33
T	12.33	12.13	11.53	11.43	11.43	12.08	12.57	13.46	14.23	15.24	16.28	17.35	18.51
U	12.45	12.25	12.05	11.55	11.55	12.20	13.10	14.00	14.37	15.39	16.44	17.52	19.09
V	12.57	12.37	12.17	12.07	12.07	12.32	13.23	14.14	14.51	15.54	17.00	18.09	19.27
W	13.09	12.49	12.29	12.19	12.19	12.44	13.36	14.28	15.05	16.09	17.16	18.26	19.45
X	13.21	13.01	12.41	12.31	12.31	12.56	13.49	14.42	15.19	16.24	17.32	18.43	20.03
Y	13.33	13.13	12.53	12.43	12.43	13.08	14.02	14.56	15.33	16.39	17.48	19.00	20.21
Z	13.45	13.25	13.05	12.55	12.55	13.20	14.15	15.10	15.47	16.54	18.04	19.17	20.39

5000 Meter – Männer

	16-17	18-19	20-24	25-29	30-34	35-39	40-44	45-49	50-54	55-59	60-64	65-69	ab 70
A	15.35	14.50	14.10	13.55	13.55	14.10	15.15	16.10	17.15	18.20	19.35	20.55	22.30
B	15.55	15.10	14.30	14.14	14.15	14.32	15.38	16.34	17.40	18.46	20.03	21.24	23.00
C	16.15	15.30	14.50	14.33	14.35	14.54	16.01	16.58	18.05	19.12	20.31	21.53	23.30
D	16.35	15.50	15.10	14.52	14.55	15.16	16.24	17.22	18.30	19.38	20.59	22.22	24.00
E	16.55	16.10	15.30	15.11	15.15	15.38	16.47	17.46	18.55	20.04	21.27	22.51	24.30
F	17.15	16.30	15.50	15.30	15.35	16.00	17.10	18.10	19.20	20.30	21.55	23.20	25.00
G	17.35	16.50	16.10	15.49	15.55	16.22	17.33	18.34	19.45	20.56	22.23	23.49	25.30
H	17.55	17.10	16.30	16.08	16.15	16.44	17.56	18.58	20.10	21.22	22.51	24.18	26.00
I	18.15	17.30	16.50	16.27	16.35	17.06	18.19	19.22	20.35	21.48	23.19	24.47	26.30
J	18.35	17.50	17.10	16.46	16.55	17.28	18.42	19.46	21.00	22.14	23.47	25.16	27.00
K	18.55	18.10	17.30	17.05	17.15	17.50	19.05	20.10	21.25	22.40	24.15	25.45	27.30
L	19.15	18.30	17.50	17.24	17.35	18.12	19.28	20.34	21.50	23.06	24.43	26.14	28.00
M	19.35	18.50	18.10	17.43	17.55	18.34	19.51	20.58	22.15	23.32	25.11	26.43	28.30
N	19.55	19.10	18.30	18.02	18.15	18.56	20.14	21.22	22.40	23.58	25.39	27.12	29.00
O	20.15	19.30	18.50	18.21	18.35	19.18	20.37	21.46	23.05	24.24	26.07	27.41	29.30
P	20.35	19.50	19.10	18.40	18.55	19.40	21.00	22.10	23.30	24.50	26.35	28.10	30.00
Q	20.55	20.10	19.30	18.59	19.15	20.02	21.23	22.34	23.55	25.16	27.03	28.39	30.30
R	21.15	20.30	19.50	19.18	19.35	20.24	21.46	22.58	24.20	25.42	27.31	29.08	31.00
S	21.35	20.50	20.10	19.37	19.55	20.46	22.09	23.22	24.45	26.08	27.59	29.37	31.30
T	21.55	21.10	20.30	19.56	20.15	21.08	22.32	23.46	25.10	26.34	28.27	30.06	32.00
U	22.15	21.30	20.50	20.15	20.35	21.30	22.55	24.10	25.35	27.00	28.55	30.35	32.30
V	22.35	21.50	21.10	20.34	20.55	21.52	23.18	24.34	26.00	27.26	29.23	31.04	33.00
W	22.55	22.10	21.30	20.53	21.15	22.14	23.41	24.58	26.25	27.52	29.51	31.33	33.30
X	23.15	22.30	21.50	21.12	21.35	22.36	24.04	25.22	26.50	28.18	30.19	32.02	34.00
Y	23.35	22.50	22.10	21.31	21.55	22.58	24.27	25.46	27.15	28.44	30.47	32.31	34.30
Z	23.55	23.10	22.30	21.50	22.15	23.20	24.50	26.10	27.40	29.10	31.15	33.00	35.00

10.000 Meter – Männer

	16-17	18-19	20-24	25-29	30-34	35-39	40-44	45-49	50-54	55-59	60-64	65-69	ab 70
A	32.40	31.00	30.00	29.00	29.00	30.00	32.00	34.00	36.00	38.20	40.50	43.30	46.40
B	33.20	31.42	30.42	29.41	29.41	30.43	32.43	34.45	36.48	39.11	41.43	44.28	47.38
C	34.04	32.24	31.24	30.22	30.22	31.26	33.26	35.30	37.36	40.02	42.36	45.26	48.36
D	34.46	33.06	32.06	31.03	31.03	32.09	34.09	36.15	38.24	40.53	43.29	46.24	49.34
E	35.28	33.48	32.48	31.44	31.44	32.52	34.52	37.00	39.12	41.44	44.22	47.22	50.32
F	36.10	34.30	33.30	32.25	32.25	33.35	35.35	37.45	40.00	42.35	45.15	48.20	51.30
G	36.52	35.12	34.12	33.06	33.06	34.18	36.18	38.30	40.48	43.26	46.08	49.18	52.28
H	37.34	35.54	34.54	33.47	33.47	35.01	37.01	39.15	41.36	44.17	47.01	50.16	53.26
I	38.16	36.36	35.36	34.28	34.28	35.44	37.44	40.00	42.24	45.08	47.54	51.14	54.25
J	38.58	37.18	36.18	35.09	35.09	36.27	38.27	40.15	43.12	45.59	48.47	52.12	55.22
K	39.43	38.00	37.00	35.50	35.50	37.10	39.10	41.30	44.00	46.50	49.40	53.10	56.20
L	40.22	38.42	37.42	36.31	36.31	37.53	39.53	43.15	44.48	47.41	50.33	54.09	57.18
M	41.04	39.24	38.24	37.12	37.12	38.36	40.36	43.00	45.36	48.32	51.26	55.06	58.16
N	41.46	40.06	39.06	37.53	37.53	39.19	41.19	43.45	46.24	49.23	52.19	56.04	59.14
O	42.28	40.48	39.48	38.34	38.34	40.02	42.02	44.30	47.12	50.14	53.12	57.02	60.12
P	43.10	41.30	40.30	39.15	39.15	40.45	42.45	45.15	48.00	51.05	54.05	58.00	61.10
Q	43.52	42.12	41.12	39.56	39.56	41.28	43.28	46.00	48.48	51.56	54.58	58.58	62.08
R	44.34	42.54	41.54	40.37	40.37	42.11	44.11	46.45	49.36	52.47	55.51	59.56	63.06
S	45.16	43.36	42.36	41.18	41.18	42.54	55.54	47.30	50.24	53.38	56.44	60.54	64.04
T	45.58	44.18	43.18	41.59	41.59	43.37	45.37	48.15	51.12	54.29	57.37	61.52	65.02
U	46.40	45.00	44.00	42.40	42.40	44.20	46.20	49.00	52.00	55.20	58.30	62.50	66.00
V	47.22	45.42	44.42	43.21	43.21	45.03	47.03	49.45	52.48	56.11	59.23	63.48	66.58
W	48.04	46.24	45.24	44.02	44.02	45.46	47.46	50.30	53.36	57.02	60.16	64.46	67.56
X	48.46	47.06	46.06	44.43	44.43	46.29	48.29	51.15	54.24	57.53	61.09	65.44	68.54
Y	49.28	47.48	46.48	45.24	45.24	47.12	49.12	52.00	55.12	58.44	62.02	66.42	69.52
Z	50.10	48.30	47.30	46.05	46.05	47.55	49.55	52.45	56.00	59.35	62.55	67.40	70.50

15 Kilometer – Männer

	16-17	18-19	20-24	25-29	30-34	35-39	40-44	45-49	50-54	55-59	60-64	65-69	ab 70
A	51.30	49.00	48.00	46.00	46.00	48.00	51.00	54.00	56.15	60.30	64.15	68.15	73.00
B	52.30	50.00	49.00	46.58	46.57	48.59	52.00	55.05	57.25	61.45	65.35	69.38	74.25
C	53.30	51.00	50.00	47.54	47.54	49.58	53.00	56.10	58.35	63.00	66.55	71.01	75.50
D	54.30	52.00	51.00	48.54	48.51	50.57	54.00	57.15	59.45	64.15	68.15	72.24	77.15
E	55.30	53.00	52.00	49.52	49.48	51.56	55.00	58.20	60.55	65.30	69.35	73.47	78.40
F	56.30	54.00	53.00	50.50	50.45	52.55	56.00	59.25	62.05	66.45	70.55	75.10	80.05
G	57.30	55.00	54.00	51.48	51.42	53.54	57.00	60.30	63.15	68.00	72.15	76.33	81.30
H	58.30	56.00	55.00	52.46	52.39	54.53	58.00	61.36	64.25	69.15	73.35	77.56	82.55
I	59.30	57.00	56.00	53.44	55.36	55.52	59.00	62.40	65.35	70.30	74.55	79.19	84.20
J	60.30	58.00	57.00	54.52	54.33	56.51	60.00	63.45	66.45	71.45	76.15	80.42	85.45
K	61.30	59.00	58.00	55.40	55.30	57.50	61.00	64.50	67.55	73.00	77.35	82.05	87.10
L	62.30	60.00	59.00	56.38	56.27	58.49	62.00	65.55	69.05	74.15	78.55	83.28	88.35
M	63.30	61.00	60.00	57.36	57.24	59.48	63.00	67.00	70.15	75.30	80.15	84.51	90.00
N	64.30	62.00	61.00	58.34	58.21	60.47	64.00	68.05	71.25	76.45	81.35	86.14	91.25
O	65.30	63.00	62.00	59.32	59.18	61.46	65.00	69.10	72.35	78.00	82.55	87.37	92.50
P	66.30	64.00	63.00	60.30	60.15	62.45	66.00	70.15	73.45	79.15	84.15	89.00	94.15
Q	67.30	65.00	64.00	61.28	61.12	63.44	67.00	71.20	74.55	80.30	83.35	90.23	95.40
R	68.30	66.00	65.00	62.26	62.09	64.43	68.00	72.25	76.05	81.45	86.55	91.46	97.05
S	69.30	67.00	66.00	63.24	63.06	65.42	69.00	73.30	77.15	83.00	88.15	93.09	98.30
T	70.30	68.00	67.00	64.22	64.03	66.41	70.00	74.35	78.25	84.45	89.35	94.32	99.55
U	71.30	69.00	68.00	65.20	65.00	67.40	71.00	75.40	79.35	85.30	90.55	95.53	101.20
V	72.30	70.00	69.00	66.18	65.57	68.39	72.00	76.45	80.45	86.45	92.15	97.18	102.45
W	73.30	71.00	70.00	67.16	66.54	69.38	73.00	77.50	81.55	88.00	93.35	98.41	104.10
X	74.30	72.00	71.00	68.14	67.51	70.37	74.00	78.55	83.05	89.15	94.55	100.04	105.35
Y	75.30	73.00	72.00	69.12	68.48	71.36	75.00	80.00	84.15	90.30	96.15	101.27	107.00
Z	76.30	74.00	73.00	70.10	69.45	72.35	76.00	81.05	85.25	91.45	97.35	102.50	108.25

20 Kilometer – Männer

	16-17	18-19	20-24	25-29	30-34	35-39	40-44	45-49	50-54	55-59	60-64	65-69	ab 70
A	1.11.20	1.08.00	1.06.00	1.04.00	1.03.00	1.06.00	1.10.00	1.14.00	1.18.00	1.23.00	1.28.00	1.33.00	1.40.00
B	1.12.40	1.09.20	1.07.20	1.05.15	1.04.15	1.07.17	1.11.20	1.15.25	1.19.30	1.24.40	1.29.45	1.34.48	1.42.45
C	1.14.00	1.10.40	1.08.40	1.06.30	1.05.30	1.08-34	1.12.40	1.16.50	1.21.00	1.26.20	1.31.30	1.36.36	1.44.50
D	1.15.20	1.12.00	1.10.00	1.07.45	1.06.45	1.09.51	1.14.00	1.18.15	1.22.30	1.28.00	1.33.15	1.38.24	1.47.15
E	1.16.40	1.13.20	1.11.20	1.09.00	1.08.00	1.11.08	1.15.20	1.19.40	1.24.00	1.29.40	1.35.00	1.40.12	1.49.48
F	1.18.00	1.14.40	1.12.40	1.10.15	1.09.15	1.12.25	1.16.40	1.21.05	1.25.30	1.31.20	1.36.45	1.42.00	1.52.05
G	1.19.20	1.16.00	1.14.00	1.11.30	1.10.30	1.13.42	1.18.00	1.22.30	1.27.00	1.33.00	1.38.30	1.43.48	1.54.30
H	1.20.40	1.17.20	1.15.20	1.12.45	1.11.45	1.15.59	1.19.20	1.23.55	1.28.30	1.34.40	1.40.15	1.45.36	1.56.55
I	1.22.00	1.18.40	1.16.40	1.14.00	1.13.00	1.16.16	1.20.40	1.25.20	1.30.00	1.36.20	1.42.00	1.47.24	1.59.20
J	1.23.20	1.20.00	1.18.00	1.15.15	1.14.15	1.15.33	1.22.00	1.26.45	1.31.30	1.38.00	1.43.45	1.49.42	2.01.45
K	1.24.40	1.21.20	1.19.20	1.16.30	1.15.30	1.18.50	1.23.20	1.28.10	1.33.00	1.39.40	1.45.30	1.51.00	2.04.10
L	1.26.00	1.22.40	1.20.40	1.17.45	1.16.45	1.20.07	1.24.40	1.29.35	1.34.30	1.41.20	1.47.15	1.52.48	2.06.35
M	1.27.20	1.24.00	1.22.00	1.19.00	1.18.00	1.21.24	1.26.00	1.31.00	1.36.00	1.43.00	1.49.00	1.54.36	2.09.00
N	1.28.40	1.25.20	1.23.20	1.20.15	1.19.15	1.22.41	1.27.20	1.32.25	1.37.30	1.44.40	1.50.45	1.56.24	2.11.25
O	1.30.00	1.26.40	1.24.40	1.21.30	1.20.30	1.23.58	1.28.40	1.33.50	1.39.00	1.46.20	1.52.30	1.58.12	2.13.50
P	1.31.20	1.28.00	1.26.00	1.22.45	1.21.45	1.26.15	1.30.00	1.35.15	1.40.30	1.48.00	1.54.15	2.00.00	2.16.15
Q	1.32.40	1.29.20	1.27.20	1.24.00	1.23.00	1.26.32	1.31.20	1.36.40	1.42.00	1.49.40	1.56.00	2.01.48	2.18.40
R	1.34.00	1.30.40	1.28.40	1.25.15	1.24.15	1.27.49	1.32.40	1.38.05	1.43.30	1.51.20	1.57.45	2.03.36	2.21.05
S	1.35.20	1.32.00	1.30.00	1.26.20	1.25.30	1.29.06	1.34.00	1.39.30	1.45.00	1.53.00	1.59.30	2.05.24	2.23.30
T	1.36.40	1.33.20	1.31.20	1.27.45	1.26.45	1.30.23	1.35.20	1.40.55	1.46.30	1.54.40	2.01.15	2.07.12	2.25.55
U	1.38.00	1.34.40	1.32.40	1.29.00	1.28.00	1.31.40	1.36.40	1.42.20	1.48.00	1.56.20	2.03.00	2.09.00	2.28.20
V	1.39.20	1.36.00	1.34.00	1.30.15	1.29.15	1.32.57	1.38.00	1.43.45	1.49.30	1.58.00	2.04.45	2.10.48	2.30.45
W	1.40.40	1.37.20	1.35.20	1.31.30	1.30.30	1.34.14	1.39.20	1.45.10	1.51.00	1.59.40	2.06.30	2.12.36	1.33.10
X	1.42.00	1.38.40	1.36.40	1.32.45	1.31.45	1.35.31	1.40.40	1.46.35	1.52.30	2.01.20	2.08.15	2.14.24	2.35.35
Y	1.43.20	1.40.00	1.38.00	1.34.00	1.33.00	1.36.48	1.42.00	1.48.00	1.54.00	2.03.00	2.10.00	2.16.12	2.38.00
Z	1.44.40	1.41.20	1.39.20	1.35.15	1.35.15	1.38.05	1.43.20	1.49.25	1.55.30	2.04.40	2.11.45	2.18.00	2.40.25

30 Kilometer – Männer

	16-17	18-19	20-24	25-29	30-34	35-39	40-44	45-49	50-54	55-59	60-64	65-69	ab 70
A	1.56.30	1.52.00	1.46.00	1.42.00	1.39.00	1.44.00	1.50.00	1.56.00	2.02.00	2.09.00	2.17.00	2.25.00	2.34.00
B	1.58.25	1.53.55	1.47.55	1.43.53	1.40.52	1.45.55	1.52.00	1.58.10	2.04.20	2.11.30	2.19.40	2.27.50	2.36.30
C	2.00.20	1.55.50	1.49.50	1.45.46	1.42.44	1.47.30	1.54.00	2.00.20	2.06.40	2.14.00	2.22.20	2.30.40	2.39.40
D	2.02.15	1.57.45	1.51.45	1.47.39	1.44.36	1.49.45	1.56.00	2.02.30	2.09.00	2.16.30	2.25.00	2.33.30	2.42.30
E	2.04.10	1.59.40	1.53.40	1.49.32	1.46.28	1.51.40	1.58.00	2.04.40	2.11.20	2.19.00	2.27.40	2.36.20	2.45.20
F	2.06.05	2.02.35	1.55.35	1.51.25	1.48.20	1.53.35	2.00.00	2.06.50	2.13.40	2.21.30	2.30.20	2.39.10	2.48.10
G	2.08.00	2.03.30	1.57.30	1.53.10	1.50.12	1.55.30	2.02.00	2.09.00	2.16.00	2.24.00	2.33.00	2.42.00	2.51.00
H	2.09.55	2.05.25	1.59.25	1.55.11	1.52.04	1.57.25	2.04.00	2.11.10	2.18.20	2.26.30	2.35.40	2.44.50	2.53.50
I	2.11.50	2.07.20	2.01.20	1.57.04	1.53.56	1.59.20	2.06.00	2.13.20	2.20.40	2.29.00	2.38.20	2.47.40	2.56.40
J	2.13.45	2.09.15	2.03.15	1.58.57	1.55.48	2.01.15	2.08.00	2.15.30	2.23.00	2.31.30	2.41.00	2.50.30	2.59.30
K	2.15.40	2.11.10	2.05.10	2.00.50	1.57.40	2.03.10	2.10.00	2.17.40	2.25.20	2.34.00	2.43.40	2.53.20	3.02.30
L	2.17.35	2.13.05	2.07.05	2.02.43	1.59.32	2.05.05	2.12.00	2.19.50	2.27.10	2.36.30	2.46.20	2.56.10	3.05.10
M	2.19.30	2.15.00	2.09.00	2.04.36	2.01.24	2.07.00	2.14.00	2.22.00	2.30.00	2.39.00	2.49.00	2.59.00	3.08.00
N	2.21.25	2.16.55	2.10.55	2.06.29	2.03.16	2.08.55	2.16.00	2.24.10	2.32.20	2.41.30	2.51.40	3.01.50	3.10.50
O	2.23.20	2.18.50	2.12.50	2.08.22	2.05.08	2.10.50	2.18.00	2.26.20	2.34.40	2.44.00	2.54.20	3.04.40	3.13.40
P	2.25.15	2.20.45	2.14.45	2.10.15	2.07.00	2.12.45	2.20.00	2.28.30	2.37.00	2.46.30	2.57.00	3.07.30	3.16.30
Q	2.27.10	2.22.40	2.16.40	2.12.00	2.08.52	2.14.40	2.22.00	2.30.40	3.29.20	2.49.00	2.59.40	3.10.20	3.19.20
R	2.29.05	2.24.35	2.18.35	2.14.01	2.10.44	2.16.35	2.24.00	2.32.50	2.41.40	2.51.30	3.02.20	3.13.10	3.22.10
S	2.31.00	2.26.30	2.20.30	2.15.54	2.12.36	2.18.30	2.26.00	2.35.00	2.44.00	2.54.00	3.05.00	3.16.00	3.27.50
T	2.32.55	2.28.25	2.22.25	2.17.47	2.14.28	2.20.25	2.28.00	2.37.10	2.46.20	2.56.30	3.07.40	3.18.50	3.27.50
U	2.34.50	2.30.20	2.24.20	2.19.40	2.16.20	2.22.20	2.30.00	2.39.20	2.48.40	2.59.00	3.10.20	3.21.40	3.33.30
V	2.36.45	2.32.15	2.26.15	2.21.33	2.18.12	2.24.15	2.32.00	2.41.30	2.51.00	3.01.30	3.13.00	3.24.30	3.33.30
W	2.38.40	2.34.10	2.28.10	2.23.26	2.20.04	2.26.10	2.35.00	2.43.40	2.53.20	3.04.00	3.15.40	3.27.20	3.36.20
X	2.40.35	2.36.05	2.30.05	2.25.19	2.21.56	2.28.05	2.36.00	2.45.50	2.55.40	3.06.30	3.18.20	3.30.10	3.39.10
Y	2.42.30	2.38.00	2.32.00	2.27.12	2.43.48	2.30.00	2.38.00	2.48.00	2.58.00	3.09.00	3.21.00	3.33.00	3.42.00
Z	2.44.25	2.39.55	2.33.55	2.09.05	2.25.40	2.31.55	2.40.00	2.50.10	3.00.20	3.11.30	3.23.40	3.35.50	3.44.50

800 Meter – Frauen

	16-19	20-24	25-29	30-34	35-39	40-44	45-49	50-54	55-59	60-65
A	2.08	2.06	2.10	2.15	2.20	2.30	2.40	2.50	3.00	3.20
B	2.11	2.09	2.13	2.18	2.23	2.33	2.44	2.54	3.04	3.24
C	2.14	2.12	2.16	2.21	2.26	2.36	2.47	2.57	3.07	3.28
D	2.17	2.15	2.19	2.24	2.29	2.39	2.51	3.01	3.11	3.32
E	2.20	2.18	2.22	2.27	2.32	2.42	2.54	3.04	3.14	3.36
F	2.23	2.21	2.25	2.30	2.35	2.45	2.58	3.08	3.18	3.40
G	2.26	2.24	2.28	2.33	2.38	2.48	3.01	3.11	3.21	3.44
H	2.29	2.27	2.31	2.36	2.41	2.51	3.05	3.15	3.25	3.48
I	2.32	2.30	2.34	2.39	2.44	2.54	3.08	3.18	3.28	3.52
J	2.35	2.33	2.37	2.42	2.47	2.57	3.12	3.22	3.32	3.56
K	2.38	2.36	2.40	2.45	2.50	3.00	3.15	3.25	3.35	4.00
L	2.41	2.39	2.43	2.48	2.53	3.03	3.19	3.29	3.39	4.04
M	2.44	2.42	2.46	2.51	2.56	3.06	3.22	3.32	3.42	4.08
N	2.47	2.45	2.49	2.54	2.59	3.09	3.26	3.36	3.46	4.12
O	2.50	2.48	2.52	2.57	3.02	3.12	3.29	3.39	3.49	4.16
P	2.53	2.51	2.55	3.00	3.05	3.15	3.33	3.43	3.53	4.20
Q	2.56	2.54	2.58	3.03	3.08	3.18	3.36	3.46	3.56	4.28
R	2.59	2.57	3.01	3.06	3.11	3.21	3.40	3.50	4.00	4.28
S	3.02	3.00	3.04	3.09	3.14	3.24	3.43	3.53	4.03	4.32
T	3.05	3.03	3.07	3.12	3.17	3.27	3.47	3.57	4.07	4.36
U	3.08	3.06	3.10	3.15	3.20	3.30	3.50	4.00	4.10	4.40
V	3.11	3.09	3.13	3.18	3.23	3.33	3.54	4.04	4.14	4.44
W	3.14	3.12	3.16	3.21	3.26	3.36	3.57	4.07	4.17	4.48
X	3.17	3.15	3.19	3.24	3.29	3.39	4.01	4.11	4.21	4.52
Y	3.20	3.18	3.22	3.27	3.32	3.42	4.04	4.14	4.24	4.56
Z	3.23	3.21	3.25	3.30	3.35	3.45	4.08	4.18	4.28	5.00

1000 Meter – Frauen

	16-19	20-24	25-29	30-34	35-39	40-44	45-49	50-54	55-59	60-65
A	2.43	2.41	2.45	2.52	2.58	3.11	3.24	3.35	3.52	4.16
B	2.47	2.45	2.49	2.56	3.02	3.15	3.28	3.39	3.57	4.21
C	2.51	2.49	2.53	3.00	3.06	3.19	3.32	3.43	4.01	4.25
D	2.54	2.52	2.56	3.03	3.09	3.22	3.36	3.47	4.06	4.30
E	2.58	2.56	3.00	3.07	3.13	3.26	3.40	3.51	4.10	4.34
F	3.02	3.00	3.04	3.11	3.17	3.30	3.44	3.55	4.15	4.39
G	3.06	3.04	3.08	3.15	3.21	3.34	3.48	3.59	4.19	4.43
H	3.10	3.08	3.12	3.19	3.25	3.38	3.52	4.03	4.24	4.48
I	3.13	3.11	3.15	3.22	3.28	3.41	3.56	4.07	4.26	4.52
J	3.17	3.15	3.19	3.26	3.32	3.45	4.00	4.11	4.33	4.57
K	3.21	3.19	3.23	3.30	3.36	3.49	4.04	4.15	4.37	5.01
L	3.25	3.23	3.27	3.34	3.40	3.53	4.08	4.19	4.42	5.06
M	3.29	3.27	3.31	3.38	3.44	3.57	4.12	4.23	4.46	5.10
N	3.32	3.30	3.34	3.41	3.47	4.00	4.16	4.27	4.51	5.15
O	3.36	3.34	3.38	3.45	3.51	4.04	4.28	4.31	4.55	5.49
P	3.40	3.38	3.42	3.49	3.55	4.08	4.24	4.35	5.00	5.24
Q	3.44	3.42	3.46	3.53	3.59	4.12	4.28	4.39	5.04	5.28
R	3.48	3.46	3.50	3.57	4.03	4.16	4.32	4.43	5.09	5.33
S	3.51	3.49	3.53	4.00	4.06	4.19	4.36	4.47	5.13	5.37
T	3.55	3.53	3.57	4.04	4.10	4.23	4.40	4.51	5.18	5.42
U	3.59	3.57	4.01	4.08	4.14	4.27	4.44	4.55	5.22	5.46
V	4.03	4.01	4.05	4.12	4.18	4.31	4.48	4.55	5.22	5.46
W	4.07	4.05	4.09	4.16	4.22	4.35	4.52	5.03	5.31	5.55
X	4.10	4.08	4.12	4.19	4.25	4.38	4.56	5.07	5.36	6.00
Y	4.14	4.12	4.16	4.23	4.29	4.42	5.00	5.11	5.40	6.04
Z	4.18	4.16	4.20	4.27	4.33	4.46	5.04	5.15	5.45	6.09

1500 Meter – Frauen

	16-19	20-24	25-29	30-34	35-39	40-44	45-49	50-54	55-59	60-65
A	4.14	4.12	4.10	4.18	4.30	4.55	5.25	6.00	6.40	7.30
B	4.20	4.18	4.16	4.24	4.36	5.01	5.31	6.06	6.47	7.37
C	4.26	4.24	4.22	4.30	4.42	5.07	5.37	6.12	6.54	7.44
D	4.32	4.30	4.28	4.36	4.48	5.13	5.43	6.18	7.01	7.51
E	4.38	4.36	4.34	4.42	4.54	5.19	5.49	6.24	7.08	7.58
F	4.44	4.42	4.40	4.48	5.00	5.25	5.55	6.30	7.15	8.05
G	4.50	4.48	4.46	4.54	5.06	5.31	6.01	6.36	7.22	8.12
H	4.56	4.54	4.52	5.00	5.12	5.37	6.07	6.42	7.29	8.19
I	5.02	5.00	4.58	5.06	5.18	5.43	6.13	6.48	7.36	8.26
J	5.08	5.06	5.04	5.12	5.24	5.49	6.19	6.54	7.43	8.33
K	5.14	5.12	5.10	5.18	5.30	5.55	6.25	7.00	7.50	8.40
L	5.20	5.18	5.16	5.24	5.36	6.01	6.31	7.06	7.57	8.47
M	5.26	5.24	5.22	5.30	5.42	6.07	6.37	7.12	8.04	8.54
N	5.32	5.30	5.28	5.36	5.48	6.13	6.43	7.18	8.11	9.01
O	5.38	5.36	5.34	5.42	5.54	6.19	6.49	7.54	8.18	9.00
P	5.44	5.42	5.40	5.48	6.00	6.25	6.55	7.30	8.25	9.15
Q	5.50	5.48	5.46	5.54	6.06	6.31	7.01	7.36	8.32	9.22
R	5.56	5.54	5.52	6.00	6.12	6.37	7.07	7.42	8.39	9.29
S	6.02	6.00	5.58	6.06	6.18	6.43	7.13	7.48	8.46	9.36
T	6.08	6.06	6.04	6.12	6.24	6.49	7.19	7.54	8.53	9.43
U	6.14	6.12	6.10	6.18	6.30	6.55	7.25	8.00	9.00	9.50
V	6.20	6.18	6.16	6.24	6.36	7.01	7.31	8.06	9.07	9.57
W	6.26	6.24	6.22	6.30	6.42	7.07	7.37	8.12	9.14	10.04
X	6.32	6.30	6.28	6.36	6.48	7.13	7.43	8.18	9.21	10.11
Y	6.38	6.36	6.34	6.42	6.54	7.19	7.49	8.24	9.28	10.18
Z	6.44	6.42	6.40	6.48	7.00	7.25	7.55	8.30	9.35	10.25

3000 Meter – Frauen

	16-19	20-24	25-29	30-34	35-39	40-44	45-49	50-54	55-59	60-65
A	9.42	9.30	9.24	9.56	10.22	11.17	12.19	13.35	15.00	16.45
B	9.54	9.42	9.36	10.08	10.34	11.30	12.33	13.49	15.15	17.01
C	10.06	9.54	9.48	10.20	10.46	11.43	12.47	14.03	15.30	17.17
D	10.18	10.10	10.00	10.32	10.58	11.56	13.01	14.17	15.45	17.33
E	10.30	10.18	10.12	10.44	11.10	12.09	13.15	14.31	16.00	17.49
F	10.42	10.30	10.24	10.56	11.22	12.22	13.29	14.45	16.15	18.05
G	10.54	10.42	10.36	11.08	11.34	12.35	13.43	14.59	16.30	18.21
H	11.06	10.54	10.48	11.20	11.46	12.48	13.47	15.13	16.45	18.37
I	11.18	11.06	11.00	11.32	11.58	13.01	14.11	15.27	17.00	19.09
J	11.30	11.18	11.12	11.44	12.10	13.14	14.25	15.41	17.15	19.09
K	11.42	11.30	11.24	11.56	12.22	13.27	14.39	15.55	17.30	19.25
L	11.54	11.42	11.36	12.08	12.34	13.40	14.53	16.09	17.45	19.41
M	12.06	11.54	11.48	12.20	12.46	13.53	15.07	16.23	18.00	19.57
N	12.18	12.06	12.00	12.32	12.58	14.06	15.21	16.37	18.15	20.13
O	12.30	12.08	12.12	12.44	13.10	14.19	15.35	16.51	18.30	20.29
P	12.42	12.30	12.24	12.56	13.22	14.32	15.49	17.05	18.45	20.45
Q	12.54	12.42	12.36	13.08	13.34	14.45	16.03	17.19	19.00	21.01
R	13.06	12.54	12.48	13.20	13.46	14.58	16.17	17.33	19.15	21.17
S	13.18	13.06	13.00	13.32	13.58	15.11	16.31	17.47	19.30	21.33
T	13.30	13.08	13.01	13.44	14.10	15.24	16.45	18.01	19.45	21.49
U	13.42	13.30	13.24	13.56	14.22	15.37	16.59	18.15	20.00	22.05
V	13.54	13.42	13.36	14.08	14.34	15.50	17.13	18.29	20.15	22.21
W	14.06	13.54	13.48	14.20	14.46	16.03	17.27	18.43	20.30	22.37
X	14.18	14.06	14.00	14.32	14.58	16.16	17.41	18.57	20.45	22.35
Y	14.30	14.18	14.12	14.44	15.10	16.29	17.55	19.11	21.00	23.09
Z	14.42	14.30	14.24	14.56	15.22	16.42	19.09	19.25	21.15	23.25

	16-19	20-24	25-29	30-34	35-39	40-44	45-49	50-54	55-59	60-65
					5000 Meter – Frauen					
A	17.00	16.40	16.30	17.20	18.05	19.40	21.31	23.45	26.15	29.45
B	17.20	17.00	16.49	17.40	18.27	20.03	21.55	24.10	26.41	30.13
C	17.40	17.20	17.08	18.00	18.49	20.26	22.19	24.35	27.07	30.41
D	18.00	17.40	17.27	18.20	19.11	20.49	22.43	25.00	27.33	31.09
E	18.20	18.00	17.46	18.40	19.33	21.12	23.07	25.25	27.59	31.37
F	18.40	18.20	18.05	19.00	19.55	21.35	23.31	25.50	28.25	32.05
G	19.00	18.40	18.24	19.20	20.17	21.58	23.55	26.15	28.51	32.33
H	19.20	19.00	18.43	19.40	20.39	22.21	24.19	26.40	29.31	33.01
I	19.40	19.20	19.02	20.00	21.01	22.44	24.43	27.05	29.43	33.29
J	20.00	19.40	19.21	20.20	21.23	23.07	25.07	27.30	30.09	33.57
K	20.20	20.00	19.40	20.40	21.45	23.30	25.31	27.55	30.35	34.25
L	20.40	20.20	19.59	21.00	22.07	23.53	25.55	28.20	31.01	34.53
M	21.00	20.40	20.18	21.20	22.29	24.16	26.19	28.45	31.27	35.21
N	21.20	21.00	20.37	21.40	22.51	24.39	26.43	29.10	31.53	35.49
O	21.40	21.20	20.56	22.00	23.03	25.02	27.07	29.35	32.19	36.17
P	22.00	21.40	21.15	22.20	23.35	25.25	27.31	30.00	32.45	36.45
Q	22.20	22.00	21.34	22.40	23.57	25.48	27.55	30.25	33.01	37.13
R	22.40	22.20	21.53	23.00	24.19	26.11	28.19	30.50	33.03	37.41
S	23.00	22.40	22.12	23.20	24.41	26.34	28.43	31.15	34.03	38.09
T	23.20	23.00	22.31	23.40	25.03	26.57	29.07	31.40	34.29	38.37
U	23.40	23.20	22.50	24.00	25.25	27.20	29.31	32.05	34.55	39.05
V	24.00	23.40	23.09	24.20	25.47	27.43	29.55	32.30	35.21	39.33
W	24.20	24.00	23.20	24.40	26.09	28.06	30.19	32.55	35.47	40.01
X	24.40	24.20	23.47	25.00	26.31	28.29	30.43	33.20	36.13	40.29
Y	25.00	24.40	24.06	25.20	26.53	28.52	31.07	33.45	36.39	40.57
Z	25.20	25.00	24.25	25.40	27.15	29.15	31.31	34.10	37.05	41.25

	16-19	20-24	25-29	30-34	35-39	40-44	45-49	50-54	55-59	60-65
					10.000 Meter – Frauen					
A	36.00	35.20	35.00	36.20	38.30	42.00	45.40	50.20	57.10	62.40
B	36.42	36.02	35.41	37.01	39.13	42.42	46.25	51.08	58.01	63.33
C	37.24	36.44	36.22	37.42	39.56	43.26	47.10	51.56	58.52	64.26
D	38.06	37.26	37.03	38.23	40.39	44.09	47.55	52.44	59.43	65.19
E	38.48	38.08	37.44	39.04	41.22	44.52	48.40	53.32	60.34	66.12
F	39.30	38.50	38.25	39.45	42.05	45.35	49.25	54.20	61.25	67.05
G	40.12	39.32	39.06	40.26	42.48	46.18	50.10	55.08	62.16	67.58
H	40.54	40.14	39.47	41.07	43.31	47.01	50.55	55.56	63.07	68.51
I	41.36	40.56	40.28	41.48	44.14	47.44	51.40	56.44	63.58	69.44
J	42.18	41.38	41.09	42.29	44.57	48.27	52.25	57.32	64.49	70.37
K	43.00	42.20	41.50	43.10	45.40	49.10	53.10	58.20	65.40	71.30
L	43.42	43.20	42.31	43.51	46.23	49.53	53.55	59.08	66.31	72.23
M	44.24	43.44	43.12	44.32	47.06	50.36	54.40	59.56	67.22	73.16
N	45.06	44.26	43.53	45.13	47.49	51.19	55.25	60.44	68.13	74.09
O	45.48	45.08	44.34	45.54	48.32	52.02	56.10	61.32	69.04	75.02
P	46.30	45.50	45.15	46.35	49.15	52.45	56.55	62.20	69.55	75.55
Q	47.12	46.32	45.56	47.16	49.58	53.28	57.40	63.08	70.46	76.18
R	47.54	47.14	46.37	47.57	50.41	54.11	58.25	63.56	71.37	77.41
S	48.36	47.56	47.18	48.38	51.24	54.54	59.10	64.44	72.28	78.34
T	49.18	48.38	47.59	49.19	52.07	55.37	59.55	63.52	73.19	79.27
U	50.00	49.28	48.40	50.00	52.50	56.20	60.40	66.20	74.10	80.20
V	50.42	50.20	49.21	50.41	53.33	57.03	61.25	67.08	75.05	81.13
W	51.24	50.44	50.02	51.22	54.16	57.46	62.10	67.56	75.52	82.06
X	52.06	51.26	50.43	52.03	54.59	58.29	62.55	68.44	76.43	82.59
Y	52.48	52.08	51.24	52.44	55.42	59.12	63.40	69.32	77.43	83.52
Z	53.30	52.50	52.05	53.25	56.25	59.55	64.25	70.20	78.25	84.45

	30-34	35-39	40-44	45-49	50-54	55-59	60-64	65-69	70-74	ab 75
					800 Meter – Jogger					
A	2.05	2.10	2.15	2.20	2.25	2.35	2.50	3.15	3.45	4.20
B	2.08	2.13	2.18	2.23	2.28	2.38	2.53	3.18	3.48	4.23
C	2.11	2.16	2.21	2.26	2.31	2.41	2.56	3.21	3.51	4.26
D	2.14	2.19	2.24	2.29	2.34	2.44	2.59	3.24	3.54	4.29
E	2.17	2.22	2.27	2.32	2.37	2.47	3.02	3.27	3.57	4.32
F	2.20	2.25	2.30	2.35	2.40	2.50	3.05	3.30	4.00	4.35
G	2.23	2.28	2.33	2.38	2.43	2.53	3.08	3.33	4.03	4.38
H	2.26	2.31	2.36	2.41	2.46	2.56	3.11	3.36	4.06	4.41
I	2.29	2.34	2.39	2.44	2.49	2.59	3.14	3.39	4.09	4.44
J	2.32	2.37	2.42	2.47	2.52	3.02	3.17	3.42	4.12	4.47
K	2.35	2.40	2.45	2.50	2.55	3.05	3.20	3.45	4.15	4.50
L	2.38	2.43	2.48	2.53	2.58	3.08	3.23	3.48	4.18	4.53
M	2.41	2.46	2.51	2.56	3.01	3.11	3.26	3.51	4.21	4.56
N	2.44	2.49	2.54	2.59	3.04	3.14	3.29	3.54	4.24	4.59
O	2.47	2.52	2.57	3.02	3.07	3.17	3.32	3.57	4.27	5.02
P	2.50	2.55	3.00	3.05	3.10	3.20	3.35	4.00	4.30	5.05
Q	2.53	2.58	3.03	3.08	3.13	3.23	3.38	4.03	4.33	5.08
R	2.56	3.01	3.06	3.11	3.16	3.26	3.41	4.06	4.36	5.11
S	2.59	3.04	3.09	3.14	3.19	3.29	3.44	4.09	4.39	5.14
T	3.02	3.07	3.12	3.17	3.22	3.32	3.47	4.12	4.42	5.17
U	3.05	3.10	3.15	3.20	3.25	3.35	3.50	4.15	4.45	5.20
V	3.08	3.13	3.18	3.23	3.28	3.38	3.53	4.18	4.48	5.23
W	3.11	3.16	3.21	3.26	3.31	3.41	3.56	4.21	4.51	5.26
X	3.14	3.19	3.24	3.29	3.34	3.44	3.59	4.24	4.54	5.29
Y	3.17	3.22	3.27	3.32	3.37	3.47	4.02	4.27	4.57	5.32
Z	3.20	3.25	3.30	3.35	3.40	3.50	4.05	4.30	5.00	5.35

	30-34	35-39	40-44	45-49	50-54	55-59	60-64	65-69	70-74	ab 75
					1500 Meter – Jogger					
A	4.15	4.30	4.45	5.00	5.15	5.35	6.00	6.35	7.15	7.45
B	4.25	4.40	4.55	5.10	5.25	5.45	6.10	6.45	7.25	7.55
C	4.35	4.50	5.05	5.20	5.35	5.55	6.20	6.55	7.35	8.05
D	4.45	5.00	5.15	5.30	5.45	6.05	6.30	7.05	7.45	8.15
E	4.55	5.10	5.25	5.40	5.55	6.15	6.40	7.15	7.55	8.25
F	5.05	5.20	5.35	5.50	6.06	6.25	6.50	7.25	8.05	8.35
G	5.15	5.30	5.45	6.00	6.15	6.35	7.00	7.35	8.15	8.45
H	5.25	5.40	5.55	6.10	6.25	6.45	7.10	7.45	8.25	8.55
I	5.35	5.50	6.05	6.20	6.35	6.55	7.20	7.55	8.35	9.05
J	5.45	6.00	6.15	6.30	6.45	7.05	7.30	8.05	8.45	9.15
K	5.55	6.10	6.25	6.40	6.55	7.15	7.40	8.15	8.55	9.25
L	6.05	6.20	6.35	6.50	7.05	7.25	7.50	8.25	9.05	9.35
M	6.15	6.30	6.45	7.00	7.15	7.35	8.00	8.35	9.15	9.45
N	6.25	6.40	6.55	7.10	7.25	7.45	8.10	8.45	9.25	9.55
O	6.35	6.50	7.05	7.20	7.35	7.55	8.20	8.55	9.35	10.05
P	6.45	7.00	7.15	7.30	7.45	8.05	8.30	9.05	9.45	10.15
Q	6.55	7.10	7.25	7.40	7.55	8.15	8.40	9.15	9.55	10.25
R	7.05	7.20	7.35	7.50	8.05	8.25	8.50	9.25	10.25	10.35
S	7.15	7.30	7.45	8.00	8.15	8.35	9.00	9.35	10.15	10.45
T	7.25	7.40	7.55	8.10	8.25	8.45	9.10	9.45	10.25	10.55
U	7.35	7.50	8.05	8.20	8.35	8.55	9.20	9.55	10.35	11.05
V	7.45	8.00	8.15	8.30	8.45	9.05	9.30	10.05	10.45	11.15
W	7.55	8.10	8.25	8.40	8.55	9.15	9.40	10.15	10.55	11.25
X	8.05	8.20	8.35	8.50	9.05	9.25	9.50	10.25	11.05	11.35
Y	8.15	8.30	8.45	9.00	9.15	9.35	10.00	10.35	11.15	11.45
Z	8.25	8.40	8.55	9.10	9.25	9.45	10.10	10.45	11.25	11.55

	3000 Meter – Jogger									
	30-34	35-39	40-44	45-49	50-54	55-59	60-64	65-69	70-74	ab 75
A	9.00	9.30	10.00	10.30	11.00	11.40	12.30	13.50	15.30	16.30
B	9.15	9.45	10.15	10.45	11.15	11.55	12.45	14.05	15.45	16.45
C	9.30	10.00	10.30	11.00	11.30	12.10	13.00	14.20	16.00	17.00
D	9.45	10.15	10.45	11.15	11.45	12.25	13.15	14.35	16.15	17.15
E	10.00	10.30	11.00	11.30	12.00	12.40	13.30	14.50	16.30	17.30
F	10.15	10.45	11.15	11.45	12.15	12.55	13.45	15.05	16.45	17.45
G	10.30	11.00	11.30	12.00	12.30	13.10	14.00	15.20	17.00	18.00
H	10.45	11.15	11.45	12.15	12.45	13.25	14.15	15.35	17.15	18.15
I	11.00	11.30	12.00	12.30	13.00	13.40	14.30	15.50	17.30	18.30
J	11.15	11.45	12.15	12.45	13.15	13.55	14.45	16.05	17.45	18.45
K	11.30	12.00	12.30	13.00	13.30	14.10	15.00	16.20	18.00	19.00
L	11.45	12.15	12.45	13.15	13.45	14.25	15.15	16.35	18.15	19.15
M	12.00	12.30	13.00	13.30	14.00	14.40	15.30	16.50	18.30	19.30
N	12.15	12.45	13.15	13.45	14.15	14.55	15.45	17.05	18.45	19.45
O	12.30	13.00	13.30	14.00	14.30	15.10	16.00	17.20	19.00	20.00
P	12.45	13.15	13.45	14.15	14.45	15.25	16.15	17.35	19.15	20.15
Q	13.00	13.30	14.00	14.30	15.00	15.40	16.30	17.50	19.30	20.30
R	13.15	13.45	14.15	14.45	15.15	15.55	16.45	18.05	19.45	20.45
S	13.30	14.00	14.30	15.00	15.30	16.10	17.00	18.20	20.00	21.00
T	13.45	14.15	14.45	15.15	15.45	16.25	17.15	18.35	20.15	21.15
U	14.00	14.30	15.00	15.30	16.00	16.40	17.30	18.50	20.30	21.30
V	14.15	14.45	15.15	15.45	16.15	16.55	17.45	19.05	20.45	21.45
W	14.30	15.00	15.30	16.00	16.30	17.10	18.00	19.20	21.00	22.00
X	14.45	15.15	15.45	16.15	16.45	17.25	18.15	19.35	21.15	22.15
Y	15.00	15.30	16.00	16.30	17.00	17.40	18.30	19.50	21.30	22.30
Z	15.15	15.45	16.15	16.45	17.15	17.55	18.45	20.05	21.45	22.45

	5000 Meter – Jogger									
	30-34	35-39	40-44	45-49	50-54	55-59	60-64	65-69	70-74	ab 75
A	16.00	16.30	17.00	17.30	18.30	20.00	22.00	24.30	26.30	28.30
B	16.20	16.50	17.20	17.50	18.50	20.20	22.30	24.50	26.50	28.50
C	16.40	17.10	17.40	18.10	19.10	20.40	22.40	25.10	27.10	29.10
D	17.00	17.30	18.00	18.30	19.30	21.00	23.00	25.30	27.30	29.30
E	17.20	17.50	18.20	18.50	19.50	21.20	23.20	22.50	27.50	29.50
F	17.40	18.10	18.40	19.10	20.10	21.40	23.40	26.10	28.10	30.10
G	18.00	18.30	19.00	19.30	20.30	22.00	24.00	26.30	28.30	30.30
H	18.20	18.50	19.20	19.50	20.50	22.20	24.20	26.50	28.50	30.50
I	18.40	19.10	19.40	20.10	21.10	22.40	24.40	27.10	29.10	31.10
J	19.00	19.30	20.00	20.30	21.30	23.00	25.00	27.30	29.30	31.30
K	19.20	19.50	20.20	20.50	21.50	23.20	25.20	27.50	29.50	31.50
L	19.40	20.10	20.40	21.10	22.10	23.40	25.40	28.10	30.10	32.10
M	20.00	20.30	21.00	21.30	22.30	24.00	26.00	28.30	30.30	32.30
N	20.20	20.50	21.20	21.50	22.50	24.20	26.20	28.50	30.50	32.50
O	20.40	21.10	21.40	22.10	23.10	24.40	26.40	29.10	31.10	33.10
P	21.00	21.30	22.00	22.30	23.30	25.00	27.00	29.30	31.30	33.30
Q	21.20	21.50	22.20	22.50	23.50	25.20	27.20	29.50	31.50	33.50
R	21.40	22.10	22.40	23.10	24.10	25.40	27.40	31.10	32.10	34.10
S	22.00	22.30	23.00	23.30	24.30	26.00	28.00	31.30	32.30	34.30
T	22.20	22.50	23.20	23.50	24.50	26.20	28.20	31.50	32.50	34.50
U	22.40	23.10	23.40	24.10	25.10	26.40	28.40	32.10	33.10	35.10
V	23.00	23.30	24.00	24.30	25.30	27.00	29.00	32.30	33.30	35.30
W	23.20	23.50	24.20	24.50	25.50	27.20	29.20	32.50	33.50	35.50
X	23.40	24.10	24.40	25.10	26.10	27.40	29.40	33.10	34.10	36.10
Y	24.00	24.30	25.10	25.30	26.30	28.00	30.00	33.30	34.30	36.30
Z	24.20	24.50	25.30	25.50	26.50	28.20	30.20	33.50	34.50	36.50

10.000 Meter - Jogger

	30-34	35-39	40-44	45-49	50-54	55-59	60-64	65-69	70-74	ab 75
A	33.00	34.30	35.30	36.30	39.00	42.00	46.00	51.30	55.30	60.00
B	33.40	35.10	36.10	37.10	39.40	42.40	46.40	52.10	56.10	60.40
C	34.20	35.50	36.50	37.50	40.20	43.20	47.20	52.50	55.50	61.20
D	35.00	36.30	37.30	38.30	41.00	44.00	48.00	53.30	57.30	62.00
E	35.40	37.10	38.10	39.10	41.40	44.40	48.40	54.10	58.10	62.40
	36.20	37.50	38.50	39.50	42.20	45.20	49.20	54.50	58.50	63.20
G	37.00	38.30	39.30	40.30	43.00	46.00	50.00	55.30	59.30	64.00
H	37.40	39.10	40.10	41.10	43.40	46.40	50.40	56.10	60.10	64.40
	38.20	39.50	40.50	41.50	44.20	47.20	51.20	56.50	60.50	65.20
	39.00	40.30	41.30	42.30	45.00	48.00	52.00	57.30	61.30	66.00
K	39.40	41.10	42.10	43.10	45.40	48.40	52.40	58.10	62.10	66.40
L	40.20	41.50	42.50	43.50	46.20	49.20	53.20	58.50	62.50	67.20
M	41.00	42.30	43.30	44.30	47.00	50.00	54.00	59.30	63.30	68.00
N	41.40	43.10	44.10	45.10	47.40	50.40	54.40	60.10	64.10	68.40
O	42.20	43.50	44.50	45.50	48.20	51.20	55.20	60.50	64.50	69.20
P	43.00	44.30	45.30	46.30	49.00	52.00	56.00	61.30	65.30	70.00
Q	43.40	45.10	46.10	47.10	49.40	52.40	56.40	62.10	66.10	70.40
R	44.20	45.50	46.50	47.50	50.20	53.20	57.20	62.50	66.50	71.20
S	45.00	46.30	47.30	48.30	51.00	54.00	58.00	63.30	67.30	72.00
T	45.40	47.10	48.10	49.10	51.40	54.40	58.40	64.10	68.10	72.40
U	46.20	47.50	48.50	49.50	52.20	55.20	59.20	64.50	68.50	73.20
V	47.00	48.30	49.30	50.30	53.00	56.00	60.00	65.30	69.30	74.00
W	47.40	49.10	50.10	51.10	53.40	56.40	60.40	66.10	70.10	74.40
X	48.20	49.50	50.50	51.50	54.20	57.20	61.20	66.50	70.50	75.20
Y	49.00	50.30	51.30	52.30	55.00	58.00	62.00	67.30	71.30	76.00
Z	49.40	51.10	52.10	53.10	55.40	58.40	62.40	68.10	72.10	76.40

20 Kilometer - Jogger

	30-34	35-39	40-44	45-49	50-54	55-59	60-64	65-69	70-74	ab 75
A	67.00	68.00	72.30	74.30	80.00	87.00	95.00	107.00	115.00	125.00
B	68.20	69.20	73.50	75.50	81.20	88.20	96.20	108.20	116.20	126.20
C	69.40	70.40	75.10	76.10	82.40	89.40	97.40	109.40	117.40	127.40
D	71.00	72.00	76.30	77.30	84.00	91.00	99.00	111.00	119.00	129.00
E	72.20	73.20	77.50	78.50	85.20	92.20	100.20	112.20	120.20	130.20
	73.40	74.40	79.10	80.10	86.40	93.40	101.40	113.40	121.40	131.40
G	75.00	76.00	80.30	81.30	88.00	95.00	103.00	115.00	123.00	133.00
H	76.20	77.20	81.50	82.50	89.20	96.20	104.20	116.20	124.20	134.20
	77.40	78.40	83.10	84.10	90.40	97.40	105.40	117.40	125.40	135.40
	79.00	80.00	84.30	85.30	92.00	99.00	107.00	119.00	127.00	137.00
K	80.20	81.20	85.50	86.50	93.20	100.20	108.20	120.00	128.00	138.20
	81.40	82.40	87.10	88.10	94.40	101.40	109.40	121.40	129.40	139.40
M	83.00	84.00	88.30	89.30	96.00	103.00	111.00	123.00	131.00	141.00
N	84.20	85.20	89.50	90.50	97.20	104.20	112.20	124.20	132.20	142.20
O	85.40	86.40	91.10	92.10	98.40	105.40	113.40	125.40	133.40	143.40
P	87.00	88.00	92.30	93.30	100.00	107.00	115.00	127.00	135.00	145.00
Q	88.20	89.20	93.50	94.50	101.20	108.20	116.20	128.20	136.20	146.20
R	89.40	90.40	95.10	96.10	102.40	109.40	117.40	129.40	137.40	147.40
	91.00	92.00	96.30	97.30	104.00	111.00	119.00	131.00	139.00	149.00
	92.20	93.20	97.50	98.50	105.20	112.20	120.20	132.20	140.20	150.20
U	93.40	94.40	99.10	100.10	106.40	113.40	121.40	133.40	141.40	151.40
	95.00	96.00	100.30	101.30	108.00	115.00	123.00	135.00	143.00	153.00
W	96.20	97.20	101.50	102.50	109.20	116.20	124.20	136.20	144.20	154.20
X	97.40	98.40	103.10	104.10	110.40	117.40	125.40	137.40	145.40	155.40
Y	99.00	100.00	104.30	105.30	112.00	119.00	127.00	139.00	147.00	157.00
Z	100.20	101.20	105.50	106.50	113.20	120.20	128.20	140.20	148.20	158.20

	25 Kilometer – Jogger									
	30-34	35-39	40-44	45-49	50-54	55-59	60-64	65-69	70-74	ab 75
A	90.00	93.30	97.00	100.00	105.00	114.00	125.00	139.00	151.00	163.00
B	91.40	95.10	98.40	101.40	106.40	115.40	126.40	140.40	152.40	164.40
C	93.20	96.50	100.20	102.20	108.20	117.20	128.20	142.20	154.20	166.20
D	95.00	98.30	102.00	104.00	110.00	119.00	130.00	144.00	166.00	168.00
E	96.40	100.10	103.40	105.40	111.40	120.40	131.40	145.40	157.40	169.40
F	98.00	101.50	105.20	107.20	113.20	122.20	133.20	147.20	159.20	171.20
G	99.40	103.30	107.00	109.00	115.00	124.00	135.00	149.00	161.00	173.00
H	101.20	105.10	108.40	110.40	116.40	125.40	136.40	150.40	162.40	174.40
I	103.00	106.50	110.20	112.20	118.20	127.20	138.20	152.20	164.20	176.20
J	104.40	108.30	112.00	114.00	120.00	129.00	140.00	154.00	166.00	178.00
K	106.20	110.10	113.40	115.40	121.40	130.40	141.40	155.40	167.40	179.40
L	108.00	111.50	115.20	117.20	123.20	132.20	143.00	157.00	169.00	181.00
M	109.40	113.30	117.00	119.00	125.00	134.00	145.00	159.00	171.00	183.00
N	111.20	115.10	118.40	120.40	126.40	135.40	143.40	160.40	172.40	184.40
O	113.00	116.50	120.20	122.20	128.20	137.20	148.20	162.20	174.20	186.20
P	114.40	118.30	122.00	124.00	130.00	139.00	150.00	164.00	176.00	188.00
Q	116.20	120.10	123.40	125.40	131.40	140.40	151.40	165.40	177.40	189.40
R	118.00	121.50	125.20	127.20	133.20	142.20	153.20	167.20	179.20	191.20
S	119.40	123.30	127.00	129.00	135.00	144.00	155.00	169.00	181.00	193.00
T	121.20	125.10	128.40	130.40	136.40	145.40	156.40	170.40	182.40	194.40
U	123.00	126.50	130.20	132.20	138.20	147.20	158.20	172.20	184.20	196.20
V	124.40	128.10	132.00	134.00	140.00	149.00	160.00	174.00	186.00	198.00
W	126.20	129.50	133.40	135.40	141.40	150.40	161.40	175.40	187.40	199.40
X	128.00	131.10	135.20	137.20	143.20	152.20	163.20	177.20	189.20	201.20
Y	129.40	134.50	137.00	139.00	145.00	154.00	165.00	179.00	191.00	203.00
Z	131.20	136.10	138.40	141.40	146.40	155.40	166.40	180.40	192.40	204.40

	30 Kilometer – Jogger									
	30-34	35-39	40-44	45-49	50-54	55-59	60-64	65-69	70-74	ab 75
A	1.50	1.54	1.59	2.04	2.12	2.22	2.36	2.58	3.10	3.25
B	1.52	1.56	2.01	2.06	2.14	2.24	2.38	3.00	3.12	3.27
C	1.54	1.58	2.03	2.08	2.16	2.26	2.40	3.02	3.14	3.29
D	1.56	2.00	2.05	2.10	2.18	2.28	2.42	3.04	3.16	3.31
E	1.58	2.02	2.07	2.12	2.20	2.30	2.44	3.06	3.18	3.33
F	2.00	2.04	2.09	2.14	2.22	2.32	2.46	3.08	3.20	3.35
G	2.02	2.06	2.11	2.16	2.24	2.34	2.48	3.10	3.22	3.37
H	2.04	2.08	2.13	2.18	2.26	2.36	2.50	3.12	3.24	3.39
I	2.06	2.10	2.15	2.20	2.28	2.38	2.52	3.14	3.26	3.41
J	2.08	2.12	2.17	2.22	2.30	2.40	2.54	3.16	3.28	3.43
K	2.10	2.14	2.19	2.24	2.32	2.42	2.56	3.18	3.30	3.45
L	2.12	2.16	2.21	2.26	2.34	2.44	2.58	3.20	3.32	3.47
M	2.14	2.18	2.23	2.28	2.36	2.46	3.00	3.22	3.34	3.49
N	2.16	2.20	2.25	2.30	2.38	2.48	3.02	3.26	3.36	3.51
O	2.18	2.22	2.27	2.32	2.40	2.50	3.04	3.28	3.38	3.53
P	2.20	2.24	2.29	2.34	2.42	2.52	3.06	3.30	3.40	3.55
Q	2.22	2.26	2.31	2.36	2.46	2.54	3.08	3.32	3.42	3.57
R	2.24	2.28	2.33	2.38	2.48	2.56	3.10	3.36	3.44	3.59
S	2.26	2.30	2.35	2.40	2.50	2.58	3.12	3.38	3.46	4.01
T	2.28	2.32	2.37	2.42	2.52	3.00	3.14	3.40	3.48	4.03
U	2.30	2.34	2.39	2.44	2.54	3.02	3.16	3.42	3.50	5.04
V	2.32	2.36	2.41	2.46	2.56	3.04	3.18	3.44	3.52	4.07
W	2.34	2.38	2.43	2.48	2.58	3.06	3.20	3.46	3.54	4.09
X	2.36	2.40	2.45	2.50	3.00	3.08	3.22	3.48	3.56	4.11
Y	2.38	2.42	2.47	2.52	3.02	3.10	3.24	3.50	3.58	4.13
Z	2.40	2.44	2.49	2.54	3.04	3.12	3.26	3.52	4.00	4.15